ECONOMIC METHODOLOGY

ECONOMIC METHODOLOGY

AN INQUIRY

SHEILA C. DOW

OXFORD
UNIVERSITY PRESS

OXFORD
UNIVERSITY PRESS

Great Clarendon Street, Oxford OX2 6DP

Oxford University Press is a department of the University of Oxford.
It furthers the University's objective of excellence in research, scholarship,
and education by publishing worldwide in

Oxford New York

Athens Auckland Bangkok Bogotá Buenos Aires Cape Town
Chennai Dar es Salaam Delhi Florence Hong Kong Istanbul Karachi
Kolkata Kuala Lumpur Madrid Melbourne Mexico City Mumbai Nairobi
Paris São Paulo Shanghai Singapore Taipei Tokyo Toronto Warsaw

with associated companies in Berlin Ibadan

Oxford is a registered trade mark of Oxford University Press
in the UK and in certain other countries

Published in the United States
by Oxford University Press Inc., New York

British Library Cataloguing in Publication Data
Data available

Library of Congress Cataloging in Publication Data
Data available

ISBN 0–19–877612–8

Typeset in Adobe Minion and Trajan
by RefineCatch Limited, Bungay, Suffolk
Printed in Great Britain by
Biddles Ltd.,
Guildford and King's Lynn

For my mother, Elizabeth Anderson
who has shown by example that women can be a
force for good outside the home as well as within.

PREFACE

This book is addressed to those who are interested in reflecting on economics as a discipline, and are curious as to what the field of methodology has to offer. Methodology is the field which is concerned with the foundations of economics: what the role of foundations is, what is meant by foundations, and what they might consist of. It provides a framework within which we can discuss a range of issues which are important for modern economics—why economics is the way it is, what are its limitations, and what are its possibilities; whether or not diversity within economics is to be welcomed; whether or not economics is moving in a constructive direction; and so on.

There is a variety of perceptions and misperceptions of what is involved in methodology. For some it is what in the methodology field is referred to as 'method'—which tool to use for which purpose, within a particular methodological framework. But methodology is concerned more with the framework within which particular methods are chosen. It requires us to dig deeper. For others methodology is associated with rule-setting from outside economics. It is a set of principles for good science; if we don't follow them, we are not good scientists. The reaction to this role for methodology tends to be either to ignore it or to argue vociferously against it. In fact it is a lively area for debate within the field itself, what degree of guidance it is legitimate for methodologists to offer to practising economists.

The fact is that methodology is not the finger-wagging exercise which many mistake it for. While over twenty years ago there was more emphasis on interpreting rules for good science, to apply them to economics, now there is much more engagement with economics itself. Much of modern methodology in fact simply aims to build up a methodological account of what economists do. But there are also issues to address, such as how economics relates to other disciplines, how economic theory can best be constructed in order to generate policy advice, and so on. It is a rich field with active debates, wide-ranging arguments, and new developments occurring all the time. It certainly includes some criticism, but then a critical attitude, it could be argued, is a common feature of scientific activity. Because methodology now attracts such increasing numbers of scholars, and has built up its own institutional structure as a field (organizations, journals, conferences, and so on), methodology is a very lively area. But this specialization also brings its costs, in that methodologists increasingly talk an internal language which is in danger of excluding non-methodologists.

Which is where this book comes in. There are many more detailed treatments of methodological subjects than is offered here. The aim here is simply to provide enough of an overview of methodology to give you an idea of what the field looks like, and to suggest, as we proceed, where you can follow up on particular questions of interest. So we spend more time on the reasons for drawing on methodology, and its implications, than do most methodology books. There is also an attempt at giving a flavour of the issues which methodology is concerned with and what the current areas of dispute are.

The book can be used as an introductory text for methodology teaching, as an entry point to the specialized methodology literature; each chapter ends with suggestions for further reading. It can also be used as supplementary reading for core theory or econometrics courses, to provide some guidance as to how to address the issues which arise in theory development and empirical work. Theories and econometrics do not appear like rabbits out of a hat— methodological principles (whether implicit or explicit) have been used to determine the direction and form of development, and how these developments are regarded. Some prior knowledge of economics is required if the methodology applications are to be understood, so that it is only suitable for advanced undergraduate courses, or postgraduate courses.

However, I would hope that the book would also have some appeal to colleagues who are curious as to what has been happening in economic methodology and how it relates to their practice. Or it could appeal to those who sense that there are some fundamental issues facing economics and are looking for some kind of framework within which to address them.

I became interested in the subject of methodology myself because I found it difficult otherwise to make sense of many of the debates within economics; there seemed to be something unacknowledged under the surface which was what the real arguments were about. Further, I was disturbed to find methodological statements being used to exclude some types of economics, for reasons which were not readily apparent; how is it established what is and what is not 'proper' economics? So my interest in methodology has always been from the perspective of practice, and in the spirit of inclusion rather than exclusion; this will be evident in the way that methodology is discussed here. Indeed, it should be made clear at the start that there is no neutral way of approaching methodology. The thinking (which we will be exploring) which led to the view that there was no neutral set of rules for economics also applies to methodology. But, as with economics, the best way of dealing with this is to be explicit about our own views, to be aware that there are other points of view, and to be open-minded.

I have benefited tremendously, in preparing this volume, from discussions with, listening to and reading the work of, many of those who work in the field of methodology, as well as many practitioners of economics over the years. Those who have helped along the way are too numerous to mention. But I would like to acknowledge in particular Victoria Chick and the Press's readers, who all commented on several chapters. I am grateful too to the many honours students at the University of Stirling, and those in the Scottish Doctoral Programme, on whom I have tried out some parts of the material presented here. They were supportive in their enthusiasm and challenging in bringing their own ideas and questions to bear. I would also like to express my appreciation to Brendan George, formerly of Oxford University Press, who had the original idea for the book and provided support and encouragement in the early stages, and to Matthew Cotton who subsequently nursed the project on its way. Finally, I would like to express my fond appreciation for the immeasurable contribution made by my husband Alistair. In addition to providing comments on several chapters, it was he who first introduced me to methodology many years ago. He has contributed more than he knows since then by many discussions along the way.

S.C.D.

CONTENTS

1

WHAT'S SO FUNNY ABOUT ECONOMICS?

Many a true word is spoken in jest. So we start this inquiry into economic methodology by looking at economist jokes.

Although economics is often referred to as the 'dismal science',[1] economists like a joke as much as anyone, and there are many 'insider' jokes by which we make fun of ourselves. We use jokes to caricature what we regard as distinctive about economics. There are other kinds of jokes which economists tend to find less funny—the 'outsider' jokes which non-economists make to express their discomfort with economics. Here we pick two of each kind of joke to get an idea, first, of economists' own caricature of ourselves, and, second, of the way others caricature us.

Three unfortunate people are shipwrecked—a physicist, a chemist, and an economist—and find themselves cast up on a desert island with little prospect of finding food. A tin of baked beans is also washed up onto the shore, but the problem is how to open it.[2] The physicist sets up a system of levers with stones and branches to exert pressure on the tin, but to no avail. The chemist tries a solution made from boiling a selection of barks and leaves, but that doesn't work either. The economist, who has been standing by all this time, smugly offers the solution: 'Let's assume we have a tin-opener.'

Yes, economists are very conscious of the fact that their theories, and applied work, are based on simplifying assumptions. Theory by definition requires simplifying assumptions—otherwise it would amount only to description.[3] These assumptions inevitably make economics unrealistic in some sense. At the same time we want economics to tell us something about the real world. The same need for simplifying assumptions surely applies also to disciplines like physics and chemistry. But are economists' assumptions distinctive in some way? Is it simply that we are more aware of them because they apply to human behaviour—something with which we are all more intimately familiar than we are with inanimate objects? Whether making assumptions raises issues peculiar to economics or general to all science, it is clearly such a central feature of economics that we will want to think about it more carefully.

An economist is on a flight from New York to London in a four-engined plane. Some way into the flight there is a muffled bang, the plane drops, and the pilot announces that one of the engines has failed. The passengers are not to worry, but their arrival in London will be delayed by half an hour. Some time later the same thing happens again—a second engine has failed. The pilot again reassures the passengers, but warns of a delay now of an hour and a half. Later, incredibly, a third engine fails; now the delay will be five hours. The economist turns to the passenger in the next seat: 'At this rate, if the last engine goes, we'll be up here all night.'

If economics is to be a guide to the future (for governments, for companies, for households), then there has to be some way of drawing on our past experience. After all, past experience is all we can go by. But how we extrapolate from the past raises challenging problems. How many readers, while reading this version of the joke, started wondering (like myself, while writing it) whether the time of travel would really correspond in this simple way to the number of engines lost? The time-delay problem raises the kind of interesting technical questions that distract us from recognizing the dire, irreversible consequences of all engines failing. Are there any serious parallels in economics? Again, since prediction on the basis of past experience is such a central feature of the practice of economics, this joke points to something else we will want to think about further.

But what about jokes made about economists by non-economists? We need to be aware of the way in which others regard economics for a whole variety of reasons, not least that most economists aim to make a useful contribution to society.

An economist post was advertised in the appointments section of the paper; the ad specified that applicants should be 'one-handed'. A mystified two-handed economist phoned the company to ask for an explanation and was told: 'We're tired of hiring economists who always answer questions by saying "on the one hand . . . and on the other . . . ".'

As economists, we don't tend to find this joke funny. Of course we answer practical (and even sometimes theoretical) questions in this way. We have to make assumptions, and it may be a matter for debate as to whether they apply to the question in hand. So our answers reflect the implications of making different possible assumptions. We can extrapolate from the past, but developments not addressed by the theory may disrupt the patterns of the past. We cannot rely on the *ceteris paribus* clause (that is, assuming other things being equal) to answer practical questions where there is no guarantee that other things will be equal. So we hedge our answers. Is this, as the joke suggests, a problem? Or is it an inevitable feature of applied economics? We need to think more carefully about why it is difficult for economists to give more definite answers to practical questions.

If you pose a problem to ten economists you will end up with (at least) eleven opinions.

This joke makes a rather different point; not only may any one economist offer at least two opinions, but also economists cannot even agree amongst themselves. Why can't economists come up with the 'right' answer, or at least a consensus as to what the 'best' answer might be? Is disagreement the sign of an immature science; given time will we all converge on the same answers? Or is there something particular about economics which makes this impossible? Indeed might there be virtue in diversity, as there is in nature? We need to think more carefully about why economists disagree, and what they disagree about.

All of these jokes have been around for a long time, suggesting a common thread in the perceptions both of economists and non-economists about the discipline. But in the meantime, economics keeps on changing, putting a new slant on the kinds of issues raised by this sample of jokes as time goes on. In the next chapter we consider this process of change, what is driving it, and why that puts a particular slant on the types of issue raised by these jokes.

Further Reading

The economics jokes website: http://netec.mcc.ac.uk/JokEc.html

Endnotes

1. This term is most closely associated with the classical economist Thomas Carlyle.
2. This joke obviously predates baked bean tins with ring-pull tops.
3. Even description itself could be seen to require some assumptions.

2

WHERE IS ECONOMICS GOING?

2.1 Introduction

Economics has a long history. In its modern form, it can be traced back to the work of Adam Smith in Scotland and François Quesnay in France in the eighteenth century, although there are plenty of earlier antecedents.[1] So why do we need to address fundamental issues now? Surely these have all been sorted out a long time ago.

The fact is that, even if economists at times consider issues to be close to being resolved, economics keeps changing, raising new issues. A cursory glance at textbooks from one decade to the next shows how both the questions asked and the tools used to answer them have changed over the years. Some would argue that this change is simply a matter of progress. If this is so, by what principles does economics progress, and be seen to progress? As practising economists, are we all aware of what it is we need to do to contribute to that progress? What are the criteria for judging progress? If we proceed by seeing what 'works', what does that mean? And do we all agree on what does work and what doesn't? There are too many questions here for us to take the notion of inevitable progress for granted.

So if we are open to the possibility of change that cannot necessarily be taken for granted as constituting progress, as well as change that occurs for reasons other than progress (by whatever criteria), then there is even more reason for considering what is driving developments in economics, and how we can each help to push it in a positive direction. This chapter therefore considers the forces behind change in economics and the issues that arise from this process. As in Chapter 1, we will draw attention to issues internal to the discipline and those that arise from outside the discipline.

2.2 Why Does Economics Keep on Changing?

2.2.1 Efforts to improve on existing theories

The force for change that is most obvious from reading articles and textbooks is perceived shortcomings in existing theories. For example, the rational expectations hypothesis was developed because the then-dominant adaptive expectations approach was claimed to be inconsistent with the assumption of rational individual behaviour. Why would individuals who were rational consistently make mistakes?

McCallum suggests that the rational expectations hypothesis:

> has one outstanding strength, namely, the weakness of its competitors. Each alternative expectational hypothesis, that is, explicitly or implicitly posits the existence of some particular pattern of *systematic* expectational error. This implication is unattractive, however, because expectational errors are costly. Thus purposeful agents have incentives to weed out all systematic components. (McCallum, 1980: 718; emphasis in original)

McCallum was right, but right within the terms of the rational expectations framework. Once rationality is defined in a particular way—in this case optimizing behaviour on the basis of complete information (including information about the structural model)—then systematic error would be recognized as such by individuals and would therefore be irrational. But this is not the only possible definition of rationality. The defence of the adaptive expectations approach was that rational individuals would only gradually adjust to new information because of inadequate information about the underlying causal mechanism (see, for example, Laidler, 1981). In other words, what is seen as an improvement to theory depends in this case on a new meaning given to a key concept, rationality. It is normal in scientific thought for terms to change meaning over time. Weintraub (1998), for example, explains how meanings have changed in mathematics. But, unless we can argue that change in meaning is always an improvement by some criterion, it does make identifying improvements in economics in general quite tricky.

It is in fact a common pattern in presenting new theoretical developments for economists to identify the shortcomings in what exists and show how the new theory improves on it. Similarly, an existing theory may be shown to be inconsistent with the evidence. For example, Lucas (1990) points out that standard neoclassical models of growth and trade would imply that the marginal product of capital in developing countries was significantly higher than in developed countries. Why then do we not see consistent capital flows from rich countries to poor countries? His article provides a good case study of how received theory could be modified to incorporate possible explanations for an apparent anomaly, for example, replacing perfect competition with imperfect competition. He concludes by suggesting that development policy should have a totally different focus—human capital. And indeed new growth theory has done just that.

Another way of trying to improve theory may be to change the way assumptions are formulated, to make them more realistic. Thus, in macroeconomics imperfect competition theory has substantially replaced theory based on the assumption of perfect competition. The field developed more from concerns at the macroeconomic level (such as persistent unemployment) than from a realist approach to microeconomics. But the route taken for finding explanations was to focus on microfoundations, and consider different formulations at that level:

[M]acroeconomics should be grounded in microeconomic principles . . . the microfoundations from which the aggregate behavior is derived can often be tested directly. A rejection of the underlying micro-hypotheses should suffice to cast doubt on the validity of the derived macro-theory. (Greenwald and Stiglitz, 1993: 24)

It is interesting that most of this literature is theoretical, or employs simulation techniques for empirical testing, rather than demonstrating evidence for the greater realism of the imperfect competition assumption. It seems that imperfect competition is presumed to be a generally accepted characterization of reality, usually without explicit reference to evidence on market structure. Backhouse (forthcoming) suggests that generalized statements about the nature of the economy are in fact characteristic of textbooks, without much reference to empirical data. This contrasts with some other areas where the realism of assumptions is challenged by counter-evidence. Experimental economics, for example, aims to test empirically whether individuals are in fact rational in the sense that we assume in the rational economic man concept.[2]

2.2.2 Technical change

While efforts to improve on existing theories are an internal source of change in economics in the line of progress, there may also be an external impetus. The most obvious one is the advance in information technology and the associated advance in the scope for data collection and analysis. Modern macroeconomics, for example, took its character from the new capacity, from the 1940s, to manipulate the increasing numbers of data series that were becoming available. Econometrics itself has undergone dramatic changes as a result of the increasing accessibility, and ease of operation, of statistical packages. Older readers may remember learning regression analysis using log tables. That is light years away from the current situation where highly sophisticated packages can be used with minimal training.[3]

The means by which the technical proficiency of economists improves may itself be understood in terms of competitive behaviour within economics. Thus Harry Johnson (1971), for example, argued that younger economists recently trained in graduate schools have become accustomed to using new mathematical techniques that many of their elders cannot grasp; they push forward with these techniques in order to improve their career prospects.

Robert Lucas (1980: 701) has specifically referred to the role of technical advances in the analysis of expectations since Keynes's day; he gives as examples the idea that 'one might describe the economy as a system of stochastically disturbed difference equations, the parameters of which could be estimated from actual time series', and the technical capacity to construct a 'mathematically explicit theory of general equilibrium'. He therefore portrays the difference between Keynes's theory of expectations, developed in the 1930s, and his own as being due primarily to technological advance:

It was a fortunate historical accident that . . . technical advances in statistical and economic theory occurred, which transformed 'Keynesian Economics' into something very different from, and much more fruitful than, anything Keynes himself had foreseen. (ibid.)

Note that Lucas is employing a notion of progress in the term 'fruitful'. This is something we need to consider more carefully in what follows.[4]

2.2.3 Changing political environment

What we have considered so far are forces for change internal to the discipline. These are perhaps the ones we are most conscious of in the day-to-day business of academic economics. But among practising economists on a day-to-day basis, and for academic economists over the longer term, external forces for change can bring about much more dramatic shifts in the discipline.

One important external impetus for change in economics is the new questions posed by the changing political environment. For example, environmental issues are important now in a way that would have been hard to imagine fifty years ago. Having assumed for years that there was a given endowment of most resources, economists now need to address the issues raised by the real possibility of resource depletion.[5] One of the old puzzles for economists was the water–diamond paradox: why is the price of diamonds so high when the need for them is so low, while, although it is essential to life, water has so low a price? The answer was identified as lying in distinguishing between the total utility derived from water (value-in-use) and its marginal utility (value-in-exchange). The supply of water was thought to be so great that the cost of production was minimal. But now we are increasingly conscious that the supply of water in specific locations, and in particular the supply of water suitable for drinking, is limited. This awareness is reflected, for example, in the fact that we now pay water rates in the UK. The pricing, or shadow pricing—using modelling to estimate what the market price would have been—of resources, and questions of resource management in general, have spawned a huge body of activity in economics (see, for example, Hanley, Shogren, and White, 1997). The large literature on the question of value in fact illustrates well the scope for different understandings of economic questions (Swale, 1993).

Similarly, European integration has encouraged a lively area for economic research. Most economics refers to the nation state. When we make judgements with reference to social welfare, we normally mean the welfare of the national society. But changing political boundaries means that that national notion of society may no longer be relevant. For the European Union (EU), social welfare refers to the welfare of Europe as a whole, with national concerns expressed in terms of distributional issues, just like regional issues within any country. Further, the dynamic nature of breaking down barriers between markets means that there will be structural change. Indeed, structural change is required by the condition for entry into European Monetary Union (EMU), that economies converge, while macroeconomics previously had been based on the assumption of a stable economic structure. The result has been a huge new literature.[6]

This political source of change in economics can also be regarded as contributing to progress in that it extends the scope of the subject to cover a wider variety of issues.

2.2.4 Change in the economy itself

Change in the economy itself could be thought to be subsumed in the discussion so far. If theories fail to predict or explain well where there has been a new development in the economy, that provides an impetus for theoretical improvement. Similarly, it is change in the economy itself that generates both the technical change, and also political change we have just discussed. But, as we shall see in the next section, by focusing on change in the economy as such, further interesting issues arise.

It is possible that, rather than changing spasmodically due to exogenous shocks, economies change as a matter of course. Such a view is suggested by looking at the background to the development of modern economics from the eighteenth century (see, for example, Deane, 1978). Looking at the broad sweep of the development of economics, we can see the classical economics of the late eighteenth to late nineteenth centuries in terms of the changes wrought by, and issues raised by, the Industrial Revolution, and the social upheaval that entailed. The focus of economic theory was therefore on economic growth and the distribution of the fruits of that growth. But then attention turned in the Marginalist Revolution period around the end of the nineteenth century to the functioning of markets, and away from production, and to focusing on economic function (provider of labour, consumer, investor of savings) rather than social class. The Great Depression in the 1930s shifted the focus onto unemployment, its causes and cures, while the stagflation of the 1970s shifted the focus onto the causes and cures of inflation. Further, the rightward shift of politics in the 1980s encouraged economists to focus their research on market issues rather than the government intervention of the post-war years.

There are also more specific changes we can identify in our subject matter. If we consider monetary policy, for example, the monetary authorities have in the past (in the UK, say, up to the 1950s) and in some economies (as in Chile in the 1970s) arguably had some success in directly affecting the money supply. But it is now widely recognized that money supply control is not feasible in modern banking systems; the monetary authorities have to exert their influence in more indirect ways. The formerly standard macroeconomic assumption of an exogenous money supply, under the control of the monetary authorities, no longer reflects reality.[7] Thus much of recent theoretical developments take the money supply to be endogenous, as for example in modern real business cycle theory (following Kydland and Prescott, 1990, for example).

Further, the structure of the economy rests on a particular structure of institutions (firms, public bodies, etc) and conventional behaviour (trust in market relations, expectations formation, drawing on tacit knowledge, and so on). Thus a significant proportion of behaviour is habitual, or routinized, by convention (see Hodgson, 1988: ch. 6). These structures and conventions too are liable to change, and to be different in different economies. This fact has been highlighted by research on European integration that requires putting a collection of different national economic structures into a single theoretical framework (see, for example, Chick, 1998; Chick and Dow, 1997).

The situation is complicated further by the fact that some institutional change is itself the product of economic theory. For example, the policy of making central banks independent of government and charged with inflation control is justified by a theoretical framework which sees monetary variables as separate from real variables (except perhaps in the short run), that is, money is neutral with respect to output and employment. The central bank is concerned with monetary variables and the general price level, while the government takes care of real variables, without much impact on each other. Similarly, European Monetary Union was designed on the basis of optimal currency area theory which specifies the conditions for a single-currency area to work well. The single market, fiscal harmonization, convergence criteria, and so on, were designed to create these conditions. The success of the institutional design therefore depends to a large extent on how good the theoretical rationale is.

Economic theory is only one force for institutional change. More generally, change in the subject matter of economics arises because economics is dealing with human beings who function within a social system. While the physical sciences are not immune to context, there is a fundamental difference in the nature of our subject matter. A comet in Adam Smith's time is essentially the same as a comet in our time, but the same cannot be said of a firm.[8] Also, while there are no doubt certain constancies in human nature, we clearly behave differently, within different institutional structures, and with different knowledge compared with people in Adam Smith's time. If theory is to refer to this changing reality, then perhaps it is inevitable that theory itself should keep changing. In these senses, economics is much more challenging than the physical sciences. Indeed Max Planck is said to have considered specializing in economics, but turned to physics instead as a less difficult subject.

Considering this most fundamental of the sources of change in economics, therefore, we are led to the view that, just as the economy inevitably changes, so too will economics. However, if the point of reference (the economy) keeps changing, it becomes much more difficult, not only to make categoric statements about the economy, but also to make categoric statements about progress in economics. Perhaps we can only hope to discuss how well economic theory is keeping up with change in the subject matter. In the next two sections we consider this and some other important issues for economists which have been thrown up by having put the spotlight on the forces for change.

2.3 Issues for Economists

2.3.1 What is meant by progress?

Economists are very persuasive, in textbooks and in articles, that the subject is progressing. Correcting an error of logic, relaxing an assumption, taking account of new evidence—surely these must all be improvements on what went before. This is the day-to-day business of economic research, and it is natural for us to think that, in the process, we are adding to economic knowledge. On the face of it, there does not seem to be much to discuss.

But as economists we are familiar with the concept of the trade-off. Even if we are happy to accept that all economic research adds to knowledge, it is hard to argue that all research adds equally to knowledge. For any one economist at any one time, pursuing the implications of relaxing one assumption is to be traded off against pursuing the implications of relaxing another assumption. Using one method of analysis is at the expense of using an alternative method. More generally, using one theoretical framework means not using another framework. How do we decide on the most productive line of research, given our limited research resources?

The fact is that there are differences of opinion on this matter. Some economists choose one framework and refinements in it in one direction (such as introducing the utility of future generations into a perfect-competition model), while others will make different choices (such as introducing more differentiation in information sets into an imperfect competition model). Who is right? Can we reach a consensus answer to that question at all? If not, is it appropriate for each economist to make her own individual choices? If so, on what basis are these choices made?

2.3.2 Is technical change neutral?

One source of change identified above was technical change. There is no question that economics has moved significantly in the direction of mathematization.[9] Backhouse (1998a), for example, reports an increase in the incidence of algebra in the two leading economics journals, the *American Economic Review* and the *Economic Journal*, from 10 per cent in 1930 to 75 per cent in 1980. This is a different sort of change from the kind of change considered above, in that it refers more to the way in which analysis is conducted than, for example, particular assumptions about economic behaviour.

It is often argued that mathematization assists progress in economics because it makes it easier to identify logical errors, and makes more clear the scope for improving on past theory by introducing new variables, altering assumptions, and so on. But it can also be argued that mathematization actually changes the content of theory. As noted above, Lucas argued that the rational expectations hypothesis was an improvement on Keynes's theory of expectations; the theory had been made operational with the aid of quantitative techniques not available in Keynes's time. But Keynes's theory rested crucially on an understanding of uncertainty as unquantifiable risk. Keynes thought that the scope for using frequency distributions to measure risk was very limited, because of the importance of the kind of changes in the economy we have just been discussing. Expectations therefore are generally held with uncertainty, that is, varying degrees of confidence. By translating Keynes's theory of uncertainty into a theory of quantifiable risk, the content of the theory had changed. Mathematizing Keynes's theory was not neutral. On what grounds, therefore, do we decide which is better? Lucas argued that his theory was better because it was operational, that is, it could be expressed in a complete mathematical system. But equally a Keynesian would argue that Keynes's theory was better because it incorporated uncertainty. Who is right? Can we even answer that question?

2.3.3 How do we handle the changing subject matter?

The fact that the subject matter keeps changing complicates matters. It raises the possibility that some theories may be better in some contexts than others, however we may decide on what we mean by 'better'. If this is the case, then the history of economic thought takes on a new light. If economics necessarily progresses, then the role of history of thought is to chart that progress. It is of purely historical interest. But if theory changes as the economy changes, then past theory provides insights into what kind of theory might best suit particular contexts. Thus, for example, a theory of monetary policy which presumed strong central bank influence on the money supply was developed at a time when this was a reasonable assumption. Theory has changed as the scope for central bank influence has changed. But modern banking systems are at different stages of development in different economies. So it may be appropriate still to use the older theory of monetary policy for some economies, while using an endogenous money supply theory for others. Such a possibility is potentially very important when considering, for example, International Monetary Fund (IMF) policy packages for debtor economies, or European monetary policy being applied equally to very different national banking systems.

A changing economy also raises issues for the content of theory at any one time. Can the economy be treated as a stable structure in the short run, or should theory itself incorporate the tendency for changing structure? Should financial markets be treated as equilibrating normally, and only unstable in abnormal periods, requiring two sets of theory? How should economic agents and their behaviour be depicted: do we as individuals, or collectively, behave normally as if our economic environment is stable, which makes our behaviour more predictable? How common is it for our behaviour itself to change and become less predictable? How do we behave when our economic environment becomes unstable?

The issues are essentially the same for us as economists as they are for us as normal human beings. How do we best make sense of our economic environment in order to predict the future as a basis for action? In the economist's case the 'action' means giving policy advice, otherwise it means taking decisions more generally. But the underlying issues are the same. How do we garner the best knowledge to help us?

2.3.4 Back to the economist jokes

Which brings us back to the economist jokes. If we are going to say anything useful at all about the economy, we have to make assumptions. There is no getting round that. But which assumptions?

There are many different types of assumption: excluding variables judged to be irrelevant, simplifying assumptions, assuming something which is known to be false in itself but which yields good predictions, assuming that relationships take a particular mathematical form, and so on. The tin-opener joke is funny because the assumption itself rules out the problem. But, as with most good jokes, it is rather close to the bone. For example, supposing it is judged that there is a problem of involuntary unemployment. A theory that rules out involuntary unemployment (because rational individuals in equilibrium by definition have made only voluntary choices) rules out the problem.

One of the purposes of theorizing is to provide policy makers (in the public sector, or in firms) with predictions about the future, and about the likely effect of particular courses of action. The aeroplane joke is funny because the extrapolation from past observations about the effect of the loss of engines didn't take account of the change in structure (to put it mildly) if all engines failed. We know that the structure of the economy does change, but in a much less predictable (though usually less disastrous) way. The characteristic *ceteris paribus* clause limits our predictions to circumstances where the structure of the model is stable. If our predictions fail because the structure of the real economy has changed, we have covered ourselves. We might have predicted, for example, that demand for British beef would rise to a particular level when the EU ban on imports was lifted in 1999, *ceteris paribus*. But the continuation of the French ban on imports, which could not easily have been predicted, held demand down below the predicted level.

We have come back to the issue of assumptions. What is it safe to assume away? Where is the dividing line between what it is reasonable to predict, and what is not? Lucas shifted that line by introducing into macroeconomic theory the possibility of private sector reactions to monetary policy announcements, just as the public choice literature opened up the black box of public-sector decision-making. In deciding what to examine and what to leave unexamined, there is a trade-off between simplicity and the extent of coverage by a theory of different possible outcomes. There is a trade-off similarly between a focus on behaviour in a stable economic environment and a focus on sources of structural change.

It is no wonder that economists end up making 'on the one hand' and 'on the other' answers to questions. We know that we are simplifying and abstracting in our research. We know that other things are rarely equal. The joke isn't very funny for economists because it is more disturbing in fact to come across categoric answers to questions. Should Britain join EMU? How many economists would answer simply 'yes' or 'no' to this kind of question? Most would hedge their answer with qualifications in terms of different assumptions about political developments, the capabilities of the European Central Bank (ECB), the entry or otherwise of Central European members, and so on. Similarly, should there be a system of public health insurance in the USA? Again we would expect any answer to be hedged about, with comments on different kinds of arrangements, the implications for fiscal policy, and so on.

Even so, economists would disagree even about their hedged answers. The theoretical framework that some economists use suggests that, by creating a larger market in order to reap economies of scale, EMU on balance will lead to industrial concentration and widening income disparities between member economies. Other economists on balance see the larger market benefiting all consumers by increasing competition, and spreading the benefits of economic growth to all member economies. As far as public health insurance is concerned, some economists' theoretical approach regards the profit motive as creating diseconomies which counteract the beneficial effects of competition for the consumer, while other economists come to the opposite conclusion.

Might it in fact be disturbing if all economists agreed? This is a possibility we need to take seriously. Our discussion so far suggests that the basis for any such agreement is not clear. That does not rule out the possibility that it is there, but the fact that it is not clear even if it is there, seems problematic. Such issues are particularly pointed now for academic economists. In many countries such as the UK, efforts are being made by public bodies to assess the quality of research and teaching (the latter raising issues of content as well as procedure). In these processes we rely on the good judgement of eminent members of the profession, and on proxies such as publication outlets, which effectively refer to the good judgement of journal editors. Judgement is clearly important, in choosing directions for research, in choosing economic policies, and in assessing the quality of others' work. There has been much written on the use of empirical evidence, for example, as a basis for such choices; how far is the number of citations a good measure of the importance of an article? But the nature and origin of judgement is more opaque. This is something we will try to bring to the fore in what follows.

2.4 The Public Understanding of Economics

2.4.1 Policy makers

The fact that economists continue to disagree also remains a problem as far as the public understanding of economics is concerned. Policy makers, whether in public bodies or in firms, are users of economics. Most economists, when asked, say that they want to provide useful knowledge for policy makers. It is therefore of particular importance that there is good mutual understanding between the two. Where, as in the UK, universities and schools are mostly publicly funded, there is even more reason for good mutual understanding.

Policy design is a testing ground for theory. If there are serious inadequacies in a theory, they will become apparent in its application to policy issues. An interesting case in point occurred when the new Conservative Government in the UK in 1979 proposed to implement monetary control in accordance with Friedman's monetarist theory. This theory required that the money supply be controlled by controlling the volume of bank reserves. Absolute control meant doing away with the lender-of-last-resort facility by which banks can, at a price, borrow from the central bank. The Bank of England made a forceful public counter-argument (Foot, Goodhart, and Hotson, 1979) that the banking system rested on confidence that banks would not run out of reserves, so that removing the lender-of-last-resort facility would seriously damage the banking system at a structural level. They won the argument, and the lender-of-last-resort facility remained in place, making it more difficult to control the money supply, of course. We shall be looking in more detail at a more recent case of the Bank of England taking a stand on applied theory, in section 3.5.

How do policy makers decide on which stand to take on applying theory? In particular, is it a problem for policy makers if economists cannot give categoric answers to applied questions? Policy makers, like individuals, have to make decisions on the basis of the knowledge available. They have to employ some criteria for choosing one theory over another.

For policy makers, the correspondence between theory and reality is a central issue, but one which we have already seen to be problematic, given that theory inevitably abstracts. Indeed, since most economists when asked say that their interest in economics is to provide useful knowledge as a basis for policy advice, the relationship between theory and reality is a central issue. More generally, this relationship, and how economists deal with it, will be a constant thread through the chapters which follow.

2.4.2 The general public

Much of economics appears to be seen, not only by policy makers, but also by the general public, as abstracting unduly from reality. The second pair of jokes in the last chapter appears to hold a particular resonance among the general public. Why can't economists be like 'proper' scientists and agree amongst themselves? Well, we know that physical scientists do disagree amongst themselves, but not to the same degree as economists. Whenever economists make bold statements in the name of economic theory, they risk appearing to be caught out whenever the *ceteris paribus* clause isn't met. Yet it is difficult to convey hedged-about statements to non-economists; much of the popular appeal of monetarism in the 1980s, for example, could be explained by the apparent straightforwardness of the message.

At the same time, economics can come across as a dry, abstract discipline, often removed from everyday issues. Economics inevitably goes beyond common sense and intuition. In his *Lectures on Rhetoric*, Adam Smith argued that the motivation of scientists is to dispel the discomfort (cognitive dissonance) caused by what appear from a common-sense point of view to be anomalies. But, to be persuasive, economists need to explain their theories in terms which are already somewhat familiar to the audience. Krugman (1998) argues specifically that the purpose of mathematical expression in economics is to yield results that are not intuitively obvious. But he also emphasizes the importance then of communicating these results to the public.

As we shall discuss in section 7.3 the way in which arguments are communicated is of tremendous importance for economics.[10] If we want to contribute useful knowledge, then it is important that the knowledge is conveyed effectively. Why do some theories capture the public's imagination and others not? If economists are not successfully communicating some important ideas to the public, then that is a problem.

Part of the solution is to put more emphasis on making it clear why it is difficult to make unqualified statements about policy issues, and why, given the range of possible abstractions which theory may make, economists will be unlikely to agree. But the solution may also lie in reflecting on the connections between economic theory and the reality it is designed to illuminate. Adam Smith argued that the physical sciences could proceed for a long time in unfruitful research because their subject matter appeared remote from everyday life. He contrasted this with what were to become the social sciences, which are more clearly concerned with everyday life, and therefore more frequently a matter for debate with the public. In light of this argument, it is worthwhile to reflect on whether the increasing mathematization of the subject has acted as a barrier to more effective communication with the general public.

2.4.3 Students

A section of the general public of particular importance is the students who will go on to be the economists of the future. The appeal of economics to potential students has become a particularly pointed issue for university economics departments also in terms of their funding and their relative positions within their institutions.

While the attitudes of students and potential students have only recently begun to be the subject of investigation in the UK (see *RES Newsletter*, April and October 1999), they have received considerable attention in the USA. The American Economic Association set up a Commission on Graduate Education in Economics, which reported in 1991 (Krueger *et al.*, 1991). Much of the report focused on the concern that the emphasis in graduate education was unduly placed on acquiring theoretical and econometric tools rather than on their real-world application, which requires creativity and problem-solving skills. Similar concerns were voiced in a related report (Kasper *et al.*, 1991), which considered only undergraduates in the elite liberal arts colleges. This report pointed to the tendency for economics undergraduates to choose more applied subjects for their postgraduate education; this 'disaffection' with economics appeared to be explained by what was seen as an undue emphasis on

technical training in graduate programmes compared with the broader education of liberal arts undergraduates. The Commission's Secretary also reported
the more general pattern of declining enrolments by home students in Ph.D.
programmes in the USA (Hansen, 1991). Further, the narrowness of the teaching programme is also reported as causing concern among teaching staff that
students are not being adequately prepared for future employment. These
findings are all consistent with an earlier study by Colander and Klamer (1987)
which had surveyed students in some of the major US graduate programmes.
These students expressed disaffection with the focus on technical matters
rather than applied economics.[11]

To the extent that what was found in the US studies reflects perceptions
further afield, it must be the case, either that we are not being persuasive
enough that the focus on technical questions is a good training for future
economists, or that the technical focus of economics training is excessive by
some criteria, or both. For the future of the discipline, which lies with our
current and future students, these are important issues to address.

2.5 Conclusion

We have reviewed here some of the reasons why the discipline of economics
keeps changing. While much of this change can be understood as efforts at
improvement, it turns out not to be straightforward to assume that all changes
are actually improvements. How do we decide on whether any particular path
is the most fruitful one, or indeed fruitful at all?

The possibility has also been raised that a major reason for change is the
changing nature of the economy itself. This could pose problems for comparing theory developed in one context with theory developed in another context. But in addition it could raise questions about the content of theory. The
individuals and institutions we analyse themselves need to address questions
about how to build up knowledge about a changing economic environment,
just like economists.

Given the complexity of the subject matter, questions of communication to
non-economists are important if the knowledge we build up is to be usefully
applied. There is considerable room for trying to explain the limits facing
economics, as well as the possibilities; there appears to be a problem of
unreasonable public expectations of economics.

One of the barriers to communication is the increasingly sophisticated
mathematical method employed to advance the subject. US studies indicate
that this is proving to be an issue for students, influencing their choice as to
whether or not to proceed to postgraduate study, and how they regard that
study. If an emphasis on formal technique is, as some suggest, necessary for

the progress of economics, then it seems that the case needs to be made more forcefully. This is an issue to which we will return.

In what follows we proceed to look at some specific theoretical issues in economics, and then some empirical issues, to see the implications of the foundational questions we have raised here. We later proceed, in Chapters 5 to 8, to review various attempts to answer these questions.

2.6 Further Reading

A good sense of the factors driving developments in economics can be gleaned from interviews with leading economists; see Klamer (1983/4), Snowdon, Vane, and Wynarczyk (1994), King (1995), and Snowdon and Vane (1999).

Endnotes

1. See, e.g. Gordon (1991) and Price (1997).
2. See, e.g. Loomes (1999) and the articles which follow.
3. See Morgan's (1990) account of the development of econometrics.
4. Lucas's view that, by changing Keynes's theory, it has become more fruitful, has been challenged; see, e.g. Lawson (1995).
5. The issue came to prominence in modern times with the OPEC action to raise oil prices in the 1970s.
6. See European Commission (1990) for a comprehensive account of research on monetary integration in Europe.
7. See Moore (1988) for a detailed account of the argument as applied to the USA.
8. The context of the comet, and how comets are understood, of course change over time; but there is not the scope as with a firm for a comet to change its nature.
9. Several scholars have provided evidence for such a statement; see for example Grubel and Boland, (1986), Mirowski (1991), McCloskey (1994), and Backhouse (1998a).
10. We will see too that communication *among* economists is a central element in the building up of economic knowledge.
11. It must be noted that the preliminary UK studies reported in the *RES Newsletter* do not support the view that the disaffection refers to the content of economics teaching; the implication is that market forces are more important.

3

SOME THEORETICAL ISSUES

3.1 Introduction

In this chapter we are going to look in more detail at some issues within economic theory. We will consider issues ranging from how we define the boundaries of the discipline to how we handle theorizing at the level of the individual in a manner that is somehow consistent with theorizing at the level of the economy. In order to theorize, we need to simplify complex reality somehow. But we will see how choices are involved; every simplification means accepting a trade-off.

The first issue we address is one that is of central importance within economics: how do we theorize about human nature? So much follows from this in terms of how we build up economic theory in general. We will see that there are important differences of opinion among economists. But it is also an important aspect of our communications with non-economists, who are after all human. Public understanding depends crucially on agreement with the way in which we take human nature and abstract from it in order to produce useful theory; it is the public's most direct contact with economic theory. The particular theory we will use as a case study is the economics of the family.

This case study throws up a more general issue, which is the relationship between economics and other disciplines; much of the disagreement over the theory of human nature has focused on how far economics should draw on other disciplines which are also concerned with human nature. Generally, economics abstracts from aspects of reality that are the subject matter of other disciplines. The case study we look at next, concerning the theory of the firm, is important for economic theory itself. It is also important for academic institutional arrangements since other disciplines (management science, business studies, marketing) are also concerned with the firm. Economics departments in many UK universities, for example, are now located in business schools, and for students there is a real choice as to where they pursue an interest in business: in an economics department or in other business-related departments. Again we see different possibilities, some of which draw on other disciplines.

The third issue arises from the relationship between theory expressed in terms of groups of households and firms and theory concerned with economic aggregates: the micro–macro distinction. Micro-theory is one form of abstraction—taking the macro environment as given. Macro-theory is another form of abstraction—assuming that the aggregations of individual markets can be understood as entities. The two levels are clearly connected in reality, but in a complex way which raises interesting issues when we try to capture these interrelationships in theory. We take credit-rationing theory as a case study of an attempt to derive macroeconomic results by reference to microeconomic behaviour. In this case, theory about individual bank behaviour with respect to borrowers is used to yield results in terms of aggregate credit creation.

The credit rationing case study puts a focus on expectations formation, so we consider this more carefully in section 3.5, in the context of monetary policy design. When economies are stable, expectations formation can rely to a great extent on past trends. But periods of instability—the most interesting periods and the ones most challenging for policy makers—pose particular difficulties for economists. Since policy must be based on expectations of what would happen with or without certain policies, we consider a particular policy-related case study: model uncertainty and monetary policy. This literature has also highlighted the potential for parallels between the expectations formation of economists and of individuals in the economy.

The final type of issue deals with what governments are taken to be trying to maximize: social welfare. This area draws on the other three: it requires a theory of human nature in order to build up to a concept of social welfare, and a theory about the building-up; and it requires a view on expectations, in the sense that economists are required to predict the implications of various actions for social welfare. The case study has been selected as one that highlights the potential for misunderstanding between economist and public: the distribution of global pollution. It also illustrates the care that must be taken in drawing policy conclusions from theory, which has inevitably abstracted from various aspects of reality.

3.2 Human Nature: Economics of the Family

Economics is concerned with the economic behaviour of individuals, and reaching conclusions about policy measures which will impact on individuals. So everyone should be able to relate in some way to economics. But, in order to construct theories about individuals, economists must abstract from reality in some way. The result can be that non-economists find our treatment of behaviour as very dry, and even offensive.

In an essay about human nature presented to the Bloomsbury Group, John Maynard Keynes (1972) described a meeting between himself, the rationalist philosopher Bertrand Russell and the romantic author D. H. Lawrence. The way they understood human nature could not have been further apart; Russell focused on reason as the ideal basis for human behaviour, while Lawrence focused on emotion. Keynes's conclusion was that reason and emotion were both essential elements of human nature. The result is potentially complex, and the difficulty for economists is how to cope with this complexity when theorizing about economic behaviour. Does economic behaviour refer only to the rational side of human behaviour, or do we need to incorporate the emotional side of behaviour too; indeed how far are they separable? And what do we mean by rational anyway?

A particularly emotive area of economic theory is the economics of the family. Traditionally microeconomic theory used the household as the unit, not enquiring about economic relations within the household. It was presumed that we optimize as individuals in the outside world (our emotions are bundled up in our preference functions), but operate on the basis of love, cooperation, and trust within the household. But the black box of the family has now been opened, and a range of theories have been developed to explain what goes on inside, using economic theory. The starting-point is that economic behaviour occurs within the family as well as without.

The pioneering 'Economics of the Family', or 'New Home Economics' of Gary Becker (1965) caused great controversy at the time by extending economic theory to what had been regarded as something falling outside the remit of economics. Becker analysed the division of labour within the family in terms of opportunity cost: household labour is undertaken by the partner who would forgo the lower earnings. Given higher average earnings for men, this provided an explanation for the pattern of women predominantly forgoing paid work in order to provide domestic services.

For this type of argument to come out of formal optimizing models, assumptions must be made about what governs behaviour in the family. Becker (1981) based his work on a hierarchical model of the family, whereby the head of the family acts as an altruist with respect to the rest of the family, with the other family members aiming to maximize their own utility. The head's utility function, U_h, is thus given as $U[Z_h, U_1(Z_1), \ldots, U_n(Z_n)]$, where Z_h is the vector representing the head's consumption, and $U_1, \ldots, U_n$ are the utility functions of the beneficiaries, defined solely over their own consumption. Perhaps this doesn't seem to capture the essence of family relations. But for optimizing models some assumptions *have* to be made about utility functions which can generate equilibrium solutions.

A variety of decisions within the family have been analysed as economic decisions, such as the decision whether or not to divorce. A particular question that has been addressed is how, as economists, we can analyse the implications for the incidence of divorce of different legal provisions. Does economic theory suggest that it would change the incidence of divorce if one party could unilaterally divorce another rather than the law requiring both parties to agree, for example? There is an argument that it would not, because what really matters is the gains and losses of the two parties. If the husband gains more than the wife loses by divorce, for example, divorce would occur under either legal system, since the husband could compensate the wife for her loss. But if the wife loses more by divorce than her husband gains, the divorce would be prevented under either system because she could compensate him sufficiently to stay in the marriage (see, for example, Becker, 1991).

Empirical studies comparing the incidence of divorce under different legal systems appear to be inconclusive, so what theoretical rationale would there be for arguing that legal structure does matter? Arguments can be produced in terms of the transactions costs (legal fees, wear and tear on nerves, and so on) involved in actually negotiating a divorce settlement, or information asymmetry (each partner misrepresenting earnings forgone, or capacity to make a settlement, for example). These are 'market imperfections' in the economic relations between the partners.

Other arguments can be constructed without resorting to explanations in terms of 'market imperfections' in this family hierarchy framework, notably using game theory. Game theory focuses on the strategy employed in decision-making processes where, unlike perfectly competitive markets, there is acute awareness of the behaviour of other players. Clark (1999), for example, considers marriage as a cooperative game between the adults in the family, where the public goods at issue are represented as expenditure on the household and expenditure on children (as a proxy for the benefits that ensue). His model suggests that the law on divorce settlements does indeed make it important whether or not one partner can unilaterally impose divorce. It depends on the way in which compensation is established, in particular whether it emphasizes earnings forgone by the partner who provides household services or child custody.

Both the Becker approach and the game-theoretic approach start from given individual preferences and work out the utility-maximizing behaviour for each individual given the particular set of legal rules under which they operate. Such analysis brings to the fore the 'economic' aspects of choices between marriage and divorce. The 'non-economic' aspects of the decision are all embedded in the preference functions, which are taken as given. 'Utility possibility sets' are specified for the two states: marriage and divorce, which, together with the legal framework, determine whether divorce will ensue; each partner aims to be on the higher set (possibly after compensation). So the initial position of the sets is crucial. In these sets are bound up all the notions of hatred, expected happiness with a new partner, continuing love, concern that the family stay together for the sake of the children, and so on. And how did the utility possibility sets reach these positions? Obviously preferences must have been different when the marriage took place. However, Stigler and Becker (1977) justify their approach on the grounds that preferences are in general stable, and can thus be taken as given.

It has thus been assumed that it is feasible to separate off economic behaviour, which we analyse, from non-economic behaviour, which we take as given; it is not the economist's business to enquire into the content of the preference function. It has also been assumed that, in their economic behaviour, individuals are rational in the sense that they optimize with respect to their own utility functions (although, in the Becker model, love enters into the utility function of the head of the household since that includes the utility functions of all the other family members). This yields definitive conclusions, given the particular assumptions made.

Other choices are possible for the economic analyst if a different focus is chosen. Much of the original impetus for exploring the economic relations within the household came from feminists. But feminist economists tend to analyse the choices involved in a way which is quite different from the Becker approach (see Nelson, 1996). While they draw attention to the economic relations between the individuals within a household, they analyse these relations in social, rather than individualistic, terms. The Becker approach suggests that it is women who generally provide household services because it is rational for the higher earner in the family to provide the outside income. Further, men on average earn more than women because of market conditions. But feminists would consider the social structure which has led to this set of market conditions, and then see the influence of social convention on the individual decision-making in any family, where convention establishes particular power relations within the family. The labour market and social conventions with respect to the family are thus seen as interdependent.

The outcome is conclusions about household choices which seem to be at odds with what would appear to be rational from a Becker perspective. For example, Wheelock (1990) has analysed the behaviour of households in de-industrialized areas where husbands are unemployed. She found a high inci-dence of wives taking paid employment, even when household income was reduced because income from the state benefit system fell by more than was earned, while the husbands took on much of the household service provision. This was explained in terms of the dignity and self-respect of the household accruing from paid employment, which in these cases was only available to women. Further, this case illustrates the capacity for conventions (for example about power relations within the family) to change with changing external conditions (like deindustrialization).

This need not be considered as conflicting altogether with the rational, optimizing approach to household behaviour. In a Becker framework, Wheelock's results might be incorporated in the preference function as utility from work. But it would not be at all straightforward; in line with much of economic theory, Becker's framework is grounded on the assumption that work causes disutility. Schumacher (1975, ch. 4) sets up what he calls a Buddhist economic framework, whereby consumption is minimized and work maximized, turning the conventional economic model on its head. So it can be done up to a point, but the repercussions for other fields in economics, notably labour economics, would be immense. Further, while the Becker approach emphasizes individual choice given labour market conditions, the feminist approach emphasizes social convention, and also social structure as a determinant of labour market conditions. It thus requires understanding of the nature of social conventions, and how and why they can change.

This highlights the importance of the *focus* of each approach; the feminist approach concentrates on what the Becker approach bundles into preferences and prices. In addition, by focusing on social convention as prior to individual preferences, the feminist approach also puts the spotlight on forces for change in the economic relationships within families. The Becker and game-theoretic approaches distinguish between what are seen as economic factors which can alter family relationships (such as changing average earnings for women) and any non-economic factors bundled into preferences. But an approach which does not separate economic behaviour out from social structure, conventions, and so on, can focus on how changes in the legal framework affect behaviour more generally. Thus, for example, Rowthorn (1999) argues that no-fault divorce itself encourages behavioural change which undermines the foundation of trust on which successful marriages depend.

Further, the *nature* of the conclusions of each type of theorizing is different. The Becker and game-theoretic approaches yield sharp, definitive results, on the basis of specific simplifications; the feminist approach (typically of those approaches which emphasize social structure) yields less definitive results, but with less strict simplifications. It is clear that the scope for formalization in mathematical models is constrained for the feminist approach by its emphasis on the social rather than the individual, the evolving nature of social conventions, and the interdependence between social structures and economic structures. The conclusions of each approach are therefore often at odds with each other, and continue to be so in spite of empirical assessment of the theories.

The contrast that has been drawn here between the different approaches used in the area of the economics of the family has been highlighted in order to draw attention to the quite fundamental questions posed by our attempts to theorize about a complex reality, which involves human beings. The focus on the individualistic nature of the model we usually use for the economic part of human nature—rational economic man—has been highlighted by its application within what is normally regarded as a social unit: the family. We have seen how neoclassical theory (based on rational economic man) has developed in order to try to capture the interactions involved. We have also seen how theory can develop without rational economic man, that is, by not separating out 'economic' behaviour from other aspects of behaviour.

While we have referred here to feminist theory, it raises more general issues as to whether, and if, we should abstract so much in economics from what is normally dealt with by other social sciences. This raises questions too about how to theorize about human behaviour in other social contexts. We turn now to a social context of particular interest to economists: the firm. This would seem to be a more obviously economic context even than the family.

3.3 Relationships with Other Disciplines: The Theory of the Firm

Just as traditional economic theory treated the household as a black box, the same may be said for the other unit of microeconomic theory: the firm. The firm was seen as a unitary, profit-maximizing entity. Even more than with the family, however, theory has been developed which looks inside the firm to try to understand the process behind, and nature of, decision-making within the firm.[1] The subject matter is less emotive than the family, but it is more complex given the sheer size of many firms and the numbers of people involved in their management.

This subject is also of interest to the economics profession in terms of its relations (both scientific and organizational) with other disciplines. Increasingly the theory of the internal workings of the firm is being developed outside economics departments, with many researchers in economics continuing to treat the firm in a unitary fashion. Is this another case, like the family, of economists taking as given something which we consider to be outside the subject? How far does it matter? In this section we consider how economists have addressed these issues.

In market economics, the price mechanism is central. So how do we analyse an entity which operates apart from the conventional market mechanism? Indeed, how do we explain its existence at all? This question is of more than academic significance. In these times of increasing out-sourcing, the boundaries of institutional arrangements for organizing production are in a state of flux. The existence of marriage is explained by the Becker and game-theoretic approaches not only in terms of economies of scale in production of household goods, but also by preferences (for companionship, commitment, and so on). On the face of it, it would seem less problematic to portray a firm in terms of economic functions; it would appear that that behaviour can be represented more clearly as based on reason than emotion.

The relevant literature originated with Coase (1937), who argued that the rationale for firms is that they are formed where it is not possible to specify complete contracts. Contracts are only complete if provision is made for all possible contingencies, that is, all developments which could affect the outcome, so that there is agreement, for example on how risk is to be shared. An insurance contract, for example, is a complete contract in that it specifies conditions for cover by the policy, and makes explicit any exclusions. The problem is that it is often not possible to think ahead to all possibilities, or how they will affect outcomes. Risk in general is not calculable in the same way as it is for insurance companies who can refer to large data sets for working out frequency distributions; even insurance companies have a catch-all exclusion under 'Acts of God'.

Where complete contracts cannot be made, firms instead coordinate resources internally for the purposes of production by means of a structure of governance, instead of by means of the price mechanism. This structure is designed to address new developments as they arise. Like marriage, this structure depends on property rights, embedded in the legal system. Williamson's (1975) interpretation of this argument was that the market mechanism entails transaction costs; where these are prohibitive, an alternative is for resource allocation to be conducted within the firm. A particular feature of the modern literature has therefore been to focus on the transaction costs where circumstances do not allow complete contracts (see, for example, Williamson and Masten, 1999).

According to this literature, where complete contracts cannot be specified in a market setting, internalizing transactions within the firm limits the scope for opportunistic behaviour. For example, suppose a new product is being developed which requires up-front costs for the supplier (a case considered by Grossman and Hart, 1986). Because this is a new product, the buyer and seller are not in a position to settle on a contract until after it is developed and the nature of the product becomes clear to the buyer. There is an asymmetry in that the contract is only made after the seller has committed resources, and yet competition between buyer and seller ensures that the gains from trade are shared between buyer and seller. Because the seller (correctly) expects that the contract will involve sharing the surplus arising from the product with the buyer, she settles on a lower level of investment than would otherwise be the case. (The level of investment is determined by equating the marginal cost of the investment with the marginal return, which is reduced by the contract with the buyer.) The seller is said to have been 'held up' by the buyer. The alternative is for the buyer to conduct the product development in-house, so that all the surplus is earned by the firm; the higher marginal return then justifies a higher level of investment. Combining separate buyers and sellers within the organization of a firm is thus justified by circumstances which rule out complete market contracts.

This view of the firm rests on the central importance of *incentives* and *conflict*, which determine the influence on and control of individual effort (in the above case, in the form of amount of investment) (see Foss, 1999). Economic actors optimize with respect to a given state of affairs by responding to price incentives and engaging in opportunistic behaviour which may involve conflict with other actors. In this sense there is much similarity with the family hierarchy and game-theoretic theories of the family, respectively. The optimal outcome may be the formation, or break-up, of economic units— firms or families. Once the formation or break-up has taken place, however, it is conventional to treat firms as unitary profit-maximizing structures which respond to external incentives—except in so far as there may be some conflict between management and ownership, in which case, principal–agent theory is employed.

Again, as with the theory of the family, this is only one of a range of possibilities in terms of the focus which economic theory may take. For example, another body of literature on incomplete contracts focuses instead on the internal workings of firms. It enquires into the learning processes and strategies within firms which determine the capacity for coordination, that is, the framework for management (or owners') influence and control. The significance of firms then is seen to lie with how effectively different organizational forms promote learning and co-ordination internally, instead of by market forces.

By focusing on the growth of knowledge and capabilities within firms as a non-deterministic process, this approach also focuses on the uncertainty of expectations. The 'hold-up' problem outlined above arose from the buyer's uncertainty about the nature of the product until it had been developed. But there is also scope for uncertainty about a much wider range of variables which impinge on the profitability of investment. There is uncertainty about production costs, and about demand for the product (which depends on the activities of competitors as well as a range of other factors). This type of uncertainty does not disappear with the formation of the firm; the question remains how organizational structure evolves to cope with this uncertainty, and if possible reduce it. As Brian Loasby, one of the modern pioneers of this approach to the theory of the firm puts it:

The imperfectly-specified contract which characterises the firm implies an imperfectly-specified structure, the central concern and dilemma of organisation theory. (Loasby, 1976, 135)

It is clear that this approach to explaining the existence of the firm leads directly into a subject matter which is also the subject matter of other business-related disciplines, in particular management science. Also, consideration of firms' capabilities in reducing uncertainty about product demand encroaches on the subject matter of marketing. The approach more generally is characterized by detailed case studies as well as abstract theories, and in some cases (for example Porter's (1980) work on strategy) by a listing approach to discussing guidelines for business behaviour rather than the traditional optimizing framework of economics. It is notable that the intermediate microeconomics textbook which focuses most on the internal workings of the firm is addressed to business and marketing students (Earl, 1995).

Does this mean that this approach to the theory of the firm more properly lies outside economics? How far are the internal workings of firms separable from the behaviour of firms as units? On the other hand, if the internal workings of the firm involve the allocation of scarce resources, should this not be treated directly by economic theory? To help us consider further the issue of contracts and their implications for economics, we consider in the next section a particular, and particularly important, contract: the debt contract between banks and borrowing firms.

3.4 The Micro–Macro Distinction: Credit Rationing

Considerable efforts have been made to try to ground macroeconomic theory in microeconomic theory, i.e. to explain macro-results as arising from rational individual behaviour. This aim lies behind many theoretical developments in macroeconomics. Thus, New Keynesian theory, for example, has sought explanations for non-clearing markets at the macro-level by appeal to the conditions facing individual decision-makers.

A bank loan contract is a market contract which is potentially complete. But the interesting issue arises from the risk facing the bank that the borrower might default on the contract. The bank contracts to lend a sum over a fixed period (or an unspecified period in the case of overdraft lending) in exchange for payment of interest at regular intervals. The interest rate may be fixed or variable, and the contract may also involve conditions, such as maintaining a minimum balance in a deposit account with the bank. But the bank faces the risk that the borrower may default on the loan; the bank may receive the return in the form of interest payments, but not the capital if the borrower's investment project fails. The bank must thus form expectations about a return on lending which is potentially highly variable when the risk of default is taken into account. The bank can protect its capital by requiring that the borrower sets collateral as backing; but this in turn requires expectations to be formed as to the future value of the collateral assets. Assessment of the risk and the consequences of default thus inevitably requires the bank to form expectations.

Stiglitz and Weiss (1981) set up a framework designed to incorporate default risk in the expected return on bank loans. Default risk was shown to rise, the higher the interest charge on the loan. Since, in equilibrium, higher risk is associated with higher returns, firms could only earn a return high enough to cover higher bank loan rates if they undertook riskier projects. It is assumed that firms conceal from banks the actual risk attached to the projects they borrow to finance; information is asymmetric. So banks operate by a rule of thumb that lower-risk (and thus lower-return) borrowers drop out when interest charges rise (this is called adverse selection) and that borrowers who continue with loan applications switch to higher-risk projects (moral hazard). On average, therefore, risk rises with interest rates, counteracting the interest return. Banks may therefore keep interest rates lower than market conditions would seem to warrant; the result is an excess demand for loans at the going loan rate, that is, credit rationing. The banks do not have full information on risk by which to distinguish between borrowers in the queue. But the normal mechanism for clearing the market, raising price, would not be in the banks' interests. This result is used to explain the macroeconomic phenomenon that a rise in market interest rates may have an unduly large impact on credit, making interest rate policy a powerful policy tool.

The issue has arisen because of the inability of banks fully to assess risk because borrowers are understood to conceal information. To the extent that the legal system, or collateral, cannot fully compensate the bank in the case of default, the contract is in that sense incomplete. It is clear that there is scope for information problems to be resolved by alternative organizational forms. Thus, for example, in Germany, a representative of the bank may sit on the board of directors of the firm; the bank overcomes information asymmetry and the firm avoids the risk of being rationed by the bank. There is some dispute as to how well these arrangements have achieved this outcome (see, for example, Edwards and Fischer, 1994). The ultimate mechanism for overcoming the asymmetry is to internalize the debt contract within the firm, and indeed it has increasingly been the practice of large corporations to develop their own treasury departments for this purpose.

As we discussed in the previous section, however, internalizing transactions does not necessarily remove uncertainty. The credit-rationing literature presumes that the firm knows the risk it is undertaking. But the organization-theory approach to the firm suggests that this is unlikely to be the case, and would focus on how firms are organized to cope with, and reduce, uncertainty. Another way of approaching the default risk issue is to consider the possibility that both borrower and lender face uncertainty about the returns on projects, possibly with differing sets of expectations and sources of uncertainty. This also opens up the possibility that borrowers and lenders may at times be over-optimistic about default risk, generating 'excessive' levels of credit, while not creating 'enough' at other times. Minsky's (1982) financial instability hypothesis, for example, is built around the consequences for aggregate credit of individual loan contracts between businesses and banks which are influenced by the confidence of each in their own expectations, confidence which fluctuates systematically over the business cycle. Underestimation of default risk encourages 'excessive' credit growth in the upswing; the resulting financial fragility creates the conditions for a downturn, which is exacerbated by the reduction in willingness to lend which comes with weak confidence on the part of the banks. This framework thus offers another explanation for immoderate changes in credit totals.

Both the credit-rationing case and the financial instability hypothesis case are relatively straightforward in their translation from the micro-level to the macro-level, because each deals with systematic changes which can be expected to apply across the economy. The Minsky approach, however, suggests that it is not only macro-events like monetary policy action which can impinge on the micro-level; confidence in expectations may not be best analysed at the individual level, but rather as responding to developments at the macro-level. How we analyse expectations is clearly of great importance. We turn now to consider expectations formation by a particularly important actor in the economy: the central bank.

3.5 Expectations: Model Uncertainty and Monetary Policy

It is becoming apparent as we proceed through different theoretical issues that the issue of expectations formation is of great importance for how we construct many theories. In particular, it appears to be significant how the concept of uncertainty is handled. Expectations are important because they influence action, by households, by firms, and by banks. But they are also important for policy makers. Any policy action must be undertaken with some expectation as to its outcome. But experience shows that, for policy makers as for everyone else, expectations can be systematically mistaken (that is, not just randomly, or stochastically, mistaken). Thus, for example, after the UK Government adopted a strategy of announcing monetary targets from the late 1970s, in the hopes that these targets would in turn be incorporated in private sector expectations, the targets were exceeded by quite large amounts.

Thus, for example, the money supply measure £M3 rose by 20 per cent in the year to February 1981, compared with a target of 7–11 per cent (see Partington, 1989, ch. 12). There were good reasons why the expected monetary growth was exceeded, but the target itself was seen as part of the mechanism to ensure that it was met.

Traditionally forecast errors have often been explained by referring to the fact that the forecasting model assumed that the *ceteris paribus* held. Since this clause is rarely satisfied in practice, systematic errors can be explained by the systematic influence of some development outside the model. The case of excessive monetary growth in the UK in 1981 could be explained, for example, by the unanticipated growth in credit due to increased competition in banking, and to the need to reduce interest rates because the pound was too strong and the economy too weak.

Ideally we would want to include as much as possible in the model on which monetary policy is based, so that the scope for such error was limited. Thus the 1960s and 1970s were characterized by the building up of vast multi-equation macro-models in the UK and the USA. But their continuing failure to perform satisfactorily (see, for example, Clements and Hendry, 1995) has led to an interesting new development in the policy-making literature (see Whitley, 1997) which is also reflected in the theoretical literature (see Blanchard and Fischer, 1989: 505). The emphasis has shifted towards using a range of small models together, as complementary lines of enquiry, rather than one large one. This pluralistic strategy raises important questions about how to choose the appropriate range of models, how to put them together, and how to incorporate different types of knowledge. We explore these questions more fully in Chapters 5 to 8, and particularly section 8.5.

However, in the monetary policy literature there is another interesting angle, where a range of possible macro-models may be regarded as substitutes rather than complements, but there is uncertainty as to which should be the single preferred model. How is the policy maker to choose between them? This predicament is called model uncertainty. It has been addressed by means of what is called robust control theory, whose approach is to minimize the loss which would result from choosing the 'wrong' model (see, for example, Sargent, 1998); the loss is the loss in the central bank's utility as a result of variance in the target variable. This theory, in contrast to optimal control theory (which identifies the one best policy), identifies the policy which is robust in the face of reality deviating systematically from the theory. Specifically, the aim is to identify the monetary policy action which minimizes loss, by means of standard formal techniques. Any model is liable to be inadequate, involving misspecification errors (which are represented by shocks with serially correlated error terms, that is, systematic errors). But in order to specify the loss-minimization function formally, certain restrictions must be placed on these error terms. Thus fairly strict conditions are applied to the relations between the model and the reality it addresses in order to make the model system operational. For robust control theory, therefore, uncertainty means not knowing which is the best model, but not knowing within very strictly quantified bounds (the known dimensions of the misspecification errors). Rudebusch (1999) has pointed out that ideally we would be able to assign probabilities to each model (the likelihood of each being correct) but this is not possible in practice. So instead rules of thumb need to be applied to a particular range of models.

There is some difference of opinion as to whether the policy advice is for more aggressive changes in monetary policy stance than if only one model were chosen outright (as Sargent's model suggests), or more gradual changes, as suggested by other US studies such as Levin, Wieland, and Williams (1998) and Sack (1998). The first of these studies shows that a gradualism rule (small, frequent interest rate changes in the same direction) best fits the optimal rules which emerge from four possible models, where it is not known which is the best model. The Sack study focuses rather on the scope for the central bank to learn which is the best model by monitoring the effects of a gradualist monetary policy; a more aggressive policy could risk compounding error.

Goodhart (1999) makes a similar argument in favour of gradualism. While he does so in the context of UK monetary policy, Goodhart points also to studies which show that gradualism is a common feature of monetary policy practice in a wide range of countries. The Bank of England does specify its uncertainty in the context of inflation forecasting by expressing the forecast in the form of a 'fan chart' (Bank of England, 1999). Rather than model uncertainty, in terms of the choice of model in any broader sense, the concern here is with uncertainty about the parameter values of the chosen 'core' model, and uncertainty about the potential for shocks. The fan is positioned around the core forecast path for inflation, and widens out over time to reflect the cumulative effect of inflation setting out on a higher or lower inflation path. The width of the fan is a measure of uncertainty as to whether the 'correct' parameter values have been chosen. Each quarter, the 'fan' is adjusted in line with actual developments. The Bank of England is thus prepared to put a measure on the relative truth-value of its model within a particular period, that is, on its vulnerability to systematic misspecification errors.

The choice of the core inflation forecast is the outcome of the application of judgement by the Monetary Policy Committee to the range of models on offer. It is interesting that this uncertainty is quantified, in the shape of the fan. But the judgement involved in applying the inflation forecast to monetary policy, and the use of different models and types of evidence, is not apparently quantified. Indeed judgement, arguably by definition, is a non-quantitative faculty; if it were quantitative, it would be possible to incorporate it into the model. This follows Brainard's (1967) early discussion of central bank uncertainty, where uncertainty as to the workings of the private sector can be captured in the 'certainty-equivalence' of stochastic models, but there is further uncertainty about how monetary policy affects the private sector.

The Bank of England (1999) is quite explicit about the partial usefulness of models for designing monetary policy, and the need to exercise judgement. There is a remarkable degree of openness about the content of the judgement exercised, with the publication of Monetary Policy Committee minutes (see Balls, 1998). But there is still much to be explored in terms of how judgement is to be understood, how different types of model can be used together on the basis of judgement, and so on. In particular, what is the relative significance of judgement, and is it something which should be explicitly taught, or for which education should explicitly provide a grounding? We return to these questions in Chapter 9.

We have seen here different uses of the concept of uncertainty. For robust control theorists it is a (constrained) randomness of the worth of a model. For the Bank of England it is something which can be measured as far as inflation forecasting is concerned, but not as far as model uncertainty is concerned. This has been a rather different type of discussion from the one we would have had if we were interested in the expectations of economic agents, but it may be that there are important implications for economic agents who we may reasonably expect to be uncertain as to how to make best sense of the economy. It is a notable feature of Sargent's work (including the study noted above) that he draws direct parallels between the economist's knowledge and the knowledge of economic agents. The focus on uncertainty about models directly focuses our minds on the question of how we, as economists, choose models, and how confident we are in the one(s) we choose. This is the stuff of methodology. But we turn now, finally, to focus on a rather different type of theoretical issue, where uncertainty is undoubtedly present, but this will not be our main focus.

3.6 Welfare Issues: The Distribution of Global Pollution

Monetary policy, like any other economic policy generally (although not necessarily), impacts on at least one group in society at the expense of another. Monetary policy which raises interest rates benefits savers at the expense of borrowers, for example, or addresses inflationary pressures in one part of the country at the expense of other, underemployed, parts of the country. Policy makers may therefore be required to take a view about the relative impacts on different groups in society, as well as the impact on the society as a whole. With government operating at several levels, what constitutes society depends on the level: for local government, concern is with the welfare of the local area, for national government it is with the welfare of the national economy, for supranational bodies, such as the European Union or the International Monetary Fund, concern is with the welfare of collections of countries.

The body of economic thought which is relevant here is welfare economics, which addresses the question of how we decide on those policy measures which are bound to affect some groups in society adversely. One of the classic results in economics, Pareto optimality, is that a policy measure is worthwhile if it increases utility for at least one party while no other party is worse off. The Kaldor–Hicks condition extends this principle to state that a policy is justified if it makes at least one party better off to such an extent that they would be able to compensate the losers and still be better off (see Boadway and Bruce, 1984). For most policies this extension is appropriate, since it is rare for any policy not to make someone worse off.

It was with this grounding in welfare economics that Lawrence Summers allegedly circulated a memo while he was Chief Economist at the World Bank, concerning the global allocation of pollution in the form of toxic waste (as reported in *The Economist*, 8 February, 1992: 66).[3] The memo made the case, on Paretian grounds, for exporting pollution-creating industry to underpopulated developing countries. The exporting developed economies would gain so much by reduced pollution that they could compensate developing countries who took on some of their pollution and still be better off. Recall that we drew on this principle in our discussion of the economic analysis of divorce, where actual compensation is a central issue. The compensation could occur through the price mechanism, with pollution effectively being traded. Since the average level of pollution is lower in developing countries, the argument goes, the marginal disutility of pollution is lower than for the more polluted developed economies. Further, there is a high income elasticity of demand for clean air. This efficiency argument is amplified by pointing out that the marginal cost of pollution in terms of health is higher the higher the life expectancy of the population; and where health was impaired by pollution, the opportunity cost in terms of forgone earnings would be lower than in developed countries. A global redistribution of pollution would thus increase global welfare.

There was a public reaction of outrage. This particular recommendation seemed to flout notions of natural justice, that the polluters should bear the full cost of their pollution. The moral question, as made explicit in the memo, is not addressed. But economists often (in introductory textbooks, for example) specify that economics is a positive subject, in the sense of being value-free; it is for the politicians to make the normative judgements based on values. Economists can make a useful contribution by pointing out the opportunity cost of particular policy actions, the consequences for efficiency, and so on, as input into the decision-making process.

Thus, for example, one area of public policy where economists have made a notable contribution is health and safety. However repellent it may seem to put a monetary value on human life, the fact is that public spending decisions effectively do exactly that. Human life cannot be given infinite value when there is a fixed health budget. The allocation of the budget to different life-saving procedures implicitly involves a finite valuation of human life. Medical procedures can be costed, and their consequences in terms of years of life saved can be estimated. Current spending on dialysis in the UK, for example, suggests that a year of life is valued at around £17,000. Other procedures imply a valuation of a year of life ranging from £15,000 to £25,000. Economists can be very helpful by bringing such judgements to the surface, pointing out any inconsistencies (one government department putting a different value on life from another department, for example) and analysing the implications. Would it be sensible, for example, within the government's budget, to consider spending on road improvements which effectively valued a year of life at £50,000, or to turn down a project which would cost only £10,000 per year of life saved? This is an area where what appears as cold and calculating is actually very helpful to the policy-making process.

Can we understand the outcry over the Summers memo in similar terms, as being due to the positiveness of economics—the economist's refusal to take sides, but simply to point out hard choices? Is it inevitable then that economists risk repelling public sympathy when addressing emotive issues like the valuation of life, just as geneticists may repel public sympathy when conducting experiments in genetic engineering?

Although the *Economist* reporter concludes that 'on the economics, [Summers's] points are hard to answer' (*The Economist*, 1992: 82), the memo does refer to potential objections to the redistribution proposal on such grounds as a lack of adequate markets. There is indeed a range of possible objections within standard economics, without reference to moral issues. Not only does the Kaldor–Hicks criterion require functioning markets, but it also requires that equilibrium conditions are met. A powerful, but underused, theorem developed by Lipsey and Lancaster (1956–7) is the Second Best Theorem, which states that if one condition for general equilibrium is not met, then it may not be optimal to use policy in order to attempt to approach as closely as possible to the general equilibrium position. What would be Pareto optimal if the starting point were Pareto optimality is not necessarily optimal if the starting point is away from equilibrium. It is a substantive question whether or not it is reasonable to treat the global economy as being in equilibrium.

But another possibility which lies behind the outcry, and which economists need to address, is that there are values implicit in economics which prevent it from being truly positive. Some argue that economics inevitably absorbs values to some extent (starting from assumptions made about human nature).

If this is the case, then the economist's advice cannot be portrayed unequivo-
cally as hard if unpalatable truths. This issue is so important, not only for how
we publicly present economics, but also for our understanding of what it is
that we do, that we will pursue this question in more depth in Chapter 5.

3.7 Conclusion

In our selective excursion through some of the economics literature we have
come across a wide range of issues which underlie how we choose to develop
our theory. Faced with an economic problem, and knowing that no model will
apply perfectly, how do we choose which one to use? If we take the pluralist
route, like the Bank of England, questions still remain as to how to choose the
collection of models and how to put together their results.

For many of us, the answer is simple—try a theory and see how well it
performs. But this begs the question of what we mean by 'perform'. For pure
theorists, 'performance' might be judged on the basis of elegance, or results
which conform to our instinctive understanding. But both of these criteria
raise further questions—about the status of the form of theorizing as opposed
to the content, and about the status of our instinctive understanding,
respectively.

You would think that empirical testing would help us choose the best theory. But it is not as easy as that. For one thing, how do we compare results
based on restrictive assumptions with a reality which is not? In any case, the
same evidence can be interpreted very differently according to different theoretical approaches, as we saw in the analysis in this chapter. It is extraordinarily
rare for empirical evidence to settle a theoretical dispute. This is clearly
important for how we understand economics. Since we have focused in this
chapter mainly on the theoretical side of issues, we devote the next chapter to
considering some of these empirical issues.

3.8 Further Reading

For further reading on the specific theoretical areas explored here, by area, see: Schultz
(1974), Papps (1980), Nelson (1996), and Blau (1998) (the economics of the family); Coase
(1937), Williamson (1975), Earl (2000), Foss and Mahnker (2000) (the theory of the firm);
Stiglitz and Weiss (1981), Dow (1998) (credit rationing); Brainard (1967), Goodhart
(1999), Bank of England (1999) (model uncertainty); and Hausman and McPherson
(1996: chs. 2, 14) (distribution of global pollution).

Endnotes

1. The study of management is much older than the study of the internal workings of the family. A classic source is Marshall's (1961/1920) *Principles*.

2. However, the Bank of England (1999) does adhere to a core model, which is supplemented by smaller models and other sources of knowledge. The series of Discussion Papers published by members of staff of the Federal Reserve Board in the USA concerning model uncertainty suggest that thinking has been moving along similar lines in the USA, although the Fed has not issued such a clear methodological statement as the Bank of England.

3. This idea is developed by Hausman and McPherson (1996), who also provide a more detailed analysis of the Summers argument.

4

SOME EMPIRICAL ISSUES

4.1 Introduction

We focused in the previous chapter very much on theoretical issues, and showed how they can be addressed in different ways. But it was not clear how we should choose between theories. Turning in this chapter to the possibility that empirical testing might provide the answer, we will in fact open up another series of issues.

We consider first how far we can use data to test theories in order to find out which one 'works best', that is, which one explains 'the facts' best.[1] We will take as an example the issue of establishing empirically the effect of education, both on earnings and on growth. We find out some clues as to why in practice the question of which is the best model is rarely settled definitively by the data, or at least not in a way such that everyone is in agreement. In fact, much applied work is done in order to decide on the best way of formulating theory (within a particular theoretical framework). Taking this approach further, empirical work can be seen as the starting point for constructing models. We briefly consider the Sims and Hendry approaches to 'letting the data speak for themselves'.

Particularly for policy makers, one of the most important uses of economic theory is to predict the future, and how the future would be different if particular policies were put in place. What is especially difficult to predict is periods of instability, as in foreign exchange crises or financial crises more generally. Predictive models require a specification of the structure of economic relationships, but this structure may change, either gradually as a result of changing behaviour patterns, for example, or more dramatically, as in the case of a financial crisis. We therefore take as an example the finance model of Black, Merton, and Scholes which was the basis for prediction of portfolio risk; the model worked well in a stable environment, but not when particular markets became highly unstable. Predictive failure in this case had dramatic consequences. But was there any alternative? How did the econometric models designed to predict currency crises fare?

Further, data can provide the basis for institutional design. One of the requirements of countries joining European Monetary Union is that the central bank is made independent of government. While some countries, like the USA, have maintained central bank independence since the modern system was introduced in 1914, other countries, like New Zealand, have only recently taken this step. The issue is whether central bank independence increases the bank's capacity to control inflation. We see in section 4.4 an account of how economists have gone about testing this proposition.

4.2 Empirical Work as Theory Testing: Education and Earnings; Education and Growth

We have seen that there is scope for different theoretical treatments of particular economic issues. One of the purposes of econometrics is to see how well theories conform to observed values of variables. This poses two challenges: expressing theory in such a way that it has an empirical counterpart, and expressing different theories in such a way that the data allow us to discriminate between them. These two challenges are related: the finer points of theories which differentiate them at the theoretical level may not have empirical counterparts which allow them to be differentiated at the empirical level.

The issue of empirical counterparts is wide-ranging. At one level, a concept may be measurable in principle, but not measured in practice. This is often the case with regional variables, for example, for which data are not available. While regional economists can develop theories without data, data are nevertheless important both for testing theories against evidence, and also in identifying the nature of the policy questions to be addressed by theory. At another level, a theoretical concept may not in principle be measurable in any case, as is the case with interpersonal comparisons of utility, or, as discussed in section 3.5, uncertainty understood as unquantifiable risk. At yet another level, there is the issue of whether the state of general equilibrium has a counterpart in reality. This was important for assessing the Summers proposal on global pollution. Coddington (1975) has explored the issue of how far there is an empirical counterpart to an Arrow–Debreu equilibrium. But it is one of the core features of rational expectations theory that every observed state is a state of equilibrium (albeit temporary); the argument is that rational agents would be irrational if they were not to respond to disequilibrium signals and move the system to equilibrium.

The solution is often to express theory in a reduced form (the result of reducing a system of simultaneous equations to one equation). This means, in microeconomics, not seeking empirical counterparts to the components of rational decision-making as such, but instead testing only the outcome of this process which theory suggests. Thus, for example, the evidence may suggest that higher product demand is associated with lower price; the demand curve slopes downwards. This 'revealed preference' can be said to justify demand theory in the absence of the scope for directly testing utility theory.

In macroeconomics, there is from the start a focus on aggregates rather than individual components (although increasingly rational individual behaviour has been embedded in macroeconomic theory). This yields a system of simultaneous equations representing the different sectors of the economy: a consumption function, an investment function, and so on. These elements of the structure of a macro-model may themselves embody (without making explicit) detailed analysis of microeconomic behaviour. But even then the empirical test may refer only to the reduced form of this system, based on the national income identity. As with microeconomics, the data which are consistent with the reduced form may not allow us to infer much about the underlying model.

The outcome of this practice of estimating reduced form equations is what is called the identification problem, highlighted by Sims (1980).[2] This is the problem that reduced form results may be compatible with a range of structural relationships. Even if the results are consistent with one theory, they may also be consistent with another. This is most clearly the case when we consider the estimation of demand and supply functions from price and quantity data, where one or both curves may have shifted during the period of observation.[3] Thus, to take a simple example, if we observe over time changing interest rates but a fixed money stock, is this evidence of a vertical money supply curve and a shifting demand curve, or of demand and supply curves which have both shifted in such a way as to keep the money stock constant? Theory can suggest the shape of demand and supply curves, and shift factors, but as long as we cannot directly estimate the structure of the model (demand and supply curves separately) we cannot be sure that we have identified the structure correctly (see Cooley and LeRoy, 1981).

The practice in much of the empirical monetary economic literature has been to put the focus on identifying the demand for money function, and shifts in it, even though there is considerable justification in alternative literatures for giving equal weight to the money supply function, or the credit supply function. The theoretical priors are that supply conditions are exogenous and that the underlying demand for money function is stable, so that the data have been able to provide estimates of this function and its shifts. As Handa (2000: 207) puts it, in his review of the literature:

This prolific variety of attempts and deviations from the standard money demand equation [during the last three decades] almost gives one the impression of a field dominated by data mining and the *ad hoc* constructions of a profession desperate at finding a stable money demand function to back its theory. While this may sound a rather harsh assessment, it does serve as a reminder of the severe difficulties in finding a stable money demand function during the ongoing innovations of the recent decades.

Let us consider the question of empirical theory-testing in more detail by looking at two related literatures: one deals with the effect of education on earnings at a micro-level; this in turn forms the basis for endogenous growth theory which assesses the effect of education on growth at the macro-level.

Human capital theory suggests that the decision made by individuals about how much education to undertake is based on an assessment of earnings forgone during education relative to the increase in earnings which would result from education, that is, a form of present-value calculation.[4] The benchmark is long-run competitive equilibrium, where supply and demand for workers at each schooling level are equated and no worker wishes to alter her schooling level. For each worker in equilibrium, the present value of education represents a return equal to the alternative return on forgone earnings, taken as the interest rate. Optimizing behaviour can then be shown to explain the optimal level of education and thus the equilibrium relationship which explains earnings-as-a-function-of-education, on the one hand, and employment-experience-rather-than-education on the other.

But it is not feasible to estimate directly the rational calculation which produces this conclusion. So, in order to test human capital theory, Willis (1986: 529) shows how studies start with the reduced form of a simple earnings function, derived from Mincer's pioneering work, whereby earnings are shown as a function of years of education and years of employment over a lifetime:

$$\ln y = \beta_0 + \beta_1 s + \beta_2 x + \beta_3 x^2 + u \qquad (4.1)$$

where y is annual earnings, s is years of schooling, x is the length of labour force experience, and u is a residual with zero mean.

This function has been highly successful empirically, in the sense that earnings are indeed closely correlated to years of education and of labour force experience (where the coefficients β_1 and β_2 are positive and β_3 negative). Willis proceeds to explore the rationale for this success in human capital theory. The decision variable for individuals is s. Logic suggests that there is a trade-off between the opportunity cost in the form of forgone earnings while gaining education on the one hand, and a higher rate of earnings as a result of education, so that embedded in the decision is an internal rate of return to education which determines the individual's choice of s. Assuming that the human capital theory explanation is correct, then the statistical estimation of the Mincer equation allows estimation of internal rates of return to education.

Griliches (1977) raised a range of issues with the estimation of earnings functions, including the issue of how the estimated coefficients should be interpreted. How far can we use estimated functions to identify the underlying causal relationship? Willis responds by giving a good indication of the extensive innovative theoretical and econometric developments designed to pin down the relationship between theory and data on earnings. But we still cannot be *sure* of what they tell us about human capital theory, that is, there is a problem with identifying the structure of the model from the reduced form. As Willis (1986: 543) points out, optimal human capital models do not typically have a closed form solution, that is, the functional form for life-cycle earnings is not known, and many of the relevant concepts (such as human capital) are not measured (or measurable?). Further he explains the extent of simplifying assumptions, such as that the data represent equilibrium outcomes, that individuals can predict the rate of return to them of education, and so on.

Blinder (1976) suggests that the Mincer equation be approached quite differently, without being tied to the specific assumptions suggested by Mincer's formulation of human capital theory. Blinder examines a range of assumptions made by Mincer which determine functional form, but which are challenged by the data. Thus, for example, Mincer assumes that years of work experience and of education are mutually exclusive, so that years of work experience can be proxied by years of schooling, plus five, subtracted from age. But Blinder points out that this formulation does not produce satisfactory empirical results for women, who may combine education and work, and also have years devoted to child-rearing rather than paid work or education. He argues accordingly that 'the choice of functional form . . . ought to be made on an *empirical* basis rather than a *theoretical* one' (Blinder, 1976: 9, emphasis in original).

The empirical analysis is essentially based on correlation, and thus cannot demonstrate anything definitive about causation. More recent work has developed dynamic extensions of the Mincer model by introducing lagged values of variables in order to identify sequencing. This gives a better indication of possible causal sequence, but there is still considerable controversy as to how far temporal sequence can be interpreted as establishing causation; both what is thought of as the cause of an effect and the effect itself may be the joint effects of another variable.

While Blinder considered different formulations within the human capital theory framework, the earnings equation can in fact be explained by a wide range of structural models, that is, a wide range of explanatory forces. For example, one alternative approach would emphasize the conventional nature of the labour market and earnings patterns in particular. Thus, the emphasis might be put on segmented labour markets, differentiating a primary market, where workers earn rents, from a secondary market where they do not (see

Gordon, Edwards, and Reich, 1982, for example). Market segmentation is also analysed in the literature in terms of gender and race. The effect of education on earnings, according to this approach, depends on the earnings conventions which apply in the relevant segment of the labour market. Much of the more recent work on earnings and education has involved breaking down aggregates in order to identify the characteristics of different segments of the labour market. Further, recent work on job satisfaction raises questions about the human capital model's presumption that utility from work derives solely from earnings (see, for example, Oswald, 1997). If job satisfaction is indeed also a significant factor, we need to consider the relationship between education and job satisfaction in analysing behaviour with respect to education plans. Valuable statistical information is being built up in order to address these questions. But the possibility of identifying the 'true' causal mechanisms underlying the data still eludes us.

The difficulty of inferring something about the 'truth' of theories from reduced-form equations applies even more forcefully in growth theory, which builds upon human capital theory to macroeconomic aggregate relationships which apply in the long run. Traditional, neoclassical growth theory is built on micro-foundations drawn from axioms of optimizing individual and firm behaviour to construct a reduced-form mathematical relationship which shows aggregate income (Y) as a function of labour (L) and capital (K) inputs. The term $A(t)$ is taken to represent the impact of technology which improves over time, t. A typical equation takes the form of:

$$Y = A(t)F(K,L). \tag{4.2}$$

Given population growth (and thus growth of the labour supply) and the state of technology, any unexplained growth in income can then only come from an increase in the capital stock. This theory has been subjected to empirical testing by estimating the coefficients of this relationship and testing to see how well it explains actual growth rates. These studies have suggested that the state of technology is empirically important (that is, labour and capital did not fully explain growth rates), putting a focus on technological change as the exogenous engine for growth.

More recently, attention has shifted from trying to endogenize technical change in general (that is, independent of capital and labour inputs) to endogenizing the other contributors to productivity, notably labour productivity. This reflects a natural drive to endogenize as much as possible, that is, to explain as much as possible. But it is much more difficult to establish the direction of causation between endogenous variables; an exogenous variable like technological change is, by virtue of its classification as exogenous, causal.[5]

We are referring here to the post-neoclassical endogenous growth theory apparently drawn on by the UK Chancellor of the Exchequer Gordon Brown.[6]

Its policy significance is that, while technological change in the long-run is available to all economies (so that all economies' growth rates would be expected to converge as technological change is globalized), labour productivity is something which is amenable to policy manipulation, allowing different growth rates across economies. Whether or not international growth rates converge is taken as an empirical test to discriminate between neoclassical growth theory and endogenous growth theory. If growth rates didn't converge, then that might be thought to contradict neoclassical growth theory, although we would still not be able to demonstrate that lack of convergence was due to different education policies. But even this kind of broad agreement is ruled out by the fact that there is not a consensus on the first question, whether or not growth rates actually converge.[7]

According to the endogenous growth approach, labour productivity may increase because of learning-by-doing (that is, as a by-product of employment), or it can increase through education outside employment. A series of mathematical models has been developed, which can be grouped around the idea that education provides a one-off increase in labour productivity, raising the rate of economic growth, or the idea that it also increases the capacity to absorb technological change into the production process. The aim is to determine the optimal level of education expenditure in terms of which would yield the highest rates of economic growth. The models inevitably require a series of assumptions to be made. Thus, for example, the Lucas (1988) human capital model portrays education as an investment decision by the individual on a par with capital investment; time spent in education means time not in employment (just as capital expenditure precludes consumption expenditure). Education yields the same increase in productivity across the board, and at all levels of education. The decision is based on a rate of time preference and a coefficient of risk aversion, but, since these are unidentifiable in aggregate, empirical application simply focuses on the coefficient of the labour variable in the reduced form equation.

Tremendous efforts have been made to get round the identification problem in areas such as this. As a result, researchers often argue that the evidence does support a particular theory relative to others. But since equally respected researchers can all be convinced that the same evidence supports quite different theories, it is clear that the identification problem has not been solved satisfactorily. Thus, endogenous growth theory is put forward as an alternative to neoclassical theories on the basis of the pure theory model which comes before the econometrics. But since the econometrics consists basically of correlation analysis applied to a reduced form of the theory which involves a similar range of variables to neoclassical theory it is not at all clear what can be distinguished.

The doyen of the neoclassical approach, Robert Solow (1994), does not accept the econometric approach to unpacking the explanation for growth. He argues that his treatment of technical change as exogenous does not mean that it cannot be analysed (his model is partial rather than general) and that such analysis must take account of the unquantifiable uncertainty associated with the innovation process. He sees the extraction of workable hypotheses from case studies as a more promising avenue than the endogenous-growth theory foundation on the intertemporally optimizing representative agent. In other words, he advocates an alternative source of evidence from standard econometrics.

Another tack was taken by Sims (1980), who advocated a quite different form of econometrics in order to address the identification problem. Rather than starting with a structural model which in most cases could only be estimated in reduced form, Sims advocated 'letting the data speak for themselves', and in particular using lag structures to tease out which variables are causing changes in which. This involves vector autoregression, or VAR, techniques which are designed to present the data in such a way as to suggest theory, rather than the other way round. The result has been a major research programme aimed at generating stylized facts. Thus if two data series are found to be 'cointegrated', then there is a strong long-run relationship between them. However, while the break from standard structural models has been refreshing, opening up possibilities for new theoretical structures, it is not clear where the theoretician goes with such results, in that they are still in effect reduced-form versions of (possibly some other) structural system. There has recently been some reversion to the traditional structural-system approach, but with enhanced techniques to address the identification problem, that is, trying to estimate the structure itself (see, for example, Hall, 1995).

A third strand in econometrics is the one pioneered by Hendry (1993), which combines a 'letting the data speak for themselves' approach with some theoretical priors.[8] These priors range from the initial selection of variables to be considered, to the theoretical understanding of long-run trends as reflecting full employment equilibrium, incorporating the classical dichotomy between nominal and real variables. The task is seen as identifying a good theoretical account of short-run disequilibrium processes, for which general equilibrium theory offers few established propositions. His 'general-to-specific' approach is designed to take account of a wide range of possible disequilibrium processes, to be narrowed down by econometric techniques. But one of the check-list of rules Hendry suggests by which to go about the narrowing-down process is to check for consistency with theory. So the data are not independent arbiters.

Experience of the Sims approach has demonstrated the limits to identifying theory from purely statistical relationships, while the Hendry approach has made the resulting issues much more explicit. It highlights the complex

combination of statistics, theoretical priors, and judgement which character-
izes applied economics. Conducting theoretical development and empirical
work independently of each other appears to be problematic whichever one
we start with. But how to integrate the two effectively is the hard question.

4.3 Empirical Work as a Basis for Prediction: Predicting
Financial Crises

Empirical work in economics is not necessarily designed to test theory or to
guide its development; it is also used for prediction. Indeed, many non-
academic economists are employed specifically for that purpose. Governments need economists to predict what will happen to the economy, and to
predict how that will be changed by government policy. Companies need
economists to predict the macroeconomic environment in which they will be
operating as well as specific market developments.

Many macroeconomic modellers refined their large structural models of
the economy in the 1980s, in an attempt to address Sims's critique, and to
improve forecasting success. One of the difficulties which Sims had addressed
was that it was difficult to identify the process of expectations formation and
learning from aggregative data. Large models, such as the Fair model in the
USA and the Minford model in the UK addressed this problem by incorporating rational expectations (see Hall, 1995). But the large structural models have
not had a good forecasting record (see, for example, Hall, 1995; Makridakis
and Wheelwright, 1979), so that disenchantment has led to recourse to different approaches (although Hall (1995) is optimistic that the problems with
structural forecasting models will eventually be resolved). Among these
approaches is the development of smaller, partial models.

In section 3.5 we saw the importance of forecasting for policy makers. But
we all rely on forecasts of some kind in all economic activity. When the
economic structure is stable, as in the hey-day of the large forecasting models,
forecasting is relatively straightforward. It is when the structure changes that
forecasters face the biggest challenge (see Clements and Hendry, 1995); the
VAR approach is more attuned to pick up structural change from the data
than are the structural models which start from a presumed structural form.

The most challenging task for economic forecasters is to *anticipate* structural change, that is, situations where what underpinned past trends is dis-
rupted. Thus for example the European Central Bank organized a conference
on model uncertainty (see Duisenberg, 1999, and section 3.5) to discuss how to
predict the outcome of monetary policy under the new institutional arrangements of EMU. Some economic relationships can be regarded as fairly stable
over time. But financial markets is one area where there is considerable scope

for structural change. We will consider here an economic model used for prediction in derivatives markets, and then the more general issue of predicting financial crises.

In 1995, the academics, Bob Merton, Myron Scholes, and (the late) Fischer Black set up the company Long-Term Capital Management (LTCM) to make practical use of a mathematical framework they had developed for pricing derivative products. This framework combined the solutions to the major, long-standing, problem of how to estimate risk (the future variance of the stock price).[9] The implication was of tremendous importance for economics, that risk was measurable in practice as well as in theory.

Options offer the possibility that risk can be hedged; they are the right to buy or sell a stock in the future at a pre-specified price. The Black–Scholes model offered a means of pricing options (the value of having such an option) on the basis of current stock prices. The key was that the risk attached to the option was already embedded in current stock prices; it wasn't necessary to estimate a separate risk premium attached to an option. This allowed a strategy of 'dynamic hedging', whereby risk is managed by active rebalancing of underlying positions rather than by arranging offsetting hedges directly. Merton and Scholes were awarded the Nobel Prize in economics in 1997 for their innovation.[10]

The company was highly successful, generating returns of over 40 per cent to investors. But this success was interrupted in the summer of 1997 when the Thai property market collapsed, with widespread repercussions for Thai assets in general. The effects on world financial markets of the ensuing financial collapse in South-East Asia were exacerbated by Russia's default on its foreign debt in August 1998. The presumed randomness of stock prices on which the Black–Scholes model relies was replaced by massive one-way movements in asset values. While other investors reacted by cutting borrowing and going liquid (adding to the downward pressure on asset prices), LTCM continued to borrow, confident in the ability of their model to eliminate risk. The result was the collapse of LTCM, and its subsequent ignominious rescue.

The official report to the US President (Working Group on Financial Markets, 1999) identified the problems which led to LTCM's downfall as threefold:

1. The scale of capital losses exceeded what conventional risk models regarded as probable.
2. Several markets were shown to be more closely correlated in their movements than was assumed.
3. The market's reaction caused a shortage of liquidity.

This experience illustrates vividly the dangers posed for prediction by structural change; the capacity for simultaneous, massive, rapid changes in value in a range of financial markets means that structural change may take the form of a crisis. But if we could predict structural change, including financial crises, then perhaps there is still scope, as the Merton–Scholes model implies, for risk to be eliminated.[11]

Clearly the 1997–8 financial crisis was not successfully predicted. Several models had been designed to predict crises, so there have been various post-mortems on how they performed. Berg and Pattillo (1999), for example, evaluate three models designed to predict currency crises by assessing how well they would have predicted the 1997 crisis on the basis of data up to 1996. The Kaminsky, Lizondo, and Reinhart (1998) model uses the signals approach; fifteen crisis indicators are selected, and threshold levels established such that, if the value moves beyond the threshold, a crisis signal is issued. Correlation analysis on past crises (up to 1995) provides estimates of the probability of crisis ensuing following the activation of each signal. But applying the estimates out of a sample (to 1996) shows the model not to be very helpful, predicting crises where none occurred, while the signals were weak for crisis countries like Indonesia and Thailand. The Frankel and Rose (1996) model uses probit regression analysis (suitable for discontinuous variables) to a wider range of countries, and performs well for in-sample crises (up to 1996), but does not satisfactorily predict the 1997 crisis. The same applies to the third model considered, that of Sachs, Tornell, and Velasco (1996), which uses a 'crisis index'. Berg and Pattillo suggest some refinement of the list of crisis indicators in the light of the 1997–8 crisis. But the conclusion is drawn that, while we can improve on our capacity to predict vulnerability to crisis by considering additional variables, it is inevitably extraordinarily difficult to predict the onset and timing of crisis.

The reasons for this difficulty are explored in greater detail by Furman and Stiglitz (1998). It is clear that the 1997–8 crisis was not, as has traditionally been considered, the outcome purely of domestic mismanagement. Indeed, as the application of currency crisis models shows, the signals for the crisis were very weak. Rather Furman and Stiglitz base their assessment on the view that financial markets are inherently unstable.[12] The implication is that, while we can improve our capacity to predict crises, and we can implement policies to reduce financial market instability, the risk of crisis cannot either be fully measured or eliminated. Referring back to the LTCM episode, risk may indeed be measurable within stable structures. But, particularly in financial markets, the risk of the kind of structural change which causes such problems for the Black–Scholes model is not itself measurable. The strong implication is that uncertainty (or unquantifiable risk) cannot be eliminated.

The problems posed by predicting structural change apply, usually less dramatically, in a wide range of circumstances. Business decisions have to be based on forecasts of demand, costs, competitor behaviour, etc., all of which are vulnerable to structural shifts. In the public sector, the Bank of England, for example, publishes an *Inflation Report*, on whose inflation predictions monetary policy is based. Account needs to be taken of the possibility of structural shifts during the forecast period. Thus, for example, in the May 2000 *Inflation Report*, account had to be taken of the fact that the pound had increased in value relative to the euro. It was widely expected at the time of publication that the pound would fall in value relative to the euro, but when and by how much was impossible to predict, not least because the underlying causes of the high exchange rate were not well understood. So the inflation forecasting exercise had to proceed without incorporating a major realignment of exchange rates, even though there was a strong possibility that one would take place in the next quarter, with direct consequences for the UK price level. This inescapable uncertainty gap contrasts with the detailed technical work which goes into those aspects of the forecasting exercise which are more confidently thought of as being based on a stable structure.

While the predicted effects of public policy require an awareness of the possibility of structural shifts which might confound forecasting exercises, the government itself may in fact initiate a structural shift as a matter of public policy. Such a policy is based on a forecast of the effect of the change in structure. We consider an example in the next section.

4.4 Empirical Work as the Basis for Institutional Design: Independent Central Banks

There has been considerable emphasis in public policy in recent years on instituting structural change, notably in the direction of liberalizing markets. European monetary integration is a particular case of instituting change in market structure generally and also promoting structural economic change in the direction of convergence. One provision of the Maastricht Treaty, which set out the final stages of European monetary unification, was that members' central banks should be independent of government. The rationale was that, if monetary policy were not compromised by political interference, then inflation control would be more effective. In other words, the prediction was that if central banks were made independent, then inflation would be reduced.

Clearly such a prediction would be difficult to make on the basis of models with fixed structures, and there is no established modelling framework by which to represent the process of such a structural change. Instead, the argument has been reinforced by a succession of empirical studies which compare the inflation performance of countries with different central banking arrangements (see Alesina and Summers's (1993) summary). These studies indicate a statistical correlation between the degree of central bank independence and low inflation, but no correlation with variability in unemployment. Central bank independence thus seems to offer governments a 'free lunch' (Grilli, Masciandaro, and Tabellini, 1991, 375). But Alesina and Summers are quite circumspect about drawing such a strong conclusion. There is, for example, the issue of how satisfactory the index of central bank independence is as a measure (see Akhtar, 1995). But many (such as Mishkin, 1992: 402) have used the empirical results as strong evidence for the benefits of central bank independence.

The empirical results in turn can draw support from rational expectations models where the central bank and the government have different rates of time preference; governments are understood to be focused on the term of government. Making monetary policy the sole preserve of central banks therefore generates confidence that the long-term goal of controlling inflation will be pursued, and this is factored into inflationary expectations.

In his review of this literature, Jenkins (1996) considers also additional factors which theory suggests may explain inflation performance, such as exchange rate regime and labour market structure. If these are important, then comparing countries which differ in other respects than just degree of central bank independence makes it difficult to interpret the results. We cannot conduct controlled experiments whereby all the subjects differ only in the factor in which we are interested, here central bank independence. Jenkins reviews studies which indicate that these other factors are indeed significant, indicating that the earlier studies suffer from the omission of relevant variables. This implies that simply making a central bank independent may not be sufficient to reduce inflation if the other relevant factors are unfavourable.

This example illustrates two recurring issues. First, correlation between a limited set of variables, while supported by a full theoretical structure, cannot demonstrate that structure to be the best one. The inflation process is a complex one, for which central bank independence may be an insufficient cure. Countries where inflation control has been most successful may be those where the will to control inflation is highest among the general population, and which therefore also have independent central banks, for example. Second, it has proved to be a persistent problem how to measure the degree of central bank independence. It is a matter not only of regulatory provision (who appoints whom, and for how long, for example), but also of practice (are there close communications between government and central bank, for example). Much effort has been devoted to constructing a satisfactory index (see, for example, Grilli, Masciandaro, and Tabellini, 1991, and Cukierman, Webb, and Neyapti, 1992). But the issue of how well the index really measures central bank independence persists, clouding the interpretation of the empirical studies.

4.5 Conclusion

Economics is a study of the economy, so you would think that, for all the difficulties we face in constructing theories, we could settle which were the best theories simply by looking at the economy. But we have seen in this chapter why this is not as straightforward as it seems. Nor is it straightforward to see empirical work as the starting-point for theory, because the way in which empirical work is done, and indeed the data themselves, require some framework as a starting point.

Among the particular issues which arose during this discussion were the following:

- It is difficult to identify the detail of structural models from data, as opposed to summary, 'reduced form' versions of the models.
- It is therefore difficult to assess the relative worth of different structural models, not least because it is difficult to discriminate between them using data.
- Since economists cannot in general conduct controlled experiments, it is difficult to isolate particular economic relationships.
- While models rely on the *ceteris paribus* clause to isolate relationships, successful prediction requires anticipation of what will happen when the clause is not met in practice.
- More generally, successful prediction relies on the structure represented in the model being stable over the prediction period. The potential for structural instability thus poses problems for prediction. If some markets are inherently unstable, then unquantifiable risk (uncertainty) is something which requires particular attention.
- The measurement issue extends also to the general question of finding empirical counterparts for theoretical concepts. Empirical work is limited to those things which can be measured, but is sensitive to how they are measured.

Given these difficulties it is extraordinary that economics has achieved as much as it has. But it should be more clear, from this chapter and Chapter 3, why there is so much scope for disagreement which cannot be settled by appeal to the facts, and why predictions need to be hedged about, and often turn out to be wrong. Theory needs to simplify, given the complexity of social systems, but it has to be compared against evidence which reflects the complexity of that system. Further, to be useful, it needs to provide the analysis and predictions to guide public policy making.

Measurement issues are crucial in a variety of respects. There are issues at the simple level of different studies using different data series. But there is the fundamental issue of finding measures for the theoretical concepts we use. Herein, I would suggest, lies much of the problem with the public perception of economics. There are some things, we could argue, which are not measurable, like happiness, or the design of institutions (like central banks). Yet, if individual welfare is what we assume individuals maximize, and if social welfare is what governments maximize, then we need to have some indication of what this is. This is why we use per capita GDP as a proxy for human welfare; the objections to the measure are well known, but it is not clear what the alternative is. Similarly, it is difficult to construct an index of central bank independence, but if we are to make an empirical study of the effects of independence, some measure has to be found.

The popular misconception is that economists only care about those things we can measure. Thus it is common for it to be asserted, with a note of resentment, that we 'should' use supermarkets because it is more *economic* to do so, even if we derive more pleasure from using small neighbourhood shops. An economist would in fact address this question by trying to *measure* the relative satisfaction gained from using small local shops rather than the supermarket, comparing actual use with transport costs and relative prices. Economists are misunderstood when they are thought of as caring *only* about what can be assigned a monetary value.

But, given the need to quantify economic variables in some form, there remains the issue of how to proceed. Thus, the degree of central bank independence, or the vulnerability to crisis, tends to be measured by an index; the measure is designed to rank rather than assign absolute values. This represents a compromise, assigning values to concepts which are difficult to quantify, but without any expectation that they can be assigned a probability distribution.[13]

But we have seen the problems that LTCM ran into from presuming that risk could be quantified (in probabilistic terms). Unquantifiable risk raises rather different issues from those discussed above. If it is in the *nature* of financial markets that they face unquantifiable risk, then it is not just a matter of the difficulty of finding empirical counterparts to theoretical concepts, but also the question of the theory itself, and whether or not it accounts for unquantifiable risk. The issue is in fact broader than financial markets in that all markets may be said to face unquantifiable risk to some degree. If it is by definition something which we cannot measure, how do we as economists deal with it?

We saw in the last chapter that the issue of uncertainty has been raised also with respect to the knowledge of economists, not just economic agents. We may be said to be uncertain as to which is the best model of the economy. Put another way, we do not in practice have certain knowledge, as economic agents or as economists. But we do have knowledge and enough confidence in it, often, to act on it. So how do we go about building up (albeit uncertain) knowledge? By now it should be apparent that there a lot of fundamental issues involved in developing economic theory, doing empirical work and providing useful advice to governments and the private sector. We turn now to a literature whose job it is to address these questions.

4.6 Further Reading

For further reading on the specific areas of empirical work explored here, by area, see: Mincer (1974), Gordon, Edwards, and Reich (1982), Oswald (1997) (education and earnings); Pasinetti (2000), Solow (2000) (growth theory); Working Group on Financial Markets (1999) (LTCM); Furman and Stiglitz (1998), Arestis and Glickman (forthcoming) (South-East Asia crisis); and Jenkins (1996), Berger, de Haan, and Eijffinger (2001) (central bank independence).

Endnotes

1. We put 'the facts' in inverted commas because we will find that what is a 'fact' is itself an issue. We will address this aspect of the question first in section 4.5, and then drawing on the methodological literature in Ch. 6.

2. The identification problem has a much longer history; see Morgan (1990, ch. 6).

3. The very notion of supply and demand curves itself presumes underlying theoretical propositions. Some economists prefer to conduct their analysis without supply curves and demand curves; see Earl (1995: 24–6).

4. See Willis (1986) for an account of the literature, and Mincer (1974) for the classic source.

5. The econometrics literature has attempted to address this issue by considering degrees of exogeneity (specifically 'weak' and 'strong' exogeneity).

6. See Aghion and Howitt (1998) for an account of the literature.

7. See Durlauf (1996) for a discussion of the technical issues involved, referring to other papers in the same issue of the *Economic Journal*; see also Barro and Sala-i-Martin (1995: chs. 11 and 12).

8. See Pagan (1987), Darnell and Evans (1990), and Gerrard (1995) for different perspectives on this range of approaches to econometrics.

9. The second innovation was Bob Merton's solution to the problem that current prices change during the time that the option price calculation is being made. He developed a method of constant recalculation.

10. The press release issued by the Royal Swedish Academy of Sciences (1997) explained the idea behind their valuation method as follows:

Consider a so-called European call option that gives the right to buy one share in a certain firm at a strike price of $50, three months from now. The value of this option obviously depends not only on the strike price, but also on today's stock price: the higher the stock price today, the greater the probability that it will exceed $50 in three months, in which case it pays to exercise the option. As a simple example, let us assume that if the stock price goes up by $2 today, the option goes up by $1. Assume also that an investor owns a number of shares in the firm in question and wants to lower the risk of changes in the stock price. He can actually eliminate that risk completely, by selling (writing) two options for every share that he owns. Since the portfolio thus created is risk-free, the capital he has invested must pay exactly the same return as the risk-free market interest rate on a three-month treasury bill. If this were not the case, arbitrage trading would begin to eliminate the possibility of making a risk-free profit. As the time to maturity approaches, however, and the stock price changes, the relation between the option price and the share price also changes. Therefore, to maintain a risk-free option-stock portfolio, the investor has to make gradual changes in its composition.

11. The thinking behind the Black–Scholes formula has application beyond options markets to any situation where the scope for flexibility needs to be priced.

12. This was a conclusion reached by Minsky in the 1950s (see e.g. Minsky 1982).

13. This type of data can be analysed using non-parametric techniques (see, e.g. Siegel and Castellan, 1988). See Finch and McMaster (forthcoming) for an explicit argument in the context of economics.

5

THE SCOPE AND PURPOSE
OF ECONOMICS

5.1 Introduction

So far, we have been drawing attention to a range of important questions in economics, concerning what economics is about (should it cover family relations, for example?), what we can reasonably hope to aim for in economics (can we use empirical testing to decide which are the best theories?), how we should go about constructing theory, and so on. These questions do not have ready answers because economics deals with a complex subject matter. Like any social science, economics deals with creative individuals (endowed with emotion as well as reason), and social systems (which are complex, and which change over time). Economists have for long grappled with these questions, within the field of what we now refer to as methodology.

Methodology is concerned with the way in which we do economics, how we build up knowledge about the economy and what status that knowledge has. The way in which methodology itself is done has also changed over the years. It in turn is not based on a fixed set of ideas; how to build up methodological knowledge is therefore itself a matter for discussion. We will proceed in the following chapters to explore this territory.

We begin by considering what the methodology literature has to say about specifying the subject matter of economics, and what we are aiming for when we build up knowledge about it. If we start with a general statement, that the primary goal of economics is to address real-world economic problems, then one of the concerns of methodology might be to assess theories according to how well they achieve this goal. So this general criterion needs to be made more concrete; how do we recognize the capacity of a theory to address real-world problems?

The approach to methodology dating from the late nineteenth century and still represented by some in the field today is indeed to consider how economics *should* be done, or at least to express judgements as to how it has been done. In discussing the concept of progress, Backhouse (2000) suggests that the characteristics of a perfect theory would be logical consistency, consistency with the evidence, and predictive success. As he points out, since no theory can come up to such a standard, it becomes a question of how to judge how far different theories fall short. We will see that there has been considerable debate over what weights to assign to the different criteria—for example, is it more important for the central bank to be able to predict inflation or for its theory of inflation to be completely logically *consistent*? We explore the way in which discussion has developed within this prescriptive approach to methodology in Chapter 6.

This approach to methodology ran into difficulties, not just because it was difficult to agree on how to assign weights, but also because each of the criteria themselves proved to be problematic. The methodology field has thus shifted to a focus on providing descriptive accounts of what economists actually do, including description of the criteria which economists actually use to guide practice (whether or not they make this explicit). We leave the discussion of these more descriptive developments in modern methodology until Chapter 7. But the element of judgemental methodology has not disappeared, and there has been renewed debate over how methodological discussion might shed light on how to apply the general criterion of capacity to address real-world problems. It may be that economists are giving priority to a different goal, which is increasing our understanding of how the economic system works. This goal is the focus of Chapter 8, where we explore the most recent literature.

But, as a way of leading into all of this literature, we grapple with the first, basic questions as to what economics is *about*, and what it is *for*. In other words, what kind of real-world issues is economics concerned with, and what does it mean to address them? How do we locate economics in relation to other subjects, particularly the physical sciences? Put another way, if we had to write a mission statement for economics, what would it be?

5.2 The Nature and Scope of Economics

5.2.1 Definitions

Most introductory textbooks define the scope of economics in terms of scarcity. Economic questions are those which address the problem of attempts to satisfy wants coming up against limited resources. But this was not always how economics was understood. In the nineteenth century, for example, when the majority of the population were living at subsistence level, economics was understood as applying to the material side of life. Alfred Marshall introduced his *Principles*, first issued in 1890, with the following definition:

Economics is a study of mankind in the ordinary business of life; it examines that part of individual and social action which is most closely connected with the attainment and with the use of the material requisites of well-being. (Marshall, 1920[1961]: 1)

This was summarized as a concern with wealth in the 1890 study of *The Scope and Method of Political Economy* written by John Neville Keynes (father of John Maynard Keynes). Keynes's study was written at the time at which economics was forming as a separate discipline in Britain, with its own department having been established by Marshall in Cambridge. Until then economics had been taught as an application of other subjects, such as moral philosophy. There had been explicit methodological discussion in economics long before this, and indeed debates over how economics should be done. But it was particularly important for the public profile of economics, at the turn of the last century, to say exactly what this new separate discipline was concerned with, and how it went about its enquiries.

Lionel Robbins (1932) pointed out that this understanding of economics as concerned with *material* well-being didn't reflect the range of problems economists actually addressed. Those living above subsistence levels can exercise some choice between work and leisure, for example. As income levels increase, the service sector increases in importance, both in production and exchange. The choice in favour of work rather than leisure, going to the cinema rather than buying clothes, or working as an artist rather than a miner, all involve non-material welfare as well as material welfare. Robbins therefore suggested that a good definition of economics would not distinguish between the material and the non-material, but would focus instead on the scarcity of resources available to meet *any* type of want:

Economics is the science which studies human behaviour as a relationship between ends and scarce means which have alternative uses. (Robbins, 1932:16)

So for example a woman's choice to be a housewife is a subject for economics, since the opportunity cost is the wage which would otherwise have been earned, less the value of services provided in the home. Similarly, the supply of clean air and water was not a subject for economics when these things were understood to be unlimited (not scarce); but now that we need to devote scarce resources to providing clean air and water, this has become a subject for economics.

Robbins's definition focuses attention on the allocation of scarce resources, not necessarily, but primarily, by means of market-based exchange. This reflected the shift in focus of economics from the concern with growth which dominated the classical period around the Industrial Revolution (up to the late nineteenth century) to a concern with markets thereafter. We have thus seen that the understanding of what were economic questions changed as the economic environment changed. The scarcity understanding of economics is now the one most commonly found.

It is worthwhile reflecting on how comprehensive this definition is for modern economics. The concept of scarcity arises because of a given endowment of resources and given preferences. It is, however, not at all clear that scarcity is the key concept in circumstances where resources and preferences are *not* given (for example where economies are undergoing structural change during the process of development), or where there is an excess supply of some resource (such as labour where there is involuntary unemployment). Robbins had intended his definition to be more general than the alternatives, and Becker adopted this view by applying Robbins's conception of economics to what was earlier seen as outside the range of economics, such as the family behaviour we discussed in Chapter 3. What is entailed is in fact more a matter of method than of subject matter:

[W]hat distinguishes economics as a discipline from other disciplines in the social sciences is not its subject matter but its approach. (Becker, 1976: 5)

If we decide to settle on a definition of economics in terms of approach, for example choosing the Robbins definition, then we need to accept that this may rule out the study of some subject matter, such as economic development or involuntary unemployment. Our definition of economics could alternatively be very general instead in terms of subject matter, but allowing a range of methods. If our purpose in studying economics is to address real economic problems, then there may be particular dangers in divorcing theory from subject matter (see Coase, 1988: ch. 1). There is in fact something quite recognizably held in common between the different approaches to economics, which is that they are all concerned with some or all of the subject matter of production, consumption, distribution (of income, or wealth), and exchange (including non-market exchange, as within the family or the firm). This definition was advocated by Boulding (1991: 33):

The old four elements of economic alchemy—production, consumption, distribution and exchange—still make some sort of sense, even though each element consists of four very diverse parts.

So let us settle on this as defining the scope of economics. In particular, we will find this definition has the advantage of encompassing the range of approaches taken to economics by the different schools of thought (neoclassical, Post Keynesian, neo-Austrian, Marxist, Institutionalist, and so on; see Dow, 1996; Mair and Miller, 1991). The economics profession offers a range of conceptions of economics along with a range of methodological approaches to economics.[1]

A different way of trying to sort out what is an economic question is to ask what is not an economic question. This amounts to asking how we can reasonably divide up the social sciences into disciplines, with each concerned with different aspects of individual or social behaviour. But then, how far *is* economic behaviour separable from other types of behaviour? This is a subject on which much has been written in the methodology literature. We review the issues in the next subsection.

5.2.2 Is economic behaviour separable?

By referring simply to 'ends', Robbins deliberately left unspecified what such ends might include; the implication was that 'ends' could be absolutely anything. What gave them economic importance was the scarcity of the means for achieving the ends. This provides a justification for what has become known as economic 'imperialism', whereby it extends the coverage of economics to areas traditionally thought to be non-economic, such as family relations.

This issue of the coverage of economics arose in the late nineteenth century, as economists built up a theory of individual economic behaviour. John Stuart Mill adapted Jeremy Bentham's pleasure–pain principle to economics, depicting economic behaviour as being driven by the maximization of pleasure and the minimization of pain, that is, utility maximization. Mill explicitly restricted utility maximization to the 'business' part of life, while Bentham had applied it to all behaviour; Mill (1863 [1979]: 100) gave self-respect as an example of something which falls outside the principle.[2] You may remember that introducing self-respect was one of the ways in which the feminist/sociological theory of the household differed from the Becker-style utility-maximizing theory in section 3.2, implying a different conception of the coverage of economics. The 'business' part of life may be thought to exclude the family and refer to such arenas as firms, or the labour market. But clearly difficulties arise if the 'business' part of life is still not fully explained by utility maximization. Is the solution to try to incorporate these other factors in utility, or to treat them as 'disturbances' to what is predicted by utility theory?

Mill (1874: 137) suggested that the solution was to *isolate* economic behaviour from other influences by means of constructing an abstract notion of a separable aspect of human nature, embodied in economic man:

It [political economy] does not treat of the whole of man's nature as modified by the social state, nor of the whole conduct of man in society. It is concerned with him solely as a being who desires to possess wealth, and who is capable of judging of the comparative efficacy of means for obtaining that end ... It makes entire abstraction of every other human passion or motive, except those which may be regarded as perpetually antagonizing principles to the desire of wealth, namely, aversion to labour, and desire of present enjoyment of costly indulgences.

Mill's abstract economic agent lies behind what we now refer to as 'rational economic man', embodied in the rationality axioms. These axioms specify that rational economic man has preferences which are complete (implying full knowledge of the possibilities) and transitive. Additional axioms are required for constructing a formal system based on economic man (for example, preferences need to be continuous if indifference curves are to be constructed) (see Hargreaves–Heap, 1989: section 3.2). It was Walras, another key figure in the development of the concept of rational economic man, who also incorporated the assumption of perfect knowledge which was required for optimizing behaviour to generate a general market-clearing solution. Like Mill, Walras regarded economic man as a fiction, distinguishing him from 'ethical man' (see Bensusan-Butt, 1978: 129).

Marshall however did not accept a (fictional) separation of behaviour into economic and non-economic:

> In all this [economists] deal with man as he is: not with an abstract or 'economic' man; but a man of flesh and blood . . . . But being concerned chiefly with those aspects of life in which the action of motive is so regular that it can be predicted, and the estimate of the motor-forces can be verified by results, they have established their work on a scientific basis. (Marshall, 1920[1961]: 26–7)

Marshall was thus prepared to analyse actual, rather than fictional behaviour. But notice that he makes clear that he regards economic behaviour as the most regular, predictable aspect of behaviour, so that the regularities we observe in actual behaviour are the economic aspects of behaviour. This is an important argument. It implies that economic behaviour can be separated from other aspects of behaviour empirically, even if not otherwise. Second, if science is concerned with regularities as the basis for prediction, then Marshall's argument implies that economics has the best chance of the social sciences of being scientific. Note also his emphasis on the criterion of prediction.

How we understand economic behaviour is thus very important for how we go about economics. If Mill is right, then economic theory proceeds by applying logical reasoning to the account of individuals' economic behaviour which involves a fictional separation from other types of behaviour. The main methodological issue then is how to apply the conclusions of this fictional theory to real problems. The primary criterion for a good theory, according to this view, is then logical consistency; consistency with the evidence is also important, but problematic. The centrality of the *ceteris paribus* clause to this approach suggests that the scope for prediction may be very limited.

If Marshall is right, however, then the empirical regularities we find define the scope for economics. Consistency with the evidence becomes central, and predictive success a reasonable goal. Logical consistency, in terms of classical logic, is secondary in Marshall's system because of his partial equilibrium method. This method involves separating off parts of the economy for analysis, taking the rest of the economy as given—the method commonly employed in microeconomics. Different micro-analyses may be inconsistent in the sense that the cheese market may be taken as given in the analysis of the sheep market, but may be endogenous to an analysis of the beef market. Consistency in this sense could only be achieved by general equilibrium analysis. But this kind of discussion depends on what we mean by 'consistency', which really depends on the kind of logic we are using.[3] We consider this further in section 8.4.

The definition of economics is thus bound up with the methodology of economics, that is, how economics is, or should be, conducted and assessed. This in turn is bound up with the question of what is seen as the purpose of economics. This question has focused around two issues, which we now consider in turn: whether the purpose of economics is explanation or prediction, and whether it is to provide a normative or positive basis for policy advice.

5.3 The Purpose of Economics

5.3.1 Explanation or prediction?

If it is indeed the case that the purpose of economics is to address real-world problems, ideally we would like to be able to provide explanations for these problems and predictions of what would happen with or without particular policy measures. But, in practice, it seems that there may be a trade-off between explanation and prediction. Theories either explain why an economy, or a market, has developed in the way it has, or predict future values of variables, but rarely do both well. Darwin's theory of evolution is a good example of a theory which offers a good explanation after the fact for a species becoming extinct, but which cannot predict very well which species will be next. On the other hand we can predict the effect on health of particular drugs on the basis of clinical trials, without understanding the process by which they work.

We have seen this juxtaposition already in section 4.2, where we considered the role of education in labour markets. Choice theory provided an explanation for why individuals undertake education. But most of that was lost in the reduced form equation used to test the theory and to form the basis for predictions, for example, of the likely outcome of a policy to further promote education. It is difficult to maintain that the reduced form equation constituted an explanation.

This issue was hotly debated after Milton Friedman (1953) published his argument for making predictive success the primary criterion for choosing a theory. Friedman takes minimum wage legislation as an example. The important issue in deciding on whether or not to support such legislation is what the predicted outcome will be—whether or not it will create significant unemployment, counteracting the desired result of raising minimum incomes. But Friedman argued that theories which predict well almost by definition rely on abstraction from reality; whether or not the abstraction is a good one can be judged by the predictive success of the theory. He addressed this argument directly to those who had objected that the assumptions about human behaviour embodied in the concept of rational economic man are unrealistic. If a rational choice model predicts well, it must be the case that economic agents are acting 'as if' they are rational economic man in the way specified by the model, whether this is in any sense 'true' or not. If theories are instruments for prediction—the methodological position called *instrumentalism*—then we need not discuss the nature of the assumptions at all (see Boland, 1979). A good prediction in effect implies a good explanation.

Friedman's argument for instrumentalism aroused a storm of protest—most economists seemed to object either to putting top priority on the prediction criterion, or questioned whether prediction and explanation were in any case substitutes rather than complements. There was clearly a strong sense among many economists that theories should have *some* explanatory content, beyond prediction. Samuelson (1963) championed giving priority to explanation (understood as the descriptive content, or empirical validity, of the theory itself) rather than prediction. His approach relies on conventional judgements about what makes for empirical validity and thus as to which is the best theory (see Boland, 1982: ch. 9). In any case, as Caldwell (1980) pointed out, Friedman himself in *practice* went beyond the simple criterion of predictive success. He sought to persuade others to accept his monetary theory by spelling out the explanation embedded in the theory, using rational choice theory to explain the demand for money (Friedman, 1956).

Friedman's notion of explanation comes from the 'covering law' model of explanation,[4] which sees explanation being based on general laws of the form 'whenever X then Y'—for example, 'whenever the money supply increases by 10 per cent, it is followed approximately eighteen months later by a 10 per cent rise in the general price level, *ceteris paribus*'. This approach requires that there are sufficient regularities in the economy to indicate law-like behaviour. But if this is the case then there are real causal mechanisms which underpin the successful prediction, and it is the role of theory to capture these mechanisms. This implies that, even if we take successful prediction as a good starting point, we still see theory as more than an instrument for prediction; it is a good instrument if it captures the real causes.

However, as we all know from introductions to econometrics, correlation does not necessarily mean causation. Friedman and Schwartz's (1963, 1982) correlation analysis between the money supply and nominal income presaged the rise of monetarism in the 1980s. Around that time a study was reported in the press which showed an even better correlation between the incidence of dysentery in Scotland and UK inflation than between UK money supply growth and UK inflation. Of course this was meant as a joke, because there was no conceivable explanation which could include dysentery in Scotland.[5] Should it matter to an instrumentalist whether or not there is a conceivable explanation?

In fact Friedman and Schwartz (1982: 13) invoked the theoretical tradition which linked money and nominal income to explain their choice of variables, and explained that this was 'the theoretical framework that guided [their] earlier study of United States monetary history but was not explicitly spelled out in that book.' The presentation of the theoretical framework involved explanation of real-world processes. Further, as Coddington (1979) pointed out, we need to have some sense of causal mechanisms even before we can decide on the domain of applicability of a theory. Friedman had argued that the short-run Phillips curve was relevant to demand-pull inflation but that we need the long-run Phillips curve for predicting the effects of cost-push inflation. But how can we even conceive of demand-pull or cost-push inflation without some prior notion of the explanation for inflation in one case or another?

There are in fact some interesting parallels between economics and medicine. It is not uncommon for a medical procedure to be suggested on the basis of a good statistical association, which is put forward as a good explanation *that* the procedure produces the desired effects, but without a satisfactory explanation of *how* the procedure actually produces its effects. As lay people, we are influenced by media reports which show a statistical relationship between eating fatty fish and brain power. For an instrumentalist, a theory which predicts well is also one which explains well, in the sense of 'explains *that*'. But an explanation of *how* the procedure works would provide insights into possible side-effects, interdependencies with other aspects of the patient's health, and so on. Similarly, while the earnings model discussed in section 4.2, for example, may predict well, there is no guarantee that the choice-theoretic model which generated the reduced form represents the true causal mechanism—there is a range of possible explanations for earnings to be correlated with level of education. There is good reason to suppose that we would predict better, the more we understood about the causal mechanisms. Further, where predictions fail, an understanding of causal mechanisms provides some guidance as to how to proceed to develop theories which will yield better predictions.

So, in spite of what Friedman said, perhaps we do need to think further about the realism of assumptions. The philosopher Nagel (1963) pointed out that Friedman had in fact been ambiguous about what he meant by assumptions being unrealistic. He suggested three possible senses of lack of realism:

- falsehood, like assuming that the money supply is under the direct control of the monetary authorities to apply to a situation where this is not the case, or that international trade occurs in a world with only two goods,
- ideal types, like assuming that economic agents are 'rational economic men', or that firms operate in perfectly competitive markets, and
- simplification, like treating an aggregate as homogeneous, although it covers some heterogeneity.

We can see that there are different senses of explanation associated with each of the three types of assumption noted above. False assumptions would seem unable to provide any insight into explaining causal mechanisms. Nevertheless they may be employed in 'thought experiments' (in the absence of actual experiments) in order to build up an understanding of causal mechanisms. Second, ideal-type assumptions are justified as an aid to explaining how causal mechanisms work. Machlup (1967), for example, used the 'as if' justification to argue that, while firms' managers don't literally equate MC and MR, they act 'as if' they do so. If not, they would not be maximizing profits and market discipline would make them fail.[6] (It is an unfortunate twist of fate that the expression 'as if' now means something rather different from what Friedman and Machlup had in mind.)

Another justification for ideal types is to treat them as benchmarks. Thus, while perfectly competitive markets are relatively rare in practice, nevertheless analysis of perfect competition provides a useful benchmark to which actual markets are an approximation. Finally, as Nagel points out, it is hard to think of any statement which does not involve some kind of simplification, so the third type of unrealism we can disregard—for the moment at least.[7]

The word 'explanation' can be used in a further sense, concerned with persuasion. Thus, we are more persuaded by theories which predict well and which also make sense in terms of what we already know (Smith, 1983). We may be persuaded of the merit of monetarist policies by film footage of Mrs Thatcher putting a firm hand on the printing press although in fact the supply of banknotes is of very limited relevance to the money supply. Or we may be persuaded of the virtues of tight fiscal policy based on the analogy being drawn with a household budget. But persuasion also occurs within academic economics—it is not simply a matter of political spin. Consider the persuasive force of an explanation based on ideal-type assumptions, for example, compared to simplifying assumptions. For example, is an explanation of household behaviour more persuasive if it is couched in terms of choice theory or in terms of empirical regularities identified in social behaviour? Or take the example of the Phillips curve. It was established by rational expectations theorists, and incorporated in many textbooks, that the short-run Phillips curve was an aberration from the vertical long-run Phillips curve, due to confused expectations. Nevertheless, the idea that there is a negative relationship between wage growth and unemployment has proved remarkably resilient, and crops up in public discussion about macroeconomic policy. Clearly the short-run Phillips curve has persuasive power. Is this in fact a good example of the benefits of abstraction, that it yields a conclusion which goes against this common understanding of how labour markets work? At what level is it persuasive as offering a good explanation for what we experience?

In a study of the history of astronomy, Adam Smith (1795) set out a psychological theory of scientific activity, explaining what motivates the enquirer. Effectively he argued that successful prediction without explanation causes a sense of wonder, but also the motivation to resolve the puzzle posed by the statistical relationship (see further, Loasby, 1995). A scientist who has developed a new theory needs to persuade other scientists to accept it; the 'truth' of a theory is not self-evident. The history of economic thought is littered with ideas which lie dormant before being chanced on subsequently by other economists who are struck by their persuasiveness, and have proceeded to persuade others. Thus, for example, the rational expectations idea that people form expectations using all the information to hand grew from a seed sown by Muth (1961), although the context of that article was a study of managerial behaviour within the firm, not optimizing individuals (see Kantor, 1979). Adam Smith also pointed out that audiences are persuaded by explanations which relate to what is already known, but what is already regarded as known depends on methodological perspective. Thus many economists would find a theory based on optimizing behaviour more persuasive than one based on the dynamics of institutional change, for example, while other economists might disagree.

We have seen, therefore, that the notion of explanation itself may mean different things depending on methodological approach, so that we are not in a position to draw any general conclusions about the relative roles of prediction and explanation in economics. It could be said that it is the policy maker who specifies what is wanted from the economist (prediction or explanation). Further, it can be argued that it is up to the policy maker to provide the value judgements to be superimposed on the economist's prediction or explanation. We explore in the next section whether such a separation of theory and values is even possible.

5.3.2 The normative–positive distinction

If the purpose of economics is to advise governments on how to improve social welfare, there is an issue as to whether the economist's job involves saying what ought to be (a normative statement), or simply saying what is and spelling out the implications of different policy measures (a positive statement). There is a widespread view among economists that economics should be positive. But there is the prior question as to whether positive economics is actually feasible. Friedman (1953) argued that the criterion of predictive success allowed economics to be positive—no matter what an economist thought of the goal of promoting a minimum living standard, for example, it was still possible to settle the question of what would be the outcome, say, of minimum wage legislation.

Classical economics was regarded as a moral science (an application of moral philosophy). But, in setting out the parameters of the new separate discipline, John Neville Keynes (1890: 46–54) advocated a separation of moral questions from positive questions:

If political economy regarded from the theoretical viewpoint is to make good progress, it is essential that all extrinsic or premature sources of controversy should be eliminated. . . . The intrusion of ethics into economics cannot but multiply and perpetuate sources of disagreement. . . . However necessary it may be to face these questions at a later stage, there is no reason why we should not have a positive science of economics that is independent of them. (Keynes, 1890: 52–3)

Robbins (1932: ch. 6) made the case even more strongly. He likened economists to economic agents, exercising rational choice. The ethical stances we bring to practical economic questions are our preferences, to which we apply rational choice based on positive economic theory.

Robbins's argument also requires that economics successfully identifies the causal mechanisms relevant to a practical problem, independent of ethical considerations. We are back to the question of the separateness of economics. Even if we were to agree that economics itself is value-free (something which is hotly debated), but we use abstraction to separate economics from the concerns of other disciplines, we are potentially excluding relevant causal mechanisms which are the business of other social sciences and which incorporate moral considerations. Hausman (1992: 261) points out that those who extend economic theory by incorporating insights from other disciplines, even if it is to represent them within the framework defined by the rationality axioms, are also thereby importing values into economic theory. Thus, for example, Akerlof (1982) introduces the idea of 'gift-exchange' into labour relations, such that workers will work harder without recompense as a 'gift' to the employer, out of a sense of loyalty which Akerlof identifies as the expectation of gifts in return. But this provides a reason for involuntary unemployment among would-be workers excluded from this mutual arrangement. Hausman points out that this theory, apparently bringing anthropological considerations within the fold of economics, introduces a moral argument for unemployment benefits. It may even be a motivation for defining the scope of economics according to the rationality axioms if the goal of making economics a positive science is paramount.[8]

But is economics, alone among the social sciences, itself value-free? Blaug (1998) points out the importance of breaking down the concept of value judgements. *Methodological value judgements* determine the choice of question asked, the means of addressing it, and the means of testing the resulting hypotheses. No scientific activity can escape this kind of value judgement. But *normative value judgements* refer to statements about whether or not some type of behaviour, or its consequences, is desirable. The normative–positive distinction tends to be used with respect to the second type of value judgement. But, having said that, Blaug also points out that there remains confusion in economics over identifying methodological value judgements. For example, do the rationality axioms reflect the facts of human behaviour; if not, does abstraction of this sort inevitably involve value judgements, and is there an implicit moral approval of the behaviour of rational economic man? Drakopoulos (1991), for example, argues that the rationality axioms are in fact an expression of hedonistic philosophy. Schumacher (1975: ch. 4) also highlights the philosophical content of standard economics by constructing a different economics for a society where work is what makes life meaningful (work is maximized) while efforts are made to conserve resources (consumption is minimized). If the underpinnings of economics are philosophical, then we get into questions of 'which philosophy'. This is clearly important, and we will address these broader questions in Chapter 9.[9]

Hutchison (1964: ch. 2) sees scope for values to enter economics through an additional route. He is concerned that theories be tested empirically (see further, section 6.3). But if we cannot demonstrate one theory definitively to be better than another, value judgements enter into the judgement as to which theory to go with. Further, if different value judgements support different methodologies, with their different questions and different means of addressing them, then it is hard to envisage values even in principle eradicated from economics. He therefore sees the scope for 'ideological bias', or less emotively the presence of values, as part of the scientific process which is particularly difficult to eradicate where theory testing cannot be definitive.

Thinking back to the example in section 3.6 of the international distribution of pollution, how far was the moral outrage at Summers's solution due to an unwillingness to accept the implications of hard economic logic? And how far was it due to the methodological value judgements intrinsic to welfare economics? Welfare economics is built round the goal of maximizing the sum of the utilities of individuals whose preferences are normally represented as greedy and selfish. The idea that social welfare is defined by such an aggregation (regardless of individual preferences) is itself a value judgement. (It would be possible to have a social welfare function which privileged the poor, or the rich, or the titled, for example.) Would economists be right who argue that welfare economics is value-free, or are the protesters right that economic arguments are inseparable from ideology, or values?[10]

Despite many statements to the contrary, therefore, it is not at all established that economics is a positive science, independent of normative judgements. Ricketts and Shoesmith (1992) used survey data on economists' opinions to attempt to identify how far different values explain differences of opinion among economists. They found that both normative and positive differences explained different views, but that there was more divergence on normative questions than on positive questions. This kind of exercise is only a start, however. As the authors admit, the classification of questions as relating to normative or positive judgements is not clear-cut. For example, whether or not inflation was a monetary phenomenon was treated as a positive question, while whether the money supply or the interest rate should be the target of monetary policy was treated as a normative question. But the first is a matter of theoretical judgement while the latter is to a large extent a matter of what is practically feasible. Values were identified primarily with such matters as income distribution, not with the values embedded in the assumptions of any theoretical analysis.

The most we can say about this for the time being is that, where values are implicit in economic theory, it would seem to be helpful for these to be made explicit when policy advice is given. But if values enter at the underlying methodological level, identifying them and their consequences is not at all straightforward. An additional issue again is whether there are value-free facts to which theory refers. If not, is science possible at all? We will come back to this, and related issues, when we consider recent developments in methodology in Chapter 7 (see also section 5.4 below).

When economists aspire to a value-free theoretical framework, they sometimes refer to the physical sciences, and particularly to physics, as a model of positive science. This has been a powerful external force in the development of economic methodology which we explore in the next section. We will see that taking the methodology of the physical sciences as the benchmark for economics has knock-on effects for the way we understand the subject matter of economics and the way it is to be analysed.

5.4 Economics and the Physical Sciences

5.4.1 The attraction of physics

As economists, we aspire to build up systematic knowledge of a particular subject matter. We could say, therefore, that economics is a science. The activity of science entails some form of organization, or system, in the building up of knowledge. Eichner (1983: ch. 9), in considering economics as a science, focuses on empirical content as the primary characteristic of science. But it is difficult to define science more closely without getting into philosophy. We have already seen that we get into some difficulties in trying to pin down scientific knowledge as providing explanation (as opposed to prediction). Indeed, the notion of knowledge itself depends on a philosophical or methodological approach. Some economists, for example, would claim to *know* that making a central bank independent increases its capacity to control inflation, while others challenge that interpretation of the evidence. If economists, as we have noted, normally disagree over what to count as knowledge, does that mean that economics is not a science? Indeed, we find some hesitation among economists in calling the discipline a science, because of the difficulty in establishing economic laws on a par with the physical sciences.

When economics was developing into a separate discipline towards the end of the nineteenth century, the physical sciences were already well-established and set a model of science to which economists could aspire. And indeed it was quite common for that model to be used explicitly. As Jevons, one of the founders of marginalist theory put it:

The Theory of Economy . . . presents a close analogy to the science of Statical Mechanics and the Laws of Exchange are found to resemble the Laws of Equilibrium of a lever as determined by the principle of virtual velocities. The nature of Wealth and Value is explained by the consideration of indefinitely small amounts of pleasure and pain, just as the Theory of Statics is made to rest upon the equality of definitely small amounts of energy. (Jevons, 1871: viii, as quoted in Drakopoulos, 1991: 55)

Similarly, Irving Fisher (1965: 85–6) explicitly likened an individual agent to a particle, utility to energy, commodities to space, and so on (see Drakopoulos, 1991: 125). Mirowski (1989) provides the most detailed account of a long history of what some term 'physics envy' in economics.[11] The influence of physics methodology continues, and can at times be very direct: economists such as Thomas Sargent, for example, have been actively involved in the Santa Fe Institute's work on complexity which had been started by physicists (see Sent, 1998: ch. 5).

Part of the agenda in establishing economics as a science on a par with the physical sciences required, as discussed in subsection 5.3.2, an explicit distancing from the previous notion of economics as a moral science. The development of utility theory, along the same lines as mechanics, was seen as having the advantage of establishing economics as a positive science. As Pareto (1927: 113) put it:

Thanks to the use of mathematics, this entire theory . . . rests on no more than a fact of experience, that is, on the determination of the quantities of goods which constitute combinations between which the individual is indifferent. The theory of economic science thus acquires the rigor of rational mechanics; it deduces its results from experience, without bringing in any metaphysical entity.

It was not surprising, therefore, that economics looked to the philosophy of science, a field which focused on the physical sciences, for methodological guidance.

The physical sciences themselves went through a process of trying to become positive, or value-free. Mathematical expression was an important part of this process, and one which key economists sought to emulate (see Beed, 1991, and section 6.5.3 below). There developed a philosophy of science called *positivism*, which was based on the power of logic to derive propositions and the power of confrontation of these propositions with facts to establish whether or not they were true.[12] Note that the word 'positive' is being used here in a different way from the distinction from normative, although the two meanings are sometimes conflated—but positivism was also seen as defining the methodology for establishing positive, as opposed to normative, statements. The most influential form of positivism was logical positivism, which very explicitly specified what marked out science from non-science. Logical positivists held that the only meaningful statements were those which were either true by definition ($2 + 2 = 4$, according to the conventional rules of number) and those which could, even only in principle, be confronted with evidence. By implication, abstract, 'ideal-type' theory in the Mill tradition was meaningless.

The important general point for methodological discussion is that logical positivism rules out all metaphysical statements, that is, those which cannot conceivably be tested. The philosopher Bertrand Russell once pointed out that the definition of logical positivism is, in its own terms, meaningless—it cannot be tested empirically. This is not just a cheap debating point. Logical positivism sets out a methodological agenda but at the same time seems to disallow methodological discussion in general, together with anything else which cannot be quantified.

The procedure of 'confronting with evidence' itself is in any case far from straightforward. We saw in the last subsection that Hutchison, who in fact was most influential as introducing positivism to economics, was himself doubtful as to how definitive testing could be in economics. We will deal with the issues it raises in much more detail in the section 6.2. But positivism also raises philosophical problems about the nature of evidence itself. Because the emphasis of logical positivism within the philosophy of science was more on the issue of meaning than on knowledge, the positivists became embroiled in a debate about whether the language we use to give accounts of observations is coloured by theoretical perspective. The general conclusion that the language of observation is not independent of the language of theory was one of the main factors which led to logical positivism being discredited within the philosophy of science. Its influence is still present in economics, but the issue of the independence of 'the facts' is relevant for economics too (see section 5.4.3).

Some physicists questioned further, not just the status of the language with which observation was expressed, but also whether observed phenomena are in any case independent of the observer, that is, whether there is a set of independent facts against which theories can be tested. The Heisenberg principle states that the properties of a subatomic particle are only defined in terms of the process of measurement itself. It is possible to 'know' either the position or the momentum of a particle, but not both simultaneously. A particle is thus an idealization—it does not exist, as defined, independent of its observation. This principle is even more clearly evident in the social sciences. It is notoriously difficult to conduct experiments, for example on rationality; students taking part in experiments may feel under pressure to give the 'correct' textbook answer in order to impress the researcher (the so-called 'professor effect'). The very act of paying attention can alter behaviour, as was found in the early time-and-motion studies of factory activity. Productivity improved as a result of workers knowing they were being studied, quite apart from changes in the way in which production was organized.

What is startling about the Heisenberg principle is that it applies to physics. Are the physical sciences then no different in kind from the social sciences? In subsection 5.4.2 we explore whether the differences between the two are significant for the way we apply the philosophy of physical science to economics.

5.4.2 Is economics fundamentally different from the physical sciences?

In Chapter 2 we explored the ways in which the subject matter of economics changes over time, as institutions evolve and creative behaviour sets economies off on new paths. This is the stuff of social science, and on the face of it distinguishes it from the physical sciences that deal with inanimate matter. It would seem that the physical sciences have much more scope for identifying law-like relationships, that is, knowledge held with a reasonable degree of certainty. The physical sciences, too, are less likely to have such significant methodological value judgements embedded in them, in that they do not refer to human behaviour.

The clearest difference in terms of how physical science proceeds is the experimental method. Experiments are a practical form of isolating some relationships on which we want to focus. A scientist can construct a theory about how some chemical reaction, say, will behave in a vacuum, to isolate the process from the influence of atmosphere, and proceed to test the theory by conducting the experiment in a vacuum. An economist cannot in the same way test a theory based on the assumption, say, that emotional state is unimportant. Other techniques need to be employed to isolate relationships from different factors. Thus statistical techniques like logit analysis can classify subjects in a data panel according to a range of characteristics other than the one of primary interest. In trying to identify the effect on earnings of higher education, for example, this type of analysis can 'remove' the effects on earnings of area of residence, sector of employment, gender, family size, and so on. A key issue of course is how far these other characteristics are independent of education, but at least there is some scope for narrowing down the extent to which the relationship between earnings and education is not isolated.

It is only partially a question, therefore, of how far experiments can be conducted isolated from outside influences, in either the physical or social sciences. We are talking here about degrees of difficulty, not absolute differences. The additional question is how the results of experiments can be applied. If the causal mechanisms identified in an experiment are, in an applied context, modified or counteracted by other causal mechanisms, then the result of the experiment may be of limited value. In airline design, for example, test flights are crucial for revealing how far the causal mechanisms identified in the modelling stage persist in the face of the multitude of outside influences in real experience; models may not incorporate random events such as birds being sucked into engines, or non-random events such as changing weather systems, for example. Economics faces the added difficulties associated with more significant non-random social disturbances from outside and behavioural disturbances within the human experimental subject, whether we are talking about an actual experiment or an attempt at statistical isolation.

We have discussed the issue for the physical sciences of whether or not there are objective facts. Potentially this is another area of difference between the physical and social sciences. Are there empirical counterparts to economic variables?

5.4.3 Empirical counterparts

In the first application of logical positivism to economics, Terence Hutchison (1938) required the outcomes of theory to be empirically testable. In particular he raised the issue of the empirical validity of assumptions, challenging the perfect foresight assumption underpinning the theory of rational choice. He argued against the way in which abstraction was used in economics to isolate 'economic forces' from the rest of experience in a way which made it difficult to test empirically (Hutchison, 1938: 119–20). Taken to an extreme, logical positivism suggests that economics should deal only with measurable entities. Again we find a methodological stance providing us with a possible definition of economics—as dealing only with the measurable aspects of life (GDP as a proxy for welfare, paid work rather than work in the home, and so on). But the measurability criterion may be unduly restrictive for the social sciences.

One of the major issues addressed by those who developed utility theory was whether or not we could measure utility. The general conclusion reached was that it was impossible to measure units of utility directly. However, it was possible to test utility theory indirectly by checking whether behaviour was consistent with it. Utility theory suggests that demand curves will generally be downward-sloping. If we observe a negative relationship between price and quantity demanded, then we have confirmation of utility theory. This is Samuelson's (1938) revealed preference theory.[13] Similarly, remember that, in section 4.2 where we looked at human capital theories of wage determination and economic growth, it was the reduced form of the theoretical systems which were confronted with the data; it was impossible to measure the values of variables which went into the deductive process of generating the 'bottom line' propositions.

Thus, while much of the subject matter of economics is clearly focused on measurable variables (inflation, unemployment, relative prices, and so on), these are analysed as the outcome of causal processes which do not have empirical counterparts (like each individual's preference map). Parts of the causal mechanism may be measurable, for example, the level of education of a panel of workers, but we apparently cannot measure all aspects of all causal mechanisms. This poses difficulties for working out how to revise hypotheses if the data do not confirm the proposition—or if the data confirm two competing propositions. Further, the ultimate concern of economics, social welfare, is only imperfectly measured. Per capita gross domestic product is a good attempt at measuring the well-being of a society, but there are many well-rehearsed shortcomings with the measure—it ignores distributional considerations, it ignores output which is not marketed (such as housework), it includes expenditure on armaments and policing (whose growth reflects increasing threats to social welfare), and so on.

The strongest position on this matter is taken by economists in the Austrian tradition.[14] Their methodology is termed *methodological individualism* because of its focus on the individual and her subjective understanding of her circumstances (see Horwitz, 1995). According to this view, data—particularly macroeconomic aggregates—have very limited meaning. The money supply, for example, should be an aggregation of what each individual perceives to be her money holdings. Somebody with an honest face, for example, may find it easier than others to have cheques accepted for amounts greater than guaranteed by her bank card. One person may treat her savings account as a liquid resource, while another may resolve to use it only for building up savings, that is, to treat it as illiquid. The conventional money supply measure, as a total of a particular range of deposits, then, doesn't make much sense as total liquidity. Given the limitations this places on empirical work, neo-Austrians tend to limit their empirical work to case studies.

It is a question really of whether or not there is such a thing as 'the facts'. Neo-Austrians think not, except at the micro-level, and even then they are subjective. But in between this view and the understanding of an objective set of facts there is another view, that facts are *theory-laden*. This means that what we choose to observe, and how we observe it, depend on our theoretical perspective. Before the late nineteenth century, for example, there was no concept of unemployment, although we can now look back and argue that unemployment existed then. Alternatively unemployment may be disregarded as a 'fact' if theory tells us that any unemployment is by definition voluntary, while others would identify unemployment which they regard as involuntary. We will need to bear these considerations in mind when we come to consider the role of empirical work in economics

5.5 Conclusion

In this chapter we have seen that, while we could find large groupings of economists at any one time who might agree on a mission statement for economics, we are unlikely to find universal agreement. While Robbins's scarcity definition of economics, for example, is probably the most widely accepted one now, it nevertheless excludes some subject matter which many economists would regard as important for economics. The definition which seems to be general enough to cover what is actually represented in the economics literature is that economics is concerned with production, consumption, distribution, and exchange.

Further, there are different views as to the relative importance of prediction and explanation as what we are striving for, and even then as to what would be a satisfactory explanation. If economics is to address real problems, is it more important to predict or to explain, and are these in any case alternatives? There is disagreement too about how far economic explanations and predictions can be independent of value judgements. Indeed, even 'the facts' may not be independent of our prior beliefs. Economists have at times looked to the physical sciences as a model for how to make economics more 'scientific', in the sense of being 'objective' or 'positive'. Quite apart from discussions as to how far the physical sciences are themselves scientific in this sense, economics as a social science clearly faces additional difficulties in generating positive conclusions.

We turn now to exploring how methodology has been employed to address these difficulties. In the next chapter we concentrate on methodological thinking which addresses the question of how economics should be done in order to generate positive conclusions. Much of the discussion centres on issues of empirical testing of theories. We leave until the following chapter the issues raised in the modern methodology literature about the limitations on positive economics and the alternative role for methodology as constructing accounts of how economists actually address the day-to-day issues they face in developing, assessing, and communicating theories.

5.6 Further Reading

For further reading on the issues explored here, see, by issue: Robbins (1932), Caldwell (1993; ii, pt. iii), the special centenary issue of the *Economic Journal* (vol. 101) and Hausman (1992: ch. 12) (the nature and scope of economics); Myrdal (1955), Hutchison (1964: ch. 2), Machlup (1969), Caldwell (1984: chs. 3, 4), Drakopoulos (1991), Caldwell (1993; ii, pt. iii), and Blaug (1998) (the purpose of economics), and Mirowski (1989) and Morgan and Morrison (1999) (economics and the physical sciences).

Endnotes

1. For accounts of these and other schools of thought, see Mair and Miller (1991), and Snowdon, Vane, and Wynarczyk (1994).

2. Mill, like Smith (1759) before him, was aware that utility maximization was an inadequate account of human behaviour in general; individuals may delude themselves about the happiness to be gained from particular courses of action, or may actually achieve happiness through self-denial. We consider behavioural economics in section 9.4 below as a modern attempt to understand behaviour which does not fit the rational economic man model.

3. Marshall continually strove for consistency in terms of his own method, at the cost of clarity of exposition; see Groenewegen (1995: 336–7).

4. This is explained, in relation to a detailed analysis of causal explanation in economics, by Runde (1998).

5. A more serious critique of Friedman and Schwartz's later work can be found in Hendry and Ericsson (1991). See also Hendry (1993: ch. 1) more generally on the issue of spurious correlation.

6. Pursuing 'as if' arguments as physical analogies is problematic. Friedman's analogy of plants acting as if they were optimizing access to sunlight is very different from the original statement of the analogy by Alchian (1950), such that plants in sunlight grow stronger than plants in the shade (see Kay, 1995).

7. For some, however, simplification is itself problematic if taken to any length at all. Economists in the Austrian tradition are concerned with the concept of aggregation (see section 5.4.3 below) on the grounds that information is thereby lost. More generally, postmodernism is based on the view that analysis should focus on the disaggregated, context-specific level (see section 7.4).

8. See Schoemaker (1991), who also distinguishes economics from other social sciences in this respect.

9. The issue is debated in terms of economics and religion in Brennan and Waterman (1994) and Dean and Waterman (1999).

10. The argument that economics inevitably incorporates some ideology or other has been most forcefully made by Myrdal (1955).

11. See de Marchi (1993) for a series of commentaries on Mirowski (1989) and a reply from Mirowski.

12. See Caldwell (1994) and Hands (1998) for fuller accounts of the development of positivism.

13. See Hausman (1992: section 9.2) for a methodological discussion.

14. The key figures in the tradition of Austrian economics are Menger, von Mises, and Hayek. An account of issues in modern, neo-Austrian economics may be found in Keizer, Tieben, and van Zijp (eds.) (1997), with a history of the school in the first chapter, and Tieben and Keizer (1997).

6

PROGRESS IN ECONOMICS

6.1 Introduction

The chapter is entitled 'Progress in Economics' because promoting progress, and identifying it when it has occurred, has been the underlying agenda for much of the field of methodology. It is also an issue that has come explicitly to the surface of much discussion with the turn of a new century: how do we characterize the development of economics in the twentieth century? What were the great achievements? Or, as Hausman (1989) opened his survey of the 'standard methodological literature', '[h]ow can one tell whether a particular bit of economics is good science?' The corollary of any answer to this kind of question is guidance for practising economists as to how to ensure progress in the future. As Hands (2001: 49) describes what he sees as the key defining objective of methodology in the twentieth century: 'to find a few clearly specified methodological rules for the proper conduct of economic science.' Put negatively, the question becomes one of deciding what qualifies as science and what does not; should some theories be rejected as unscientific?

The criteria for identifying good theories within the methodological tradition we consider in this chapter have generally been some combination of logical consistency, consistency with the evidence, and predictive success. Logical consistency has tended to be regarded as the most straightforward criterion, although we will discuss in Chapter 8 the implications of choosing different forms of logic. However, what consistency with the evidence actually means has been more clearly seen as problematic. Even predictive success turns out not to be straightforward. And there is in any case the issue of the priority to be placed on the different criteria.

So we need to consider ideas as to what this tradition means by progress in more detail—what are we looking for in a progressive economics?—and then how do we know it when we see it? We start with the debate, between inductivism and deductivism, which dominated the field of methodology for many years.

6.2 Inductivism and Deductivism

6.2.1 Introduction

The most clear focus of debate in the history of methodology has been the relative merits of induction and deduction. There was fierce debate between Malthus and Ricardo in the eighteenth century, and again between the German Historical School and the Austrian deductivists in the nineteenth century. The relative importance of building up theory from econometric work on the one hand and from pure theory on the other continues to be a central issue in methodology.

The underlying debate stems from debate over what is ultimately the source of knowledge. The inductivists like the German Historical School saw experience as the source of knowledge. Experience is captured in empirical data; this position is called *empiricism*. Deductivists in contrast see reason as the basis for knowledge; this position is called *rationalism*. We will explore rationalism in more detail later in the chapter (section 6.4). We will find that rationalism underpins much of the literature explored here, whether deductivist or inductivist, to the extent that *methodological* knowledge is understood to be based on reason rather than observation. The methodology considered in this chapter is rationalist in the sense that it is primarily derived from philosophical reasoning rather than a study of practice. But first here we explore what is meant by inductivism and deductivism.

6.2.2 Inductivism

Induction involves detailed empirical study out of which emerges the idea for a hypothesis. Theory is induced from the data as shown in Figure 6.1.

An early example of inductive reasoning was Adam Smith's (1776) extraordinarily detailed study of historical material drawn from a range of periods and places, out of which he identified his general principle of the division of labour: the scope for increasing productivity, and thus the basis for economic growth, was increased by specialization in production.[1] Similarly, modern

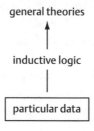

Figure 6.1 Induction

endogenous growth theory used extensive empirical studies to identify a key factor which correlated with different growth experience: expenditure on education, particularly education in early childhood.

But, while it is clearly useful in suggesting empirical regularities on which theory may be built, induction does not provide a complete methodology (see Boland, 1982: ch. 1). There is a logical problem: no matter how many observations we have to support a theory, there is no inevitability that future observations will continue to bear out the same theory. Just because the only swans you have seen are white doesn't rule out the possibility that sometime you might come across a black swan; this is the empirical version of the *problem of induction*.[2]

More generally, the problem of induction is that, just because a theory has been consistent with the facts from which it was induced does not demonstrate it to be a true representation of causal mechanisms which can be used to predict the future. For example, Friedman and Schwartz (1963) inferred from a close correlation in historical data between the money supply and nominal income that monetary growth was the key factor explaining inflation. But when this conclusion was used as the basis for restrictive policy action, the financial sector responded by changing its behaviour and innovating in new money-assets in such a way as to alter the relationship between money and nominal income. This outcome was enshrined in Goodhart's Law, that any attempt to control money defined as one collection of assets encourages substitution with other assets such that the usefulness of the original definition of money declines.

Induction thus scores well on consistency with the evidence, but not on prediction. This is particularly likely when an inductive argument is the basis for policy action which itself changes the underlying relationships, that is, violates the *ceteris paribus* clause. A theory based on induction *may* predict well, but there is no assurance that it will continue to do so unless there is some reason for expecting the causal mechanism captured in the theory to continue to be relevant. In other words, for successful prediction, some element of explanation is required.

While not generating demonstrable truth about causal mechanisms, induction does nevertheless make very effective use of detailed experience. It provides a means of identifying the regularities which could be said to define the subject matter of economics (see section 5.2). Empiricism starts with our experience of the world, and thus potentially the basis for identifying and analysing the real problems which economic theory is designed to address. But, as far as demonstrating true knowledge is concerned, the logical problem of induction remains an insuperable methodological obstacle. Grounding theory in evidence is seen by empiricists as being better than not doing so; if true or certain knowledge is unattainable, then it is a matter of judgement how best to proceed. This is the second-best argument applied to method-ology itself (see section 3.6). However, the desire to demonstrate truth, as a scientific exercise, is a powerful force, and encouraged support for an alterna-tive methodology—one which focused on how to construct certain know-ledge. The priority shifted from consistency with the evidence to logical consistency.

6.2.3 Deductivism

The alternative to inductive logic was to start instead with axioms which were taken to be true, apply deductive logic, and only then (but not necessarily) consult the data in relation to the propositions which emerge to see if they were consistent. This approach is termed *deductivism*, illustrated in Figure 6.2. Thus, for example, addressing the real issues of household behaviour, the Becker approach involves starting with the rationality axioms, making some further assumptions (such as the the head of the household behaving as an altruist and the other family members as self-interested) in order to frame the optimizing analysis. Conclusions may then be drawn, such as that wives are more likely to be housepersons than husbands. As long as the deductive logic is sound, and the assumptions taken to be true, then the logical truth of the conclusions follows. Since the conclusions are always qualified by the *ceteris paribus* clause, however, the empirical truth of the conclusions cannot be guaranteed. In the case of this example, historical data may confirm the conclusion, but social, behavioural and economic changes may affect its predictive power.

Deductivism was the approach advocated by Mill and, later, Robbins. The secondary role given to data was not just because of the problem of induction, but also because of the method of abstraction. If economics was concerned with economic behaviour abstracted from other behaviour as an 'ideal type', then induction could not work anyway, since the data refer instead to

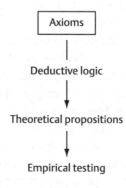

Figure 6.2 Deduction

composite behaviour. Even if the rationality axioms were to be taken as self-evidently true, relating the conclusions of theory based on the axioms to data could not be seen as in any way 'testing' the theory (see Blaug, 1980: 81).

In the modern methodology literature, Hausman (1992) continues this tradition. As he puts it, economics is inevitably an inexact science, in that actual economic behaviour is subject to influences outside the ambit of any set of theoretical economic principles. This means that we need the *ceteris paribus* clause to take account of any additional forces ('disturbances'). Thus, since empirical evidence includes all forces, accounted for or not, he argues that theory should be constructed deductively. This means starting with a set of axioms and deducing, by means of classical logic, a set of theoretical propositions. This is what we do in intermediate microeconomics when we start with the axioms of rational individual behaviour (such as complete, transitive preferences) and derive indifference maps, then downward-sloping demand curves. This framework then generates propositions about the effect, say, on the market for cheese of a rise in the price of crackers, *ceteris paribus*. The *ceteris paribus* clause is crucial. It refers not only to the assumption, for example, that the macroeconomic environment is given for any individual product market, but also to the nature of the individual decision-making assumed to govern market behaviour. This latter follows inevitably from the deliberate abstraction from non-economic influences.[3]

According to the deductivist approach, therefore, the assumptions lack realism because they refer to ideal types (they are not just simplifications). Empirical evidence therefore is of limited relevance. Consistency with the evidence and predictive success would support the notion that real agents act 'as if' they were ideal types, but the problem of induction remains. The emphasis in the deductive approach is therefore on the logical consistency criterion. Since the logic employed in the deductivist approach is classical logic, then, if the logic is correct, the conclusions can be taken to be certainly true—given the truth of the assumptions. Of course, it is this 'given' which is most controversial for this approach. But equally important is the reliance on classical logic, which relies on certainty as to the truth or falsity of assumptions. We will explore other approaches to logic, which allow for uncertainty about the truth value of assumptions, in Chapter 8.

6.2.4 The hypothetico-deductive method

As with most dichotomies, the induction–deduction dichotomy is in fact misleading. It is not clear that either pure induction or pure deduction is even possible. At the very least, the identification of facts for induction requires some theoretical perspective. Why, for example, would endogenous growth theorists choose to include education expenditure variables as a potential causal factor in growth theory unless there was some prior expectation that this was the case? Further, Becker constructed his model of family employment behaviour with the fact in mind that women were less likely to take paid employment than their male partners.

More fundamentally, if deduction is based on application of logic to 'self-evident' axioms, there must be some basis in experience for the judgement of self-evidence. If not, then the justification for the choice of axioms is a matter of defining the scope of economics by specifying a particular abstraction, that is, the axioms are only true by definition. But then, if this is the case, it remains unclear how the results of theory are to be interpreted in relation to practical problems. We consider this particular question in Chapter 8.

We can clearly see in the work of most of the great economists a combination of induction and deduction. Marshall, for example, made detailed studies of firms and social welfare conditions. His focus on actual behaviour accorded well with the inductive tradition in economics of constructing theories by distilling relationships from detailed observation. It also accorded well with the emerging tendency to test theories empirically. But Marshall also employed deductive logic, using the principles he had derived from observation. In other words he went back and forth between induction and deduction; this is called the hypothetico-deductive method, and was set out in Keynes (1890) as an answer to the question of whether to concentrate on induction or deduction in economics.[4] It involved formulating hypotheses, deducing propositions, and testing these propositions against the data; if the data don't confirm the proposition, then the hypothesis needs to be revised, and further propositions tested, and so on. The process is represented in Figure 6.3.

An example of this methodology is the evolution of the Phillips curve framework. Phillips (1958) initially estimated the statistical relationship between the rate of change in wages and the rate of unemployment in order to find the basis for a theory of inflation. Since he found a strong empirical

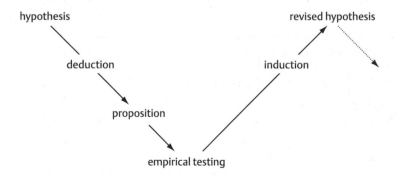

Figure 6.3 The hypothetico-deductive method

relationship, a low-unemployment-induced wage-push theory of inflation was developed, suggesting a trade-off between inflation and unemployment. But the evidence of the 1970s, of high inflation and high unemployment, suggested that the theory needed revision, and so the expectations-augmented Phillips curve was developed to account for stagflation. And so on.

The hypothetico-deductive procedure implies that the hypotheses from which theories are deduced are contestable, and subject to periodic revision. This differs from the deductivist approach, which is based on deriving theories from axioms which are explicitly abstract. Although the axioms are taken as 'self-evidently true', they are not contestable on the basis of empirical testing. But some do contest the truth of the axioms, claiming that rational economic man is not only fictional but significantly at variance with the reality of incomplete knowledge (see Hutchison, 1938, for example) or of human nature (see Nelson, 1993; England, 1993, for example). Indeed, there is a significant literature on rationality within economics, which is not surprising given its centrality to much of economic theory (see, for example, Hargreaves-Heap, 1989, and Gerrard, 1993). In Chapter 8 we will consider further how rationality is understood.

In fact, in the case of the Phillips curve, the revision of Phillips's hypothesis included the incorporation of the rationality axioms explicitly into the theory, but with mistaken expectations in the short run. The labour market deviated from the long-run Phillips curve along short-run curves only while expectations adjusted to new circumstances. But the full rationality axioms, with perfect foresight, apply in the long run. The rational expectations theory developed on the presumption that actual (not abstract, economic) behaviour was always rational (in the sense of complete, transitive, continuous preferences), but that random shocks periodically drive expectations, and thus rational behaviour, off-course. We see thus an uneasy combination of deductivism and hypothetico-deductivism, whereby the axioms are generally exempt from the revision process when hypotheses are being revised—but the perfect foresight axiom has had to be refined in the light of the expectations literature.

In practice, the situation has developed in economics where pure theorists employ a more deductivist methodology while econometricians employ a more inductivist methodology, with little cross-over between the two (but a pure version of neither is feasible in practice). The axioms of the first group are in general incontestable while the empirical work of the second group cannot provide adequate tests of pure theory, because it is expressed in terms for which there are not clear empirical counterparts. Hutchison (1998) has chastised the deductivists for not addressing the data, while Mayer (1993) argued for a twin-track approach, with each following their own separate agenda. But Backhouse (1997, 1998*a*) is less willing to give deductivism its head. He argues that logical consistency on its own is not a sufficient condition for progress in economics—if it is to improve its capacity to address practical problems, that is, build up knowledge of the real world, then economics must also have significant empirical content.

A high proportion of the twentieth-century methodology literature was concerned with how this should be done, given that there appears to be an irreconcilable problem with maintaining a set of axioms as incontestable (as a way of separating off economic from non-economic behaviour, or else as a matter of fact), while allowing empirical observation to be used to challenge the theory which derives from the axioms. But then this is only an irreconcilable problem if the axioms are not necessarily true. Rational expectations theory is put forward as a way of conflating axiomatic theory with empirical observation. If economic behaviour is rational, then data necessarily reflect equilibrium states; otherwise rational individuals would be missing opportunities to increase utility. There is then, in principle at least, a direct correspondence between theory and data.

The resulting exercise in identifying empirical regularities in economic behaviour is consistent with Marshall's view that economics should be concerned with actual behaviour, not with an abstraction from reality. But Marshall would have been uncomfortable with the assumption of complete information at the macroeconomic, as well as microeconomic, levels. Rational expectations theory depicts rational individuals as having full knowledge of a macroeconomic model—in the case of the strong version of the rational expectations hypothesis, the correct model. But Marshall saw the growth of knowledge through learning as central to economic processes, like the life cycle of the firm (see Loasby, 1989: ch. 4). This was why he developed the method of partial equilibrium analysis, where a wide range of variables (and knowledge of them) are taken as given, as in actual decision-making. Rational expectations theory, rather, depicts the state of knowledge for decision makers as the outcome of optimizing behaviour applied to information acquisition itself. Individual agents are depicted 'as if' they equate the marginal cost of acquiring information with the marginal benefit they derive from it. This requires the strong assumption that the marginal benefit of information is known before it is acquired.

One of the major figures in the development of rational expectations theory has stated explicitly that his motivation has been to put theory and empirical work on the same logical footing, that is, to resolve the *impasse* between induction and deduction. Sent (1998) documents how Sargent has changed from one tack to another in an attempt (unsuccessful to date) to resolve the difficulties he faces in doing this. He turned for example to predictive models, then to engineering models, then to complexity models in an attempt to deal with the problems which kept arising with each successive method, challenging the conceptual integrity of theory and method which he strove to maintain. In particular, he was grappling with how to represent uncertainty and learning (issues arising from induction from observation) in terms of the rationality axioms. Marshall's theory of knowledge alluded to above would explain why Sargent's search for a formal model of knowledge and learning has proved so elusive. This is something which we will explore more in section 8.3.

Since the rational expectations solution therefore does not seem to have resolved the difficulties of reconciling deductivist theory and induction, in spite of the best intentions of the rational expectations theorists, we turn now to consider the issues as they have been understood in the traditional methodology literature. These concern empirical testing of theory, however derived.

6.3 Empirical Testing

6.3.1 Verification, confirmation, or falsification?

We have seen, between Chapter 5 and the discussion above in this chapter, that the methodological questions about how to do economics are tied up with how we define the subject matter. It is hard to separate the two issues—particular methodological approaches allow economics to deal with different subject matter, and each prevents economics from dealing with some subject matter. There are trade-offs. Deductivism allows us to separate off economic behaviour, defined axiomatically. Inductivism can only do so if Marshall is right, that the empirical regularities we pick up coincide with economic forces. The kind of theory suggested by a deductive approach (based on axioms taken as true) may not be the same as the type of theory suggested by an inductive approach (based on observation of a reality which keeps evolving at the level of individual learning as well as at the societal level). And which seems more appealing depends on the weight we attach to such criteria as logical consistency, empirical confirmation, and prediction.

In this section we consider the issues which arise when we try to confront theory with evidence, whether that theory originated in an inductive or a deductive process. Logical positivism had specified that science be concerned with quantifiable statements, so that 'the facts' could determine which were the best theories. The criteria of 'consistency with the evidence' and 'predictive power' are thus given top priority.

The philosopher of science Karl Popper was highly critical of logical positivism. Inevitably, we will always be uncertain if an applied theory is a good one simply because it has been confirmed by the evidence (as opposed to a pure theory, which can be a good one simply because the internal logic is correct). There could be another, equally good explanation. Although seeking confirming evidence is normally called *verification*, this term is inappropriate since it means 'showing to be true'. It would be better to refer to it as a process of *confirmation*. We cannot even be certain of a theory being proved wrong if the theory is contradicted by the evidence; Popper was a fallibilist in that he did not see any possibility of establishing the truth.

Nevertheless Popper (1959) suggested a strategy for addressing the problem of induction. On the other hand, theory rejection is more constructive than theory confirmation in that it encourages the scientist to be critical of theory and consider how to improve it. Relying only on confirmation encourages complacency. Popper was particularly concerned that scientists should not engage in immunizing stratagems, that is, means of protecting hypotheses from contradiction by evidence. In other words, instead of a process of empirical verification, Popper advocated *falsification*. Science should therefore proceed by actively seeking to falsify theories, gradually whittling down the range of theories which might be true, and thereby getting closer to the truth, although attaining truth (or even knowing that it had been attained) was not possible. Progress would then be measured by the number of rejected hypotheses.

Logically Popper had a good point. But working out what has actually been shown to be likely to be false is the difficult part. Supposing a theory predicts that a fall in the standard rate of income tax will increase work effort, *ceteris paribus*. On economists' advice, the government reduces the standard rate of income tax and work effort doesn't change. Should the theory be rejected? Well, for a start, *ceteris paribus* may not have been satisfied. The government could point to something like the increasing relative attractiveness of employment outside the UK (for example, because of some change in EU labour market conditions). But, even if *ceteris paribus* were satisfied (and how do we prove that it has?), perhaps there is some shortcoming with the data used—perhaps they do not measure work effort well.

Even if the data are satisfactory, and we agreed that the theory has been falsified, how should it be improved? Did the problem lie with the technical specification of the labour supply function (is it in fact twice-differentiable?), with the information assumptions (do workers actually know their marginal rate of income tax?), or the institutional arrangements (are workers free to vary hours of work?), and so on. Most theories are conjunctions of hypotheses, rather than a single hypothesis; if the theory is refuted, which of the many conjoint hypotheses is at fault? This is called the *Duhem–Quine problem*, after a physicist and a philosopher, respectively, who raised and expanded on the issues involved (see Harding, 1976; Cross, 1982). As Quine (1951: 42–3) put it:

[T]otal science is like a field of force whose boundary conditions are experience. A conflict with experience at the periphery occasions readjustments in the interior of the field. . . . Having reëvaluated one statement we must reëvaluate some others, which may be statements logically connected with the first or may be statements of logical connections themselves. But the total field is so underdetermined by its boundary conditions, experience, that there is much latitude of choice as to what statements to reëvaluate in the light of any single contrary experience.

Popper was aware of the problem and so argued that only very narrow hypotheses should be tested so that only a very narrow range of possibilities could account for falsification.

The falsification criterion is very strict. It implies that most scientific activity would be negative, rejecting theories. Indeed, in studying what economists actually do, Blaug (1980) saw that the practice was very far from what Popper had advocated. Caldwell (1991) argues that there may be good reason for this. Popper had ignored the relevance for accepting or rejecting theories of the weight of evidence. If theories are consistently confirmed by the evidence (without immunizing stratagems), we should have more confidence in them, even though the confirmation does not prove the theory to be true.[5]

The methodology implied by Imre Lakatos's theory of scientific research programmes appealed to economists much more than Popper's approach. Lakatos (1970), another philosopher of science, suggested a more moderate version of falsification, effectively applying an infant industry argument to theories. New theories should be allowed protection from falsification until they have had time to evolve and develop, with reference to the data. Only at a relatively mature stage would contradictory evidence be taken as a signal to reject the theory. Thus, for example, when there is a bright new idea, such as applying choice theory to households, economists should be given the latitude to try out different variations in the light of reference to the evidence. Progress for Lakatos was put in a more positive way than for Popper. A scientific research programme would be progressive if it could explain 'novel facts', that is if it survived in the face of the problem of induction. Thus a body of theory would be progressive if it could explain a novel fact like the South-East Asia crisis, even though it had not predicted it. However, if the body of theory had to undergo ad hoc adjustments (like Popper's immunizing stratagems) to explain the crisis, then it would be degenerating.[6] This was the way to identify what was most 'scientific'.

We saw in section 2.2.1 how Lucas addressed what he took to be a novel fact, that capital was not systematically flowing to developing countries. He considered a range of possible explanations, and concluded that introducing imperfect competition was the best way of adjusting theory in order to explain the novel fact. Was this or was it not an ad hoc adjustment? Some would argue that, for a theoretical framework founded on perfectly competitive markets, this was indeed an ad hoc adjustment, while others who believe that markets are in general only imperfectly competitive would disagree. Still others who believe markets to be in general imperfectly competitive might still regard it as an ad hoc adjustment if the theoretical framework were not completely over-hauled to build up from imperfectly competitive markets. How Lakatos's criterion is applied clearly depends on prior methodological judgements.

6.3.2 Econometrics

Strict falsificationism also met a challenge in the practice of theory testing, that is, in the field of econometrics, which had continued to evolve with its own methodological agenda. A particular issue for falsificationism was the increasing treatment of economic relationships as stochastic. Whether this random element in relationships was due to a randomness in the subject matter, or to a random failure in theory to capture reality, it was no longer clear-cut whether evidence did or did not contradict theory. The issue became whether or not observations fell within a confidence interval. But then what size of confidence interval should demarcate between confirmation and contradiction?

The methodological agenda in econometrics therefore focused on other questions to do with the role of empirical evidence, with an emphasis more on verification than falsification. In particular, different approaches to econo-metrics have developed according to different views as to the relationship between theory and data. We introduced these approaches in section 4.2 in terms of empirical work on education, earnings, and growth. Here we con-sider econometrics explicitly in terms of the methodological issues we have been discussing in this chapter.

The traditional approach to econometrics had been the hypothetico-deductive approach. It was associated with the US Cowles Commission and sometimes called the Average Economic Regression, or AER, approach. Theor-ies were constructed deductively and then the values of parameters estimated econometrically in a process of seeking confirmation. Diagnostic tests, such as measuring the Durbin–Watson statistic, or testing for multicollinearity, are the indicators of whether or not the evidence confirms the theory. The Duhem–Quine problem is narrowed down to refer only to what the diag-nostic tests can identify. It is assumed that the underlying structure of the theory is correct, on the basis of deductive logic. So failure of any diagnostic test calls, not for a respecification of the theory, but for a change in estimation procedure. Various procedures, such as dropping variables, or introducing different lag structures, are used on a trial-and-error basis until a good specifi-cation is found. Empirical evidence, according to this approach, contributes by finding the empirical specification which best fits the theory. This specifica-tion can then be used for policy purposes. If, for example, the lag structure which fits best suggests that the price level in time t is most directly affected by the money supply in time $(t-2)$, then the implication is that the central bank has an idea of how long it takes for monetary policy to have an impact on the price level.

However, along with growing support for positivism in economics, the argument gained force for a more inductive approach which held no theoretical priors, that is, one which does not start with the belief that one particular theory is the best one. Then the purpose of empirical work is to provide independent evidence by which to judge theories. Sims (1980) in particular argued that it was in general impossible to test the full structure of theories, and there were particular dangers in what he called 'one-equation-at-a-time' specification of large models. For example, supply and demand curves in theoretical analysis are assumed to be independent of each other. But in practice they may be interdependent, which makes it difficult to identify the two functions separately from market data. Sims gave the example of the possibility of American consumers stockpiling coffee after they hear news of a frost in Brazil which they would expect to affect future supplies of coffee. Supply and demand would be interdependent through the expected price variable.

So instead Sims developed time-series analysis using vector autoregressions (VARs) as a way of identifying relationships from the data themselves, rather than from deductive theory. It is a way of drawing generalized descriptions from the data. But because the data analysis deliberately avoids referring to theory structure, the kind of descriptive information it provides relates to theories only at the reduced-form level. Thus, for example, we discussed in section 4.2 the reduced-form testing of theories about the effects of education on earnings based on choice theory. VARs can confirm or deny that a relationship exists between education and earnings, and say something of the form of the relationship. But the deductive reasoning is otherwise left untouched.

The third approach was developed in the 1970s and 1980s at the London School of Economics and Political Science (hence the 'LSE approach') by Hendry (1993). This approach does allow some theoretical priors. In particular, it is assumed that the causal structure conforms to some kind of general equilibrium framework. But there is then no presumption about the nature of short-term disequilibrium relationships. The data are used in such a way as to gradually narrow down the range of possible detailed relationships; it is accordingly also referred to as the 'general-to specific' approach. If a particular specification fails the diagnostic tests, the response is not, like the AER approach, to re-estimate, but rather to respecify the model. The aim then is to use the data to help to specify the theory, in an application of the hypothetico-deductive method. An empirical model is a good one, according to this approach, if it can explain rival models, and it can predict 'out of sample'. Traditional estimation uses the entire data set to estimate the model. The LSE approach uses only part of the sample, keeping some data back to see how well the model fits. This is a way of testing for whether the model can predict novel facts. If it does, then in Lakatosian terms it is progressive.

Econometric modelling and forecasting techniques continue to evolve, primarily in the direction of reinstating an interplay between theory, models, and forecasting practice, that is, addressing the Sims critique (see, for example, Hall, 1995). In econometric methodology therefore, as in methodology more generally, a central issue is how to handle the relationship between deduction and induction, or, more generally, the relationship between reason and reality (for economists as well as economic agents).

6.4 (Critical) Rationalism

6.4.1 Rationalism

The philosophy of science within which Popper and Lakatos put forward their versions of falsificationism is called critical rationalism. Rationalism is a philosophy, developed in the seventeenth century, which sees reason rather than experience as the source of knowledge. It is more normally associated with deductivism than the empirical issues addressed by Popper. But we will see that Popper's critical rationalism was designed to promote theory development by the critical use of observation, as a way of getting round the problem of induction. Popper was concerned to specify what was science and what was not science, and wanted to put in the latter category what he referred to as 'historicism', the identification of long-run trends from historical experience (notably in Popper, 1944–5). Lakatos, as we shall see, was more sanguine about the knowledge which could be gleaned from induction.

It is worthwhile to consider rationalism itself briefly before proceeding to critical rationalism. Since rationalism provides a philosophical foundation for deductivism, it is important for economics. As we have seen, the particular characteristics of economics, that is the particular requirements for abstraction, have encouraged the persistence, and indeed importance of Mill's deductivist approach. In core economics textbooks, for example, empirical content generally tends to be very much secondary to logical argument (see Backhouse, forthcoming).

But rationalism is also important for how we discuss methodology. In particular, there is the fact that we are here discussing philosophy. Rationalism implies that scientific knowledge arises from a hierarchy of philosophy-methodology-science. First, we use reason to establish the best philosophy of science. This philosophy suggests principles for conducting science, that is, methodology. These principles are then presented to the scientist, who puts them into practice. So rationalism as a philosophy can also be seen as justifying empiricism as a methodology. Indeed, this chapter is an enquiry into methodological rules founded in reason rather than practice, although we can question this separation (section 8.3).

Rationalism raises questions which Popper (1982) himself addressed. First, part of Popper's argument against inductivism was that rationalism was empty if the real world was governed by universal laws. If the real world is deterministic (so that we can identify universal laws empirically), then our belief in these laws is simply part of the predetermined whole, not the outcome of rational argument. Instead he put forward various arguments against

'scientific' determinism, that is to say, the doctrine that the structure of the world is such that any event can be rationally predicted, with any desired degree of precision, if we are given a sufficiently precise description of past events, together with all the laws of nature. (Popper, 1982: 1–2)

Popper suggested that, in order to understand human freedom (as opposed to determinism) we need to consider the reality of social life in terms of three 'worlds'. World 1 is the physical world (as studied by the physical sciences) and World 2 is the psychological world (as studied by those concerned with the mind of humans or of animals). World 3 is of a different sort, being the product of the human mind; it extends from works of art, ethical values, and social institutions to theoretical knowledge. Focusing on scientific knowledge, Popper saw knowledge as being rationally constructed with reference to objective observation of Worlds 1 and 2. Popper argued that World 3 is open in the sense that it is not deterministic; knowledge is fallible. But it is not just that rational knowledge is limited because there is an element of randomness in the object of knowledge; human creativity itself makes the universe indeterminate. Further, World 3 interacts with Worlds 1 and 2 in a real sense, so that, if World 3 is open, the universe is in general open. He gives as an example a man drawing a highly detailed map of the room in which he sits. This exercise combines World 1 (the physical pen and paper) with World 2 (the perception of the scene to be mapped out) and World 3 (the map). But it is impossible to complete the exercise. When he draws a rectangle to represent the map, he then needs to draw a rectangle within it to represent the drawing of the map, and so on *ad infinitum*.

Popper thus chose to retain rationalism while rejecting determinism. Rationalism keeps philosophy at the top of the hierarchy in terms of generating methodologies for science. But inevitably the rejection of determinism colours the kind of scientific knowledge we can hope to construct, and how far it can be justified. Popper's open world perspective (with the real world, our perception of it, and the knowledge we construct about it all being interdependent), is reminiscent of Marshall's analysis. Marshall had argued that the knowledge which firms build up about the business environment plays a part in the way in which the firm is organized, which determines the type of knowledge which can be built up, and so on. To understand the firm, therefore, Marshall argued that what we need to study is processes, rather than end-states (see section 6.2.4 above). We will return to some implications of indeterminism in Chapters 7 and 8.

6.4.2 Critical rationalism

In this section we explore Popper and Lakatos's critical version of rationalism in some more detail. Critical rationalism involves, in addition to reason, what Popper (1974: 68) called 'the *critical method*, the method of trial and error: the method of proposing bold hypotheses, and exposing them to the severest criticism, in order to detect where they have erred.' While Popper saw reason as being limited in terms of prediction (because of indeterminacy) it was not limited in terms of criticism; it is the exercise of criticism which marks out science from non-science. Non-scientific knowledge is maintained in the absence of critical exposure to reason and testing.

Popper (1963) saw the origins of theory in 'conjectures', arrived at deductively, or rationally. They are tentative theories suggested as a solution to a particular problem. These conjectures should be 'bold' in the sense that they are narrowly and precisely expressed, and thus open to refutation. Refutation was to be an empirical exercise, whereby conjectures were confronted by 'the facts'; this critical confrontation was the hallmark of science. So at the same time as apparently defending the role of deduction, Popper's critical rationalism also defended a form of empiricism. Where he departed most notably from the logical positivists (see section 5.4.1) was that, through aiming to falsify theories, scientists would have the best chance of identifying error and thus the best way for working out how theory should then be developed. He argued that scientists should avoid 'immunizing stratagems', or ad hoc adjustments to their theories to protect them from falsification. The detail of Popper's philosophy of science was then addressed to the question of how to construct theory in such a way as to allow falsification without being hampered unduly by the Duhem–Quine problem.

We keep coming up against the problem in economics of how to relate abstract theory to empirical evidence. Unusually for a philosopher of science, Popper explicitly considered the methodological issues facing economics. (This was a product of the two-way influence between him and his friend, Hayek.) In subsection 6.2.3 we considered the issue, for empirical testing, of the status of the axioms used in deductivist theory. Popper concluded that the assumption that individuals behave rationally should be taken as a non-testable starting point for theory (Popper, 1994). By that he meant that it was necessary to assume that individuals would behave appropriately to the situation in which they found themselves; this was his *situational logic*. Rationality should then be understood in terms of aims and constraints. Social science was concerned with the unintended consequences of human action, which is analysed in terms of behaviour which is rational at the individual level.

Although the rationality axioms in economics are much more restrictive than is required by this definition of rationality, Popper was prepared to argue that these axioms should be treated as logically necessary for economic analysis, and thus not to be subjected to empirical testing. Falsification of a theory would not hold any implications for the rationality axioms, since these were to be treated as a 'zero principle'. In fact Popper accepted that actual behaviour is not always appropriate to the situation. But, because of the Duhem–Quine problem, it would be impossible to implement falsificationism in economics if the assumptions made about individual behaviour in general were contestable along with the content of the theory.

As we have already seen, the justification for the rationality axioms has been a matter of much discussion. What we might think of as 'appropriate' behaviour may not be the same as optimizing behaviour. The notion of 'behaviour appropriate to the situation' would normally imply not stealing from a blind beggar because it would be inappropriate, although the rationality axioms might justify it on utility-maximization grounds. The normal usage of the term 'appropriate' refers to social conventions which may override individualistic optimizing considerations. We have thus come back to the separateness issue. Should we still use the rationality axioms to define economically appropriate behaviour, as a means of separating off the subject matter of economics? There has been much discussion as to how to square Popper's situational logic for economics with his falsificationism for the natural sciences (see Caldwell, 1998). Just as important, but not the focus of much discussion, is the question of how to square Popper's indeterminism and emphasis on creative individual behaviour with the rationality axioms. This issue has been a focus for neo-Austrian economics.

The idea of unchallenged assumptions also can be found in Lakatos's version of critical rationalism. He argued more on sociological grounds that any research programme would have a hard core of assumptions which were not to be challenged. This refers to the sociology of the economics profession. It is ironic that economists might use this justification for retaining axioms which abstract from the sociology of the subject matter. Theory development, according to Lakatos, consists of the evolution of the body of theory built up around this hard core, in what he called the protective belt. Unlike the core assumptions, the hypotheses yielded by theories in the protective belt would be subjected to empirical testing. Since at some stage it would be accepted that some theories were falsified by the evidence, and new theories would be developed, the protective belt would shift over time. The process was therefore one of the growth of scientific knowledge. Lakatos, like Popper, was a fallibilist in accepting that science could not establish truth. Nevertheless, scientific activity (namely that which satisfied the strictures of critical rationalism) would ensure that knowledge grew. Lakatos carried forward Popper's situational logic, with scientific research programmes themselves evolving to address new situations. Lakatos had thus shifted the falsification programme from the level of individual, tightly specified theories, to 'the problem of appraising historical series of theories, or, rather, of "research programmes"' (Lakatos, 1974: 318). In order to be appraised, research programmes were to be 'rationally reconstructed', that is expressed in terms of a rational system defined by a hard core and protective belt.

The hard core of a research programme is defined by various propositions (HC), and also by positive and negative heuristics (PH and NH) to guide theory development. Let us consider Weintraub's (1985: 109) Lakatosian definition of the neo-Walrasian (general equilibrium) research programme, in terms which go beyond the rationality axioms (which are represented by HC2, HC3, and HC5):

HC1   There exist economic agents
HC2   Agents have preferences over outcomes
HC3   Agents independently optimize, subject to constraints
HC4   Choices are made in interrelated markets
HC5   Agents have full relevant knowledge
HC6   Observable economic outcomes are coordinated, so they must be discussed with reference to equilibrium states

PH1   Go forth and construct theories in which agents optimize
PH2   Construct theories that make predictions about equilibrium states

NH1   Do not construct theories in which irrational behaviour plays any role
NH2   Do not construct theories in which equilibrium has no meaning
NH3   Do not test hard core propositions.

A key feature of how Lakatos identifies progress is whether novel facts are explained within the research programme's heuristics or by ad hoc adjustments. An ad hoc adjustment would be something inconsistent with this hard core. Considering again the South-East Asia crisis, this was, for many theories, a novel fact. Were it not, then it would have been more widely anticipated. Many of the explanations after the fact pointed to inadequate information. If markets had known about the fragility of the financial structure in the affected economies, they would not have supplied as much capital inflow in the first place. This explanation violates HC5 in Weintraub's schema, implying that it was at best an ad hoc adjustment.

But, as Backhouse (1991: 404–5) argues, HC5 no longer fits more recent neo-Walrasian theory, where information limitations play a key role. Instead he suggests that HC5 be replaced by a positive heuristic, PH3: 'Construct theories in which agents have a well-defined set of information about relevant phenomena.' This raises two issues. One is that it seems that, in practice, the hard core itself can evolve, not just the protective belt, so that it is no longer clear-cut what is ad hoc and what is not. But, even apart from the changing hard core, we see that the meaning of the research programme specification, and thus of what is and is not ad hoc, is not unambiguous. If, as in the neo-Walrasian programme, knowledge is understood as an 'information set' which can be 'well-specified', then identifying a set of relevant information which was not known is an empirical matter—it is not necessarily ad hoc. But one of the competing explanations of the crisis is that it was an unsurprising, endogenous outcome of the financial fragility created by an excessive expansion of capital inflows encouraged by financial liberalization (see, for example, Arestis and Glickman, forthcoming). The object of knowledge is thus created endogenously, and so information held cannot be well specified. To explain the crisis by information limitations, according to this alternative approach, is ad hoc.

Lakatos's scientific research programme framework has attracted much attention in economics, with the capacity to explain novel facts being seen as an important vehicle for appraising theories (see Hands, 1991). But it was eventually concluded that the capacity of the Lakatosian framework to allow theory appraisal was quite limited (see de Marchi and Blaug, 1991). In particular, as we have seen, it was difficult to decide whether a novel fact was explained fully by an existing theory, or only after ad hoc adjustments, without first having a clear specification of research programmes. It was only latterly that efforts were made to try to set out what exactly were the hard core and protective belts of different research programmes. But by this time there was a consensus that the Lakatosian framework was more suited to constructing descriptive accounts of what economists do rather than appraising what they do. And indeed the framework has been used descriptively to good effect (see, for example, Mair and Miller, 1991). The framework designed for theory appraisal, the methodology of scientific research programmes, was being replaced by the methodology of historiographical research programmes, which is concerned with how economists actually (often implicitly) appraise theories (see Blaug, 1991).

In terms of the methodology of historiographical research programmes, the idea that the hard core could reasonably be protected from challenge, and new theories could be protected from falsification, allowed theories to survive persistent falsification.[7] Popper's strong injunction to develop theory explicitly to make it testable, in the sense of falsifiable, had been watered down. What had held the promise of resolving the issue for economics of relating theory to evidence ended up by disappointing, falling far short of Popper's idea of critical rationalism. Nevertheless, Lakatos held out the prospect of the growth of knowledge through science, by means of empirical testing of theories in mature research programmes. The central importance of the empirical criterion for theory appraisal is still maintained by Hutchison, Blaug, Klant, Boland, and Backhouse. We will consider the relation between theory and evidence further in the next section.

6.5 Modelling, Mathematics, and Economics

6.5.1 Introduction

We have been talking so far mainly in terms of theory, but much of economics actually takes the form of models. As Morrison and Morgan put it, in their aptly named book *Models as Mediators* (Morgan and Morrison, 1999), models are intermediate between theory and data, mediate between them, and have their own autonomy. Further, economic models are usually, though not necessarily, mathematical. They are seen as a particularly useful vehicle for relating (mathematical) theory to (statistical) evidence.

But how do models differ from theories? We start by considering what we mean by models, and the role they play in economics in relation to theory and data. Since economic models are normally expressed diagrammatically or mathematically, we consider the mathematization of economic theory in the following section.

6.5.2 Models

(a) Models as a vehicle for testing theories
In everyday language, a model is a simplified representation (often smaller in scale) of something more complex. A model railway cuts out the detail of such things as locomotive mechanism, interior carriage design, passengers, and outside environment in order to focus on the layout of the track, the signalling system, and the motion of the trains. In designing the engines of real trains, a very different model would be constructed which focuses on the mechanism of the engine.

In the model of the engine itself we can see the embodiment of a theory about how engines work. The model engine can then be put through a range of tests to assess whether the theory is a good one. Similarly a model in economics is a particular expression of a theory which potentially allows the theory to be tested. The neoclassical theory of the firm, for example, is based on the principle that firms aim to maximize profits, along with a variety of general assumptions (about knowledge available to the firm, about the existence of individual products whose costs of production can be separately identified, and so on). But the theory has different implications depending on what is assumed, for example, about the structure of the industry. Once the theory is broken down according to the assumptions made about industry structure, it is possible to construct models according to each set of assumptions.

The perfect competition model makes specific assumptions about the number of firms, the homogeneity of the product, and so on, which allows for a model which suggests definite conclusions which are in principle testable. The model makes predictions such as: 'If, starting in equilibrium, a firm in a perfectly competitive industry experiences a rise in the market price for its product, it will expand production until marginal cost equals marginal revenue again, and make supernormal profits. In the long run, *ceteris paribus*, new firms will enter the industry and the increased supply will drive the product price back down again.' If the evidence in a particular case were consistent with this prediction, it would confirm the perfect competition model. This would lend weight to the theory of the firm which generated the model, as would confirming evidence for the monopoly model. However, evidence which contradicted the model's conclusions would suggest that the theory needs to be revised. The models are acting as mediators between the theory and the evidence.

(b) Models for applied economics

Boland (1989: ch. 1) points out that the criteria for constructing a model, or assessing it, depend on its purpose. He draws the distinction between pure theorists, who construct models to improve their understanding, and applied economists who construct models to help them address practical questions.[8] Similarly Mayer (1993) discusses the idea that different criteria are relevant to the different purposes of pure and applied economics. But both types of model either stand or fall ultimately, according to Boland, on how well they stand up to empirical testing.

For example, in Chapter 4 we discussed how economists have addressed the relationship between education and earnings. The choice theory models are designed to improve our understanding, and are developed by incorporating ever more complicated 'real world' factors. But it is impossible to test the models directly because so much of the theory doesn't have empirical counterparts. The models can only be tested indirectly in terms of their reduced-form equations. For applied economists, the reduced forms are central. There is a presumption that the underlying theory provides an adequate explanation for why there should be a positive relationship between education and earnings. But in order to advise governments about the consequences of a policy like charging student fees, the important thing for the applied economist is to estimate the parameter values which fit the situation at hand, and then predict the outcome of the policy. For example, when the Scottish Parliament was considering the appropriate level of university tuition fees, evidence was submitted to the Cubie Committee which estimated rates of return to higher education in Scotland directly from the labour force data (Bell, 2000). The reasoning offered was consistent with, but did not require, the optimizing model.

(c) Models as thought experiments

The models of pure theory can be seen as thought experiments. As in the case of the model railway, models are a means of isolating particular features of a theory for close attention. Abstraction is one form of isolation which involves creating an abstract, or 'ideal' type for study. But there are other forms of isolation, such as removing from consideration a range of factors which would be present in a real-life situation.[9] The model railway isolates the structure from snow and rain, for example. This is material isolation, the characteristic of physical experiments. But physical experiments are not normally possible for economists, so we rely on theoretical isolation whereby we conjure up an imaginary experiment. Lucas (1980: 696) for example is quite explicit that:

[o]ne of the functions of theoretical economics is to provide fully articulated, artificial economic systems that can serve as laboratories in which policies that would be prohibitively expensive to experiment with in actual economies can be tested out at much lower cost.

The implementation of monetarist policies in the UK in 1979 was nevertheless referred to as a 'Monetarist Experiment'. But, as experience showed, the transition from thought experiment to policy implementation is so fraught with pitfalls that the policy maker cannot be sure at all of the outcome of the policy in practice.

(d) Models as a means of communication

Models also, as any student knows, are a means of communicating ideas. Much of the teaching of economics focuses on models as a means of getting across core ideas. Thus introductory courses are constructed around learning the supply and demand framework at the micro- and macro-levels. Indeed, these models are so important to the discipline that Leijonhufvud (1981) wrote a spoof anthropological article about the two castes within the tribe of the Econ: the Micro-caste and the Macro-caste. While each caste had very different preoccupations (market coordination and market failure, respectively) each had its own totem, represented by two crossed carved sticks (see Figure 6.4), which looked remarkably similar to each other.

Models need not in fact be diagrammatic or mathematical. Morgan (1999) shows how Fisher's quantity theory model of inflation was built up from a mechanical balance model, duly illustrated with pictures of scales with coins at one end balancing real goods like bread and cloth at the other. This model was only later translated into mathematics. Similarly Phillips built a physical

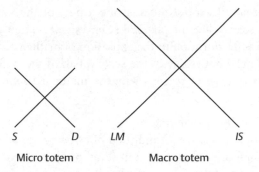

Figure 6.4 The totems of the Micro-caste and the Macro-caste

hydraulic model in order to teach Keynesian macroeconomics. He constructed a system of pipes, baths, and pumps to represent the Keynesian income–expenditure model. This model made it visually clear that, as the flow of investment expenditure increased, the income flow increased until it reached an equilibrium level where the new injection into expenditure was matched by outflows (literally) of saving. Indeed, much of the language we use—inflows, outflows, equilibrium, and so on—draws on our understanding of these physical mechanisms. Phillips's hydraulic model is a metaphor for Keynes's conceptual model of the workings of the macroeconomy.

(e) Theory without models
But not all economic theory is expressed or communicated by means of models as we commonly understand them. Much of economic theory is developed verbally. Thus for example one approach to the theory of the firm which we discussed in section 3.3 is expressed or communicated instead by means of case studies. Of course even language involves isolation, both in terms of isolating the discussion from certain features of a real-world case and in terms of abstraction. But, as we will consider later, language generally involves less isolation than the greater formality which we associate with models. While we consider these issues in greater depth in sections 7.3 and 8.4, we proceed now to consider the role of mathematics, the most common vehicle for modelling in economics.

6.5.3 Mathematics

Models do not need to be expressed mathematically. But since the alternatives (other than language) are either mechanical models, or diagrammatic models, and these can normally be expressed mathematically, we will focus on the mathematical expression of economic theories, through models. There has been much discussion about the role of mathematics in economics, not least because so much of economics is now expressed mathematically. The move towards mathematical expression was one aspect of the drive to build up economics as a science like the physical sciences (see section 5.4.1), led by the work of Walras and Cournot. But the explosion of mathematics in economics really occurred most noticeably in the second half of the twentieth century.[10] We can identify a range of reasons why the mathematization of economics was so appealing.

(a) Mathematics and theory testing

The appeal of logical positivism, and then of critical rationalism, in economics put the emphasis on empirical testing of theories as the means of promoting progress. Popper himself identified a 'Newtonian revolution' in mathematical economics (see Hutchison, 2000: 104). Indeed the very notion of testing with empirical data leads a discipline into mathematical expression. Data themselves are a form of abstraction (Mirowski, 1991).

In particular there was a concern that economics, as a positive science, should be seen to be independent of the subjectivity of individual economists and free of value judgements (see Morgan and Rutherford, 1998b). Mathematics was thus seen as a means of presenting all propositions on an equal footing, that is, the propositions were clear and commensurate (all expressed in the same terms). Further, the statements arising from theories needed to be sufficiently precise that tests could be seen as definitive, and mathematics provided precision (see Hahn, 1973a). Mathematics was thus seen as an effective mechanism for building up scientific knowledge within economics, and is still seen by many in this light (see, for example, Backhouse, 1998a).

However, there were signs that mathematics did not ensure commensurability. Even within mathematics, there is scope for terms to have different meanings (see Weintraub, 1998). But the debates over macroeconomics in the 1970s illustrate how mathematical expression and empirical testing of mathematical propositions may not be sufficient to settle disputes. The arguments between Keynesians and Monetarists was often presented as an argument over the slope of the LM curve (see Laidler's (1981) discussion). How interest-elastic was the demand for money? On the face of it, this should have been resolved easily by recourse to the data. But the Duhem–Quine problem meant that the data could not discriminate between the two theories to everyone's satisfaction. There was more to the differences than the slope of the LM curve, and this coloured the way in which the models were set up and the data interpreted. The issues arose from theoretical differences which could not be translated into a common framework (IS–LM analysis). This difficulty therefore reflects the problems we have already identified with empirical testing, which throw our attention back to the formulation of the theories themselves. Here too there has been a tremendous impetus for mathematization.

(b) Mathematics and the formulation of theory
A major problem with empirical testing is the specificity of any context from which data are drawn. This makes it difficult to establish economic laws. The argument in favour of deductivism was that abstracting from specific contexts, and non-economic factors in particular, gave us the best chance of coming up with economic laws. Since deductivism was built on classical logic, mathematics derived from classical logic seemed to provide the best mechanism for such a project. As Debreu, a leading force in the mathematization of economics put it:

[Mathematics] ceaselessly asks for weaker assumptions, for stronger conclusions, for greater generality. ... Mathematics also dictates the imperative of simplicity. ... [E]conomic theory was helped by greater abstraction ... [which] led to the study of fundamental problems of great generality, but also to a broad range of applications. (Debreu, 1991: 4–5)

By making clear what the issues are (the specification of precise assumptions, exposing the logic to scrutiny, and so on) mathematical expression is seen as pointing the way to the proper future path of development of economic theory (Krugman, 1998; Backhouse, 1998a). Further, the more complex the theories become, the more useful is mathematics as a language for representing that complexity and allowing theory to be analysed and exposed to criticism. Put another way, mathematics was seen as a means for promoting rigour in economic analysis.

The issue of the role of mathematics in economics adds another layer to the issue of abstraction in general. Abstraction of economic behaviour from other behaviour deliberately separates economic analysis off from correspondence with the real world, posing particular problems for empirical testing, as well as application to real-world problems (see Hutchison, 2000; Mayer, 1993). The structure of economic theory then is driven by the internal logic of the form of abstraction. Mathematics clearly has tremendous benefits for economic theory. But these benefits do not come without a cost. The benefit of greater generality offered by mathematical expression may be offset by the fact that precision of mathematical expression increases the degree of abstraction; if this precision is not matched in the real world, we may only be able to draw conclusions about how theory may *not* be applicable (see Coddington, 1975). Hahn (1973b) for example sees general equilibrium theory as specifying the conditions which must obtain if markets are to coordinate successfully. Rigour in terms of a particular form of logic may not mean rigour in terms of correspondence with the subject matter (Chick, 1998).

There is a particular issue for the assumptions underpinning the deductive structure. It is often argued that, for the mathematics to be tractable, and solutions to be generated, restrictions need to be imposed, for example, on the representation of individual rationality. Thus, while interdependent utility may be something we would like to incorporate in theory, it is generally left to one side as being too difficult. Similarly, knowledge limitations need to be specified in some formal way; we normally assume complete knowledge, or else limit knowledge according to probability distributions.

Since mathematical expression comes with costs as well as benefits, how we view it is ultimately a matter of judgement (Katzner, 1991). We will consider the issues further in section 8.4, where we open up the discussion to the possibility of different types of logic and different types of mathematics, and in section 8.5 where we consider mathematics as one of a range of tools rather than the primary tool.

6.6 Conclusion

In this chapter we have explored the issues which dominated methodological discussion in much of the twentieth century. For all the difficulties in finding satisfactory criteria for choosing good theories, and offering guidelines for the future of economics, there was among many a (more or less wistful) optimism that the project could still yield fruit. But other methodologists were critical of how little seemed to have been achieved in the field (see, for example, Salanti, 1987). The achievements seemed to have been negative ones of recognizing the severe limitations to the type of methodology explored in this chapter, which was geared to establishing the basis for identifying progress in economics. There had been, in particular, a drawing back from seeing empirical testing as defining the growth of economic knowledge.

Hands (1990) put a positive construction on these developments in methodology, arguing that understanding of the limitations had grown over the 1980s, so that there was at least some consensus on a range of important points. Perhaps the best way of summing up where we have got to is by listing some of these points of consensus, all abstracted from Hands (1990: 73–4)[11]:

1. Econometric work does not 'test' fundamental economic theory in a way which would satisfy most philosophers of science or in the way suggested by the standard rhetoric of economic testing.

2. Falsificationism, the methodology of bold conjecture and severe test, is often preached in economics but is almost never practised.

3. Though 'hard cores' and 'positive heuristics' abound, 'novel facts' as defined by the Lakatosian school have been few and far between in the history of economic thought.

4. The 'Duhemian Problem' is particularly difficult in economics; the

complexity of economic phenomena and questions about the empirical basis of the discipline make empirical testing an extremely complex affair.

5. It is not the case that one particular general theory or research program in economics (neoclassical micro, Keynesian macro, American institutionalism, Marxian economics, etc.) is clearly 'science' while the others are clearly 'nonscience'.

6. The axiomatic mathematical structure of modern general equilibrium theory (the Arrow/Debreu/Walras model) does not relate to empirical economics in the same way that mathematical physics relates to empirical work in its domain.

7. The maximization assumption is a basic methodological presupposition of neoclassical economics (it is not a tautology [that is, it is not necessarily true] but it is seldom falsifiable).

Hands (2001) later revisited this assessment, taking account of developments within methodology in the 1990s. Given the disillusionment with the positivist approach to methodology, he detected a revival of interest in the deductivist approach. At the same time he identified the emergence of a more sophisticated understanding of Popper than the simple falsificationist reading which had had the greatest impact on economics, and indeed a more sophisticated reading of positivism in general.

Two further points of consensus which he had already identified as having been reached by the 1990s introduce questions which we have not yet directly addressed, since they refer to two important currents of thought which developed in the last two decades of the twentieth century as departures from the kind of methodology we have been considering in this chapter:

8. Discussions in economics, like discussions everywhere, have a fundamentally rhetorical component.

9. Regardless of how modern theorists view neoclassical microeconomics, the founders of the theory (in the 1870s) viewed the theory from a realist perspective.

The way in which arguments and theories in economics are expressed—the rhetoric used—is something which has attracted significant attention since the 1980s. Further, the question of realism, while something we have touched on in a variety of ways in Chapters 5 and 6, also came to prominence again recently, since the 1980s. But ever since the 1960s there had been a growing groundswell of opinion that the traditional twentieth-century methodology covered in this chapter was unsatisfactory—either it was unduly ambitious in seeking criteria for identifying growth in scientific knowledge, or it was unduly narrow in defining the role of methodology in this way. In the next two chapters we focus on the different approaches to methodology which emerged late last century (but not without historical precedents), including the rhetoric and realist approaches. We will find a more optimistic set of views as to the useful contribution which methodology, in some form or other, may make to economics.

6.7 Further Reading

For further reading on the topics explored here, see, by topic: Hutchison (2000), Hausman (1992: Appendix) (inductivism and deductivism); Blaug (1980/1992: chs. 1, 3, 4, 16), Caldwell (1984), de Marchi and Blaug (1991), Mayer (1993), Backhouse (1997) (empirical testing); Boland (1998b), Caldwell (1991), de Marchi and Blaug (1991), Caldwell (1993: vol. iii, parts I and II) (critical rationalism); Boland (1989), Morgan and Morrison (1999), and the four articles published together in the *Economic Journal* as a Controversy: Weintraub (1998), Krugman (1998), Backhouse (1998), and Chick (1998) (modelling, mathematics, and economics); and Salanti (1987), Hausman (1989), and Hands (1990) (summings up).

Endnotes

1. Smith and his contemporary, David Hume are often thought of as empiricists. As we shall see (section 6.2.4) it is in fact impossible to be either a pure inductivist or a pure deductivist. Smith and Hume were both philosophers whose philosophy of science was more complex than is implied by the label 'empiricist', and indeed has much in common with many of the modern developments in philosophy of science discussed in Ch. 7 and 8 (see Dow, 2000).

2. Although this way of putting the problem is commonly associated with the philosopher-economist David Hume, his problem of induction was very different: it was that the natural and social worlds are so complex that it is part of the human condition that we cannot hope to identify with any degree of certainty all the causal mechanisms at work.

3. Hausman (1992) addresses the issue of the separateness of economics from 'non-economic' influences on behaviour. How far this is connected to the inexactness of economics is debated in Mäki (1996, 1998a) and Hausman (1997, 1998).

4. The second half of the nineteenth century saw the battle lines being drawn between the deductivists of the Austrian school (notably Menger) and the inductivists of the German Historical School (such as Roscher and Schmoller). The ensuing debate was called the *Methodenstreit* (see, e.g. the account in Screpanti and Zamagni, 1993, sect. 5.4.1).

5. See also Salanti's (1987: 368–92) critique of Popper's fallibilism and falsificationism.

6. We have raised some questions in subsect. 5.4.3 about the status of 'facts', in particular whether they are 'theory-laden'. So we might raise similar questions about whether what is thought of as a 'novel fact' and an 'ad hoc adjustment' might also be theory-laden. We will consider these questions further in Ch. 7.

7. The notion that the facts against which theories would be tested were independent of the theories themselves was open to challenge (Rosenberg, 1986). See sect. 5.4.3 and Ch. 7.

8. This corresponds to the distinction between explanation and prediction we discussed in sect. 5.3.1.

9. See Mäki (1992) for a full discussion of the different senses of isolation in relation to realisticness; we will focus on issues of realisticness and realism later in Ch. 8.

10. See Morgan and Rutherford (eds.) (1998a) and Blaug (1999) for analyses of the forces which promoted mathematical formalism in this period.

11. The title of the article refers to thirteen theses, but three do not relate so directly to the discussion in this chapter, and the last one is Hands's own argument rather than a point of consensus.

7

UNDERSTANDING ECONOMICS

7.1 Introduction

The last chapter was rounded up with Hands's (1990) listing of areas of consensus in the methodology literature which revolved around the agenda of identifying criteria for progress in economics. The most stark illustration of the extent to which the field of methodology was changing is the listing which Hands constructed a decade later. He concluded that, in terms of the objective of methodology as being 'to find a few clearly specified methodological rules for the proper conduct of economic science' that 'if followed, would guarantee that the resulting economic theory constituted legitimate scientific knowledge', the result had to be judged 'a failure' (Hands, 2001: 49).

Admission of this failure, allowed methodology to develop in new and fruitful directions, including drawing on a more general development called 'science studies' which we explore in section 7.4. Hands defines the 'new economic methodology as any inquiry that substantially involves both economics and science theory' (Hands, 2000: 51). This new methodology allowed a broadening of horizons, encompassing a better understanding of how economics is actually conducted, drawing on developments in the more general area of science theory. It is the purpose of this chapter to chart the thinking which led to this state of affairs, and in the process to explain the routes by which many methodologists now approach their subject. While the prescriptive approach outlined in Chapter 6 is now often referred to as 'big m' methodology, or 'Methodology', the descriptive approach outlined in this chapter is often referred to as 'small m' methodology. As we shall see, however, seeing methodology as pure description is seen as unsatisfactory from the point of view of helping economists in their quest to address real-world problems; this aspect of modern methodology is the subject of the next chapter.

We start with the work of Thomas Kuhn, which promoted a new line of enquiry in the philosophy of science, and raised important issues for economic methodology. Kuhn's approach focuses on the way in which economists function as members of communities of economists. A key issue in Kuhn was the language used to convey ideas in science; this finds an echo in the work on the rhetoric of economics, which we explore in section 7.3. Kuhn was a historian of science, and thus set an agenda for what is now known as science studies, the study of scientific activity in its social context. Having explored this approach in section 7.4, we turn to another development in the context of ideas in which economic methodology develops: postmodernism.

7.2 Economics as a Social Activity

7.2.1 Kuhn

In Chapter 6 we discussed the contributions of Popper and Lakatos, who were conscious of the significance of scientists working in scientific communities. Popper's critical rationalism took a rather individualistic view of how individual scientists behave, while Lakatos emphasized the hard core of a research programme as being something shared, and sustained, by the community. In considering restricting the scope of the falsificationist programme, he was addressing the observation that scientists don't as a general rule reject theories when they are falsified. Lakatos was in fact reacting to the ideas of Thomas Kuhn, but still within the rationalist agenda of seeking criteria for identifying good science. Like Popper, he sought criteria for the growth of scientific knowledge which were specified in terms of empirical testing, so he fits into the subject matter of Chapter 6. But Kuhn in the meantime had opened up the field of philosophy of science, not just to new answers, but also to new questions.

While Kuhn's ideas set the philosophy of science off on a new path, his ideas did not come out of the blue. There had been growing concern about positivism, much of it due to Popper. As we have seen, Popper saw the capacity for establishing true knowledge to be very limited. In particular, he had highlighted, in his three-worlds framework, the interplay between the real world, how it is observed and recorded, and how we construct theories about it. While Popper insisted that the best way to construct knowledge was still to set up propositions to be falsified empirically, there were growing doubts, not only about the capacity to test successfully (because of the Duhem–Quine problem), but also about the independence of the 'facts' against which theory was to be tested. Further, the experience in physics in the first half of the twentieth century suggested that whole bodies of theory, which previously had been held as good foundations for physical laws, could be overthrown by an entirely new way of looking at things—as with Einstein's theory of relativity and Planck's quantum physics. This period also saw the emergence of

Heisenberg's principle which raised very specific questions about the independence of observation (see section 5.4.1). Without a reliable empirical criterion, it was becoming less clear that it was feasible to develop rules for good conduct in science which were independent of current practice.

Kuhn was a historian of science, which meant that his aim was to provide an account of scientific activity. Like Adam Smith (1795), he chose astronomy as his focus of attention, showing how thought evolves discontinuously, with new bodies of thought bringing with them new meanings.[1] Astronomy has had a dramatic history, notably with Galileo being charged by the Inquisition with heresy for challenging the Aristotelian view that the earth is the centre of the universe (once this had been drawn to the Church's attention by Galileo's fellow academics); Galileo was initially imprisoned because he would not recant, and ended his days under house arrest. This inhibited the further development of Galileo's ideas, in Italy at least, until much later. Thus we see that scientific ideas (like the earth being fixed at the centre of the galaxy) can persist in the face of falsification, in this case with the aid of institutional arrangements.

But once the new set of ideas had taken hold within Newtonian physics (the planets moving round the sun), meanings changed so that there was no neutral ground on which to compare the old and new theories. Kuhn wrote later (Kuhn, 1999) that what had motivated the development of his own ideas was an attempt, as a graduate student, to make sense of Aristotle in order to set the scene for a study of Galileo. He encountered some passages in Aristotle which made no sense:

> My difficulty was not that these anomalous passages were more obscure than the others I had read, for they were not. My problem was rather that I could not believe a person of universally acknowledged intelligence could have written them: they seemed not so much obscure as absurd. (Kuhn, 1999: 33)

It was only when he experimented with changes in meaning of concepts used by Aristotle, by identifying patterns in the texts, that the passages made any sense. From this experience, Kuhn had realized that meaning is not fixed, and there is great scope for talking (or reading) at cross purposes, that is, for incommensurability. Out of this understanding of history, requiring the historian to understand the meaning of the terms intended by those expressing ideas, Kuhn (1962) developed his theory of scientific revolutions.

7.2.2 Paradigms

The key concept is the *paradigm* which represents the focus of scientific research for a particular community. (Lakatos's concept of the scientific research programme was based on the paradigm concept.) Kuhn was criticized for using the term 'paradigm' too loosely. This is in itself an issue.

Precision of definition is a requirement of rationalism, but Kuhn was himself addressing the possibility that even precise meanings may change with changing ideas and perceptions in the body of thought within which the definition is applied. There may even be virtue in 'vagueness'; we will explore this idea further in section 8.4.[2]

However, Kuhn accepted that further refinement was needed in order to make his argument more clear, so he consolidated the different facets of paradigms within the concept of a 'disciplinary matrix'. This matrix encompasses not only the particular range of methods and models used by the community of scientists, but also their world-view (Kuhn, 1974). A world-view includes not only how reality is understood but also values (such as the importance to be attached to consistency in judging theories, for example). We discussed in section 5.3.2 the question of how far economics could be positive, or value-free; Kuhn's framework suggests that science is organized in communities where to a considerable extent values are held in common, with the implication that it is not normally deemed necessary to separate out their shared value judgements from positive statements. Specifically, successful puzzle-solving activity in a scientific community requires consensus on methodology (see Kuhn, 1970: 184–5).

A paradigm is taught and thus solidified by means of exemplars. Most of the scientific activity within the community involves what he called 'normal science', taking the fundamentals of the paradigm as given, and refining the theories and models built on these fundamentals. While Popper (1970) abhorred this characterization of normal science for being uncritical, Kuhn (1970) argued that it was necessary for the growth of knowledge within a paradigm to take the shared foundations as given, albeit provisionally. His argument is based on a historical study of what scientists actually do; Popper saw his role as prescribing what scientists should do, while Kuhn, in describing actual practice, could identify how scientists saw themselves as adding to knowledge in spite of all the methodological difficulties they face. Popper's critical rationalism accords more with what Kuhn characterized as 'extraordinary science' which involves a reassessment of the fundamentals of the paradigm and the exploration of alternative paradigms. The development of science is the outcome of the interplay between normal science and extraordinary science.

The growth of knowledge *within* the paradigm is a matter of refinement in response to internal logical 'puzzles', and confirmation by evidence. Puzzle-solving is an effective vehicle for knowledge to grow *according to the criteria of the paradigm*. Puzzle-solving may however come up against contrary evidence. Falsification of some feature of the paradigm may then either be ignored (not necessarily wilfully, but as a matter of what is 'seen'), or, if acknowledged, encourage adaptation of the paradigm to accommodate this new evidence.

But if this paradigm-defence is unsuccessful, there is a scientific revolution and a new paradigm takes over. But then what was regarded as growth of knowledge in the old paradigm may not be so regarded from the viewpoint of the new paradigm.

Implicit in any paradigm is a methodology in the sense of a set of principles to guide theory development and to assess new theories. But each paradigm has its own principles. There is no set of principles outside a paradigm which can be brought in to settle inter-paradigmatic disputes. This would explain why the search by methodologists for a set of principles to apply to any new theory was seen to be doomed—any principles we could consider are specific to some methodological paradigm or another. There is certainly the basis for discussion, but no neutral territory.

Further, building on Kuhn's understanding of the importance of language, the scope for discussion is hampered by the fact that meaning varies from one paradigm to another. For example, we saw that one of the negative heuristics of the neo-Walrasian research programme is:

NH1   Do not construct theories in which irrational behaviour plays any role.

But 'irrational' in that programme means not conforming to the rationality axioms of that programme, while in another paradigm it could mean 'self-deluding', and be an important motive force in the economy which is thought worthy of study.[3] This type of theory would fare poorly by the criteria of the neo-Walrasian paradigm, but not necessarily by the criteria of the other paradigm's own criteria. Finally, and perhaps most fundamental with respect to the empirical testing of theories, what we observe is 'seen' differently by members of different paradigms. Thus, for example, a rational expectations theorist cannot 'see' involuntary unemployment. Or, where a Becker-type analysis of household behaviour sees only self-serving or altruistic behaviour, a sociological approach might see behaviour conforming to the social conventions of the context.

In summary, paradigms are *incommensurate*; there is no neutral basis on which to compare them. One of the virtues we identified (in section 6.5.3) with the use of mathematics was that it put all sources of knowledge on a par, for ready comparison between models and for ready testing by data which corresponded to the mathematical variables. What Kuhn's framework suggests is that, even if all theories were expressed in terms of the same type of mathematics, the meaning of terms might differ, the meaning of the data might differ, and in any case different weights might be attached to different attributes of the theory (logical consistency, consistency with the facts, and so on). In this sense theories of family behaviour based on choice theory are incommensurate with sociological theories of the family. We have no independent set of rules by which to decide which is better. We can certainly discuss which we think is better, and why, but the methodologist cannot arbitrate other than from the perspective of some paradigm or other.

Indeed, readers of economics texts where new theories are justified as improvements on the old may have recognised Kuhn's puzzlement as to how Aristotle could have said what he was alleged to have said. Did economists before the rational expectations revolution *really* think that people are irrational? Or take the representation of general equilibrium theory as the completion of Adam Smith's project:

One of the main theorems of Welfare economics formulates precisely the principle enunciated by Adam Smith (1776): If all the agents of an economy are in equilibrium relative to a price system, then they utilize their collective resources optimally. The proof of that theorem ... has become so simple that it can be given without mathematical symbols. (Debreu, 1991: 4)

Was Smith really so hampered by lack of modern tools that it took such effort to show something which can now be demonstrated so simply? Is Debreu's language and mathematical method simply an improvement on Smith's, or is there some incommensurability between Smith and Debreu? Is optimizing behaviour as defined on the basis of the rationality axioms consistent with the way in which Smith analysed the economy? Winch (1997) argues convincingly that the two are in fact incommensurate. Similarly it is easy to come away from reading Lucas's (1980) account of Keynes with some puzzlement as to how Keynes could have been regarded as such a great economist. Kuhn's framework offers an explanation: Lucas and Keynes are best understood in terms of different paradigms (Vercelli, 1991). Each is bound to fare badly by the criteria of the other's paradigm.

Kuhn's framework itself can be seen as an exemplar of his paradigm in the philosophy of science. We can see that his ideas did not emerge in a vacuum; there is some continuity from earlier ideas. Nevertheless, he constructed a view of science which was quite at odds with the dominant, rationalist, approach. Concerns with rationalism had been growing within the philosophy of science, and with positivism in science. Developments in the physical sciences such as quantum mechanics did not seem to fit the positivist agenda, and so Kuhn's work can be seen as an exercise in extraordinary science within the philosophy of science, which attracted support, allowing the emergence of a new paradigm. While we can identify continuities in the process of the emergence of this paradigm, what actually emerged was incommensurate with what had gone before. In rationalist terms, Kuhn's paradigm was irrational. In Kuhnian terms, 'they would say that, wouldn't they'. Critical rationalism does not have the status of ultimate arbiter of science, but is simply one paradigm in the philosophy of science which was dominant for many years, but which has now been dropped by much of the philosophy of science community (Caldwell, 1982). To think of critical rationalism as the sole representative of the growth of knowledge in the philosophy of science is to ignore other paradigms, such as that which prevailed in the Scottish Enlightenment and which had much in common with the Kuhnian paradigm and other modern developments in the philosophy of science.

7.2.3 Scientific revolutions

Against the background of social change in the 1960s it is understandable why Kuhn's ideas took hold. He had sought to describe the conduct of science in terms of a series of paradigms with no ultimate arbitrating authority. In a social environment where authority was being challenged more generally, Kuhn seemed to legitimize the rejection of authority. We will see the outcome of pursuing this train of thought to its limits in section 7.4.

The use of the term 'revolution' was also significant. In assessing whether his ideas fitted economics, much of the focus was on the question of whether or not there had been any revolutions in economic thought (see Coats, 1969; Bronfenbrenner, 1971; Kunin and Weaver, 1971; Dobb, 1973: ch. 1; and Blaug, 1976). The consensus that emerged was either that revolutions had been quashed or that change had been evolutionary rather than revolutionary. Keynes had set out to 'revolutionize' the way we think about economic problems. But it was concluded either that the neo-Walrasian research programme had adapted to encompass what it understood as Keynes's ideas, or else it was concluded that, while Keynes's ideas were indeed revolutionary, there had in fact been no discrete shifts in economic thought (Laidler, 1994). Although there had been nothing so dramatic as a confrontation with the Inquisition, the institutional context may have been just as effective in preserving traditional ways of thinking about economics.

Nevertheless, regardless of whether or not there had been any revolutions in economics, Kuhn's conception of scientific communities seemed to capture well what became an increasingly significant phenomenon in economics from the 1960s on. The post-war years had been characterized by a strong movement towards mathematical formalism (see Blaug, 1999) which was seen as promoting commensurabilty: a common language for economics. Up to a point this allowed a range of ideas (and value judgements) to flourish (see Morgan and Rutherford, 1998b). But overall it cemented the identification of mathematical formalism with the dominant paradigm, making very apparent the incommensurability with alternative paradigms which did not adopt mathematical formalism. Thus, for example, neo-Austrian economics, which has methodological objections to mathematical formalism, was incommensurate with the mainstream. Similarly, when Post-Keynesians engaged with the mainstream, the debates focused on those aspects which were commensurate, that is, expressed mathematically (such as the slope of the LM curve), to the neglect of other more fundamental areas of dispute (such as the meaning and role of money). The professed methodology of the mainstream was mainly still some form of positivism, which provided grounds for making judgements about non-mainstream theory as if they were commensurate (in terms of deductive logic, exposure to econometric testing, and so on). In this climate, Kuhn's framework opened up the possibility that such judgements were only valid in terms of one methodological stance, and thus did not have general validity. Each school of thought in economics could legitimately establish its own methodological stance. Obviously these were up for discussion, but there was no independent arbiter. Kuhn's framework implied that, in a mature science, one paradigm would be dominant at any one time; in other words a proliferation of approaches would only occur during periods when extraordinary science came to the fore (that is, revolutionary periods). It is a matter for debate as to how far this model fits the physical sciences rather than the social sciences. But Kuhn's framework can be adapted readily to address a discipline characterized by a proliferation of paradigms as the norm.

7.2.4 Relativism?

At the methodological level, there were very mixed feelings about Kuhn. While some saw his ideas as fruitful (see, for example, Loasby, 1982), others saw Kuhn's move away from the rationalist agenda of specifying criteria for the growth of knowledge as potentially undermining the scientific status of economics (see, for example, Blaug, 1980). Kuhn was charged with *relativism*, seen as the only alternative to rationalism in the philosophy of science. To a dualist either there are criteria for good science or there are none. Paul Feyerabend (1975) expressed Kuhn's arguments in a more extreme fashion, arguing that any change in theory involved incommensurability, changing both the meaning of theoretical terms and the understanding of facts, so that no two theories could be compared on the same ground. Feyerabend therefore criticized Kuhn for presenting a linear picture of one paradigm succeeding another. He positively welcomed the proliferation of theories as providing the most fruitful climate for promoting understanding. Indeed, Feyerabend argued that the experience of science (both physical and social) justifies this stance. On the one hand, it is through changing meanings and practice that new ideas emerge. On the other hand, debates within science as to which theory to accept involve non-rational argument. This stance invited Blaug's (1980: 44) charge that Feyerabend was putting forward the 'philosophy of flower power'.[4] 'Anything goes', as Feyerabend himself put it, became associated for many also with Kuhn. Since the only possibilities were seen as either rationalism or relativism/irrationalism, not surprisingly, this philosophy of science struck most economists as highly unsatisfactory.

Nevertheless, Kuhn's ideas more generally have been very influential and productive of further ideas. His idea of science being constructed around a range of incommensurate paradigms addressed the issue of how we deal with the limitations on human understanding, which became apparent as we proceeded through Chapter 6. Further, the notion of incommensurability focused on the role of language and meaning in the development of knowledge, which we discuss further in section 7.3. Incommensurability is if anything more important for the social sciences than the natural sciences. Up to a point, the subject matter of the physical sciences is the same, but is understood differently by different paradigms. But the subject matter of economics keeps changing, as we discussed in Chapter 2. A paradigm may well suit a particular context (that is, not be faced with significant anomalies), but cease to be suitable (face insurmountable anomalies) when that context changes. Thus a theory which treats the money supply as exogenous, or assumes that workers don't save, for example, may be appropriate for one set of circumstances, but not be appropriate with a more developed financial system and rising incomes.

Perhaps most influential for the path which much of economic methodology took from the 1980s was Kuhn's descriptive approach (albeit in terms of a powerful conceptual framework), with its emphasis on the social environment of the scientist. Much of this work has been couched in terms of Lakatos's scientific research programmes; as we saw, Lakatos's attempt to reinstate the empirical criterion for identifying progress was not as successful as many had hoped. But this focus on scientific communities paved the way for a major new development in the methodology of economics which for some time was referred to as the 'sociology of scientific knowledge', and now goes under the umbrella of 'science studies' or 'science theory'. The attempts (discussed in Chapter 6) to prescribe good practice for economics had failed, so many economic methodologists turned to description instead. We consider this development in section 7.5.

But conceptually the key element of Kuhn's work was incommensurability. It held profound implications for methodology which we will explore more fully later in this chapter and in Chapter 8. As we have noted, Kuhn's focus in considering incommensurability was on language. There was an important development in the economics literature in the 1980s which focused on the language which economists use to persuade. We consider this rhetoric approach next.

7.3 Rhetoric

7.3.1 Pragmatism, hermeneutics, and literary theory

Kuhn had addressed the question of how some theories come to dominate the discipline while others fall from sight, given that economists cannot demonstrate the truth of their theories. It must be the case that most economists have been persuaded of the advantages of the successful theories but not of the neglected theories. Much of this has to do with convention within a paradigm. If it is conventionally regarded as preferable for theories to be expressed in terms of neo-Walrasian choice theory, for example, then this type of theory has a better chance of being accepted than one which does not. But it may be more than simply a preference for being in line with a Lakatosian positive heuristic (as set out in section 6.4.2). There is the prior question of the language used to express the theory, on which heuristics also depend.

The groundswell of thought of which Kuhn was a part included an increasing attention to the importance of language for scientific communities, both in philosophy and in literary studies. In philosophy, there is a long-standing tradition termed *pragmatism* which seeks a practical (philosophical) resolution to the failure of rationalism to generate truth. Quine, whose work we have already referred to in Chapter 6 as challenging the feasibility of applying falsificationism to individual statements (rather than bodies of thought), was part of this tradition, as were Dewey and Peirce (see Hoover, 1994). Also in this tradition is Rorty (1979), who developed the argument that philosophy does not mirror nature, but is rather a social construction, understood by means of interpretation—there is no neutral vantage point from which to view nature. As a pragmatist, Rorty suggests that the value of science-as-a-social-construction lies in its usefulness, since we cannot satisfactorily judge it in terms of how well it represents reality.

We can see here some philosophical foundation for Friedman's instrumentalism. Friedman had argued that theories should be judged according to how well they predict, not according to their form or content (see section 5.3.1). However, Friedman's positivism goes against Rorty's argument that there is no independent set of 'facts' by which to assess theories. This consideration of pragmatism therefore lends a certain irony to the debate between Friedman and Samuelson. Unlike pragmatism, Friedman argued that nature (actual values of the predicted variables) would determine which was the best theory, while Samuelson had argued that there were conventions about the form and content of theories by which to judge a theory. While Samuelson did not express it in these terms, conventions are community-based, and fit in well with the pragmatist's view that scientific knowledge is socially constructed.

Rorty argued that the search for rules for the building up of scientific knowledge should be replaced by *hermeneutics*, the exercise of interpreting socially constructed accounts. Like others, he referred to the episode in astronomy where Galileo conflicts with the Church's account of the position of the earth in the universe. According to Rorty, to say that Galileo was right and the Church wrong is to import a perspective from later years, without understanding the Church's notion of truth. A hermeneutic analysis would try to make sense of the strong positions held in the debate in terms of the perspective of the protagonists themselves. Well yes, you may be thinking, but surely it is empirically established now that the sun is the centre of the galaxy. But it is worthwhile reflecting on the fact that that statement is at least partly a matter of perspective. If we wanted, we could specify a system with the earth at the centre of the galaxy; the paths the other planets would take would be very cumbersome compared with the ellipses of the normal system, with the sun defined as the centre. But it is less obvious that one system is true and the other false. In economics, the basic unit of analysis for a Marxian is class, while the basic unit of analysis for a neo-Austrian is the individual. The resulting theoretical structures are very different; difference of perspective is not neutral. But are we in a position to say that one is true and the other not? Further, do these need to be alternatives (either/or), or could they be complements (both/and)?

As Kuhn noted, historians are naturally hermeneutic, but it does not come so naturally to economists in their formal writing. In his Introduction to a collection of essays on hermeneutics and economics, Lavoie (1990b: 1) defines hermeneutics as follows:

Hermeneutics, or interpretive philosophy, is essentially a philosophy of understanding, which elucidates how it is that one person comes to understanding the actions or words, or any other meaningful product, of another. It takes the case of reading a text as paradigmatic of all forms of interpretation, throughout the arts and sciences, and in everyday life.

Lavoie contrasts human communications with the 'copy' approach. If a fax or an e-mail fails to get through because of telecommunications breakdown, the solution is to send it again exactly as before. However, if a human argument fails to communicate, 'we say it differently the next time, we explicate hidden assumptions, anticipate possible objections, deploy different examples' (Lavoie, 1990b: 1). Thus economists unwittingly employ hermeneutics in informal discussion.

Hermeneutics can be applied not only as a means of interpreting what economists say and do, but also as a means of interpreting the economy itself (see Brown, 1994; see also Henderson et al., 1993). Thus, it is not just the case that meaning is specific to a context of ideas, but also to an interpretation of reality. As Rorty had argued, the 'facts' we use in science as the reference point of theory are themselves socially constructed.

Meanwhile, within literary theory, Fish (1980) was pursuing a similar agenda by focusing on the interpretation of literary texts. Fish focused on the role of interpretive communities as putting some constraints on the range of possible interpretations; this is an important factor when we consider the charge of relativism. While in principle any interpretation is possible (casting doubt on the whole idea of building up knowledge), the need to communicate to an audience requires that audiences (different communities of scholars) have shared interpretations. So the range of interpretations is limited; these interpretive communities correspond to Kuhn's paradigms.

While Peirce was concerned to distinguish science from non-science by its greater precision and its critical approach, other pragmatists were concerned to emphasize the commonalities between science and other forms of know-ledge. This has been a key feature when this approach has been applied to economics. The focus on the rhetoric of economics has been led by Deirdre McCloskey, who draws on both Rorty and Fish in order to analyse the lan-guage used by economists. The argument that we would do well to pay atten-tion to economic rhetoric is accompanied by an argument that any attempt at prescriptive methodology—capital 'm' Methodology—is doomed to failure. What is possible is small 'm' methodology—studying the methodological principles which economists actually follow.

7.3.2 Metaphor

McCloskey (1985: 3) points out that, contrary to popular perception, there is in fact a remarkable degree of agreement among economists, and that much of this stems from a shared use of language. She argues that we can gain a much better understanding of economics by studying the language that is used, with the aid of concepts taken from literary studies (McCloskey, 1985: 84 ff). Of these perhaps the most important is the use of metaphor (see Henderson (1994) for a full discussion). 'A metaphor is a use of language in which what is said is not literally what is meant' (Henderson, 1994: 344). It may be viewed as a 'surface' linguistic decoration of a logical argument; the language of a first-year textbook is less formal, for example, than an article in the *Journal of Economic Theory*. But more fundamentally, the use of metaphor may influ-ence the direction of inquiry and the logic of the argument. Indeed, Solow (1988) argues that use of language can itself be used to ensure the continuance of one methodology at the expense of others.

Studying the metaphors used in economics adds depth to our earlier dis-cussion of 'simplification' in economics; the language we use is the vehicle for capturing a complex reality in simpler form. If a metaphor were literally true, then it would no longer be a metaphor, and would not serve the purpose of simplifying reality for the purposes of theorizing. But the metaphors are tied up with the choices made as to *how* to simplify reality for the purpose of theorizing. Rational economic man is a powerful metaphor; few would argue that people literally maximize utility on the basis of complete preferences; the use of the metaphor is designed to capture the essence of economic behaviour. But inevitably there will be disagreement as to whether it does so successfully or not. Similarly, when Becker represents children as 'durable goods' (see section 3.2) he is not saying that they are literally durable goods, but he is guiding our thoughts in the direction of transferring arguments applied to capital equipment to an analysis of children. The metaphor may be used ironically—we may laugh when we first come across it—but once we use it in analysis, the focus on the chosen features of children (those akin to capital goods) suppresses those aspects which are unlike capital goods. Even the variables we use involve the literary device of symbolism, or metonymies. The variable 'L' stands for labour, and is measured by hours of work, which we all know suppresses much of what is involved in work; modern labour economics is struggling to deal with that suppression, referring, for example, to 'work effort' rather than 'labour hours'. But given the power of symbolism, it is inevitably a struggle, constrained by well-established meanings. Symbols are powerful devices which aid thought, but they need to be open to discussion as to how useful they are, given their power also to direct thought.

Further, thinking back to our discussion of values in economics (section 5.3.2), we can see that metaphors provide a vehicle for values to be embedded in theory. A downward-sloping marginal productivity curve (which involves a whole collection of metaphors) tips us towards a theory of income distribution according to value of marginal product. Or using the term 'natural', for a rate of unemployment, or an interest rate, makes it sound unassailable. Or who could object to a theory which portrays individuals as being rational? A study of the language used can help us to identify where the values are embedded and what they are (see Heilbroner, 1988).

This understanding of metaphor as permeating economics is central to Mirowski's (1989) analysis of the relationship between economics and physics. The early development of utility theory was explicitly expressed using a physical analogy. Mirowski argues that the subsequent development of the discipline has been governed by the sustained use of metaphor drawn from physics because it was held to be the archetypical science on which economics should be modelled. When we discussed the relationship between economics and the physical sciences in section 5.4.1, a major issue was the nature of the subject matter; what is the significance of the differences between an economy and a physical object? As noted above, Brown (1994) develops the metaphor of the economy itself as being a text. This metaphor suggests that, when we try to understand the economy, it is like trying to understand a text. Literary theory points to the possibility of different readings of texts; markets or firms can be understood in different ways (see for example the discussion of the theory of the firm in section 3.3). Brown identifies a strong force in academic disciplines to unify the reading of the text, one mechanism being the induction of students into 'the literature'. This discussion parallels Kuhn's analysis of paradigms: the emergence of dominant paradigms, paradigm-specific language, and the propagation of the paradigm by means of exemplars. By learning supply and demand analysis in introductory courses we learn to use the metaphor of a supply-and-demand diagram, which colours much of the economics which builds on the metaphor. This is why Leijonhufvud (1981) lighted on the supply-and-demand diagram as the totem of his mythical Micro-tribe, and the visually very similar IS-LM diagram as the totem of the Macro-tribe (see Figure 6.1).

7.3.3 Economics as discourse

McCloskey argues that the language of economics is best understood if we think of the process of theory development in economics as a dynamic process consisting of a conversation. Even at an individual level, thought progresses as a process of internal negotiation between different considerations. The exercise of judgement is a form of internal conversation. But even more so in scientific communities, and in the economy itself (as a social structure), developments can be understood as negotiated positions. An individual economist may have a brilliant new insight, but it only impacts on the discipline if others are persuaded that it is so; it has to be expressed in language with which others can connect. McCloskey (1985) takes Muth's (1961) article as a case study of a piece of writing which inspired the emergence of rational expectations theory, and considers it in terms of persuasiveness of language, noting particularly the way it rests the argument on a positivist methodology.

The basis of McCloskey's approach is that it is hard to understand the persuasiveness of a piece of writing purely in terms of its internal logic; in addition we need to pay attention to the literary devices which lead to persuasion. It is a good exercise in fact to consider the most influential pieces of economic writing, and to try to work out what it is about them which stands out. Klamer (1995) for example analyses a pivotal article by Samuelson in this way. Klamer's (1983/4) book of interviews with leading economists was motivated by wanting to understand what made them tick, to understand theory by understanding the process of the development of these individuals' thinking, through the medium of conversation with an interviewer. The tremendous success of that book, and the fact that it spawned innumerable other interviews, testifies to the fact that economists want to know what the interviews can tell us, which academic writing cannot.

A formal piece of writing, like an academic journal article, may not seem like part of a conversation, and indeed that may be one element of its persuasiveness. McCloskey distinguishes between the 'official' rhetoric of most academic publications and the 'unofficial rhetoric' of the actual process of communication and theory development. Clearly great weight is attached to formal publications as authority to be cited. But how much do we understand from reading an article in isolation? It is normally necessary to know the related literature, that is, to become familiar with a particular discourse. But in addition, normally we understand better and are thus persuaded to accept some idea or another, through informal discourse: seminar discussions, asking questions of the lecturer, arguing with colleagues. It is often remarked that the question-and-answer session following the presentation of an economics paper is the most useful part of a seminar or conference session. As Lavoie pointed out, if we do not communicate successfully putting an argument one way, we change tack and put it another way. Unless we are already embedded in a particular discourse about a formal model, it is only when the cold logic of the model is embellished by a good introduction and conclusion that we begin to understand both its meaning and its significance.

McCloskey therefore presents strong arguments for improving our under-standing of economic discourse, as a means of understanding why economics develops in the way it does. It offers a 'thick' account compared to the 'thin' account of economics offered by, say, a Lakatosian approach, which rationally reconstructs what economists do. But in addition, McCloskey argues that a study of the rhetoric of economics reveals problems which are not otherwise apparent. In particular, she notes the pervasive reference to a positivist scien-tific method in the official discourse (as in Muth's (1961) article), while the actual process of persuasion which is conducted by means of unofficial rhet-oric is not positivist; persuasion in unofficial rhetoric is not based purely on rational logic exposed to challenge by the evidence, but includes use of rhet-orical devices, such as appeal to authority, and a range of expressions of arguments. This is so because positivism could not provide economics with a methodology which would allow us to demonstrate truth, for all the reasons we explored in Chapter 6.

This juxtaposition between the official and unofficial rhetoric is seen as a problem not just because contradictions are problematic, but because the nature of the positivist official rhetoric is such that it stifles conversation and thus the development of the discipline. McCloskey argues that the language has been unified to such an extent that the metaphors used are not up for discussion. The resulting intolerance of non-mathematical discourse, of openness to other disciplines, and so on, unduly limits the scope of the con-versation. McCloskey is not arguing against mathematical economics *per se*, or indeed against mainstream economics, but against their insulation from criticism:

The invitation to rhetoric is not, I emphasize, to 'replace careful analysis with rhetoric', or to abandon mathematics in favor of name-calling or flowery language. The good rhetorician loves care, precision, explicitness, and economy in argument as much as the next person. Since he has thought more carefully and explicitly than most people have about the place of such virtues in a larger system of scholarly values, he may even love them more. A rhetorical approach to economics is machine-building, not machine-breaking. It is not an invitation to irrationality of argument. (McCloskey, 1985: 36)

McCloskey, like Popper, thus sees openness to criticism as crucial, but empirical testing for her is only one part of the rhetoric. And by focusing on rhetoric, McCloskey is departing from Popper's individualistic approach to scientific activity. Further, McCloskey is concerned not to demarcate economics (or science) from other activities on the grounds that that too impedes conversation. Models in economics are simply one type of metaphor, not a sign of the scientific status of economics.

Boylan and O'Gorman (1995: ch. 6) discuss McCloskey's position as one of 'global rhetoric', and contrast it with a more moderate position termed 'local rhetoric', which gives rhetoric a less all-encompassing role. It is an aspect of conversation, for example, that it is not global, but takes place within institutional groupings and among self-forming groups. Thus, while McCloskey sees the concept of schools of thought (or paradigms) as unhelpful because they set up barriers to conversation, they could rather be seen, from a local rhetoric perspective, as a helpful shorthand for conversational groupings where the use of language is held in common. This form of segmentation is a matter of practicalities and need not prevent conversation between groupings, if it is aided by some prior understanding of the typical use of language by each grouping. Thus, if the Austrian focus on the individual and the Marxian focus on class were thought of in 'both/and' terms, rather than 'either/or' terms, then constructive discussion is possible between the two schools of thought.

7.3.4 Rhetoric and methodology

In order to promote good conversation, McCloskey (1994: 99) advocates Habermas's *Sprachethik* (rules for good conversation): 'Don't lie; pay attention; don't sneer; cooperate; don't shout; let other people talk; be open-minded; explain yourself when asked; don't resort to violence or conspiracy in aid of your ideas.' These are surely rules which no one could object to. Indeed, Redman's (1991: 173) characterization of critical rationalism is very similar, other than referring to the 'advance of science'. Otherwise McCloskey argues fiercely against any notion of rules for how to conduct economics. Because previous attempts to establish rules have failed, and yet these attempts still crop up in the rhetoric of economics as an important element of persuasion, she regards them as a pernicious force in economics:

The claims of an overblown methodology of Science merely end conversation. (McCloskey, 1983: 515)

Yet some have criticized this rejection of methodology as throwing economics open to relativism; 'he who persuades best wins.' There has been criticism in particular from those still concerned with providing guidance for progress in economics, expressed in critical reviews of McCloskey's first book on rhetoric (McCloskey, 1985), and in particular in a symposium published in *Economics and Philosophy* (see McCloskey, 1988, and Rosenberg, 1988). While Rosenberg (1988) argued that rhetoric disallowed any form of criticism of practice, McCloskey (1988) replied that rhetoric added new criteria by which to decide on which were 'good' theories and which 'bad' theories. The criticisms are generally addressed to McCloskey's global rhetoric. Boylan and O'Gorman (1995: ch. 6) classify the other leading figure in the rhetoric approach, Klamer, as taking a local rhetoric approach. While McCloskey emphasizes the common ground of economic discourse, Klamer emphasizes more the arguments within economics, thus casting the net wider than rhetoric alone. In particular, this approach draws attention to the possibility of a range of interpretive communities in economics. As Klamer (2001: 74) puts it:

Whereas McCloskey tends to play down differences between discursive practices, I accentuate them. The point of the rhetorical approach is for me the ability to bring out and to characterize differences. By considering the narratives and metaphors that Keynes employs we can quite easily show that he is not a Keynesian.

Once methodological differences are addressed, albeit by the rhetoric approach, methodology inevitably comes back into the picture.

It has been an interesting factor in the success of the rhetoric approach that McCloskey's emphasis on commonalities reflects her espousal of mainstream economics, although she is highly critical of the divergence between the official rhetoric of mainstream methodology and the unofficial rhetoric. Friedman (1953), a Chicago economist, had used his instrumentalist argument (see section 5.3.1) to deflect criticism of his macro-money model and to shift the focus to its apparent predictive success. So McCloskey (originally also a Chicago economist) seemed to offer a rhetorical argument for deflecting criticism of mainstream economics. It was another argument against interference in practice from the progress-oriented methodology. In section 7.6 we will see what has come of that development. But first we look to another wide cultural trend which lent further support to McCloskey's ideas.

7.4 Postmodernism

McCloskey had criticized the official methodological rhetoric as being that of positivism, or 'modernism'. Modernist science tends to be expressed mathematically, built up from axioms referring to the smallest element. It is ahistorical, in that its objective is to identify universal laws of nature (or society). It is to be assessed rationally, in terms of its logic and empirical testing, independent of how the ideas originated or for what purpose. McCloskey argued against this form of rhetoric as closing off conversation, demarcating between science and non-science, between good science and bad science.

The philosophy which more generally departs from modernism is post-modernism. It is an outgrowth of the challenge to scientific authority which came to prominence in the 1960s, and has been most apparent perhaps in social behaviour. Before the 1960s it was often socially acceptable to make sexist or racist remarks (to invoke social demarcations within a single, authoritative framework). But over the next few decades these demarcations were subject to increasing challenge and there was an increased focus on language. The sentiment was a good one—to treat all human beings with equal respect regardless of gender, race, religion, or age—and to be wary of applying judgements based on the majority experience to members of minorities with different experience. Any judgements needed to be context-specific.

Postmodernism was evident more generally in a wide range of disciplines, from architecture to literary criticism. In philosophy, it focused, among other things, on the fragmentation of the self (see Amariglio, 1988). As McCloskey had picked up, the notion of conversation applies even to individual choice: individual actions are the outcome of a negotiation within the self, as much as persuasion by others. Postmodernism focuses on fragmentation in general, encouraging attention to shift from the general to the particular. In economic geography, for example, it took the form of a reaction against Marxism, which was seen as presenting universal laws of motion of capitalism regardless of local context (see Lash and Urry, 1987). Economic geography turned against the idea that there might be general theories and focused on case studies of local communities. If there are no universal laws, then there is much less justification for government intervention and greater attention to local decision-making. Again we can see these ideas developing within the new liberalism which led to the move away from demand management, privatization of public sector activity, and so on. Further, within economics specifically, rational expectations theory was challenging the idea that government had superior access to knowledge which would warrant government activism and also allow it to be effective.

We can see similar developments in economics (see Dow, 1991). Over the last few decades, there has been a gradual project to build up the microfoundations of macroeconomics, that is, to express aggregate outcomes as the result of rational individual behaviour. At the same time, there has been a substantial body of macroeconomics which has discouraged the idea of macroeconomic intervention by government. Also in recent years there has been a fragmentation in economics itself; twenty years ago it was reasonable to classify mainstream economics in terms of general equilibrium—as Weintraub (1985) did in his Lakatosian reconstruction (see section 6.4). But perhaps the approach to economics closest to postmodernism is neo-Austrian economics, which is primarily microeconomic, and is conducted by means of case studies (see Lavoie, 1990*a*; Cubeddu, 1993).

But what exactly is postmodernism? Postmodernism is not just anti-modernism, because it is seen as emerging out of modernism over a period of time, and thus embodying some of the features of modernism. But beyond that, it is notoriously difficult to define. It manifests itself differently in different fields, but in any case, part of the point of postmodernism is to get away from general definitions and categorizations. There is therefore scope for different understandings of postmodernism, not helped by paradox being one of the postmodern characteristics (see Graham, 1992). Thus, for example, Keynes is sometimes portrayed as the archetypical modernist and sometimes as a postmodernist.

Postmodernism can perhaps be best understood in terms of the incommensurability we encountered in Kuhn's framework and the focus on discourse we encountered in the rhetoric approach. As two of the leading postmodernist economists put it:

> [P]ostmodernism focuses on and emphasizes the discursivity and plurality of knowledges—and thus the potential 'incommensurability' of such different knowledges—as well as related sensibilities of the fragmentary, discontinuous, undecidable, contextual, and decentring. (Amariglio and Ruccio, 1995)

Each context (in terms of the economic situation, and also of the economist studying it) is particular and generates its own knowledge. Each of these knowledges is incommensurate in that the concepts and language used to account for each situation may have different meanings from when applied to another situation. There is no independent means of deciding which account is 'best'. Further, 'decentring' means not making 'Man' central to economic analysis; in postmodern philosophy, individuals themselves are on the one hand part of their social context and on the other fragmented. Individuals are not themselves independent unities with given information sets.

Postmodernism supports the rhetorical approach to understanding economics. Like McCloskey, for example, Rossetti (1990) offers a deconstruction of some economics writing (in her case, two pieces of work by Robert Lucas) to demonstrate the power of this approach in forming judgements about economics:

> If economics progresses in a Popperian fashion, by the discovery of facts and the testing of theories relating to facts, then the vocabulary, metaphor and style of argumentation economists use are irrelevant to economists' acceptance of the theory or model in question. (Rossetti, 1990: 225–6)

However, for postmodernism:

[l]anguage and meaning are seen to be completely interdependent and unavoidably context-dependent. We are always trapped within some context; we can never step outside of it to attain an objective basis for our thought and our models. (Rossetti, 1990: 226–7)

Postmodernists contrast the use of discourse analysis as a search for meaning with the positivists' rationalist programme of searching for truth.

Postmodernists insist that postmodernism is not the dual of modernism:

I have said and will say again that 'post-modernism' signifies not the end of modernism, but another relation to modernism. (Van Reijen and Veerman (1988: 227) interview with Lyotard, as quoted in Ruccio, 1991: 495)

A dual is a mutually exclusive, all-encompassing pair of categories which have fixed meanings. Good examples of duals in economics are: rational/irrational, endogenous/exogenous, determined/random, and known/unknown. The habit of expressing categories as duals was one of the features of modernism which McCloskey (1983) had identified. It is also more generally a powerful characteristic of rationalist methodology, which explains much of the reaction to postmodernism (and the rhetoric approach).

If postmodernists study meaning, but meaning is inevitably context-dependent, then the project seems to be inadequate as a basis for science. Blaug (1994) and Backhouse (1995, 1997: chs. 3, 4) have put forward a critique along these lines. Methodologies are categorized as being either rationalist or relativist, the latter taken to mean that 'nothing may be said'. Postmodernists have not helped by using the term 'nihilist' to apply to postmodernism; nihilism is a philosophy promoting the state of believing in nothing and having no purpose. Thinking dualistically, it is the only alternative to a set of absolute values (as expressed in traditional methodology), but there is no reason for postmodernism to be dualist.

Postmodernism has in fact been concerned to go beyond dualism in other respects. Thus, for example, there is a concern to get away from demarcation between science and non-science, to consider economics in terms of how well it serves the needs of society, and more generally to see a two-way connection between science and society (Garnett, 1999). Indeed, as a plea also for tolerance and an open-mindedness to different meanings arising from different contexts (in the economy as well as among economists) postmodernism is surely to be welcomed. But there is a danger inherent in the approach, that the injunction to be tolerant be enforced in an intolerant manner. In social relations, what began as civilized behaviour in respecting differences of gender, race, and so on turned into the tyranny of 'political correctness'. It has become difficult to address real social issues in conversation when it is branded inappropriate even to refer to gender, religious, or racial differences. The same danger applies to economics. If respecting different approaches to economics—different meanings of terms, different interpretations of economic problems, and so on—means that disputes are not addressed, then it is not clear how to regard the discipline of economics. The move within the methodology of economics to flip over from one side of the prescriptive/descriptive dual to the other (because rationalist prescription was seen to be flawed) creates its own problems, which we explore in the next section.

7.5 Sociology of Scientific Knowledge/Science Studies

The type of methodology explored in Chapter 6 focused on translating principles from the philosophy of science for application to economics. In so far as economic practice was investigated, it was for the purpose of judging it in relation to these methodological principles. Thus, for example, Blaug's (1980) influential book on methodology chastised economists for falling short of Popperian principles. But, methodologists began to recognize the scope for studying what economists actually do in order to understand why they departed from standard methodological principles, even when these principles are explicitly professed (as in the introduction to many first-year textbooks). This development was inspired by Kuhn's history of science, but more particularly by Lakatos's notion of rational reconstruction of practice.

But economics has not been alone in grappling with the problems of adopting rationalism/positivism/modernism. More generally a body of thought has been built up which, like Kuhn's framework, focuses on the fact that science is practised within communities. Seeing scientific knowledge as being socially constructed, sociology is drawn on to understand scientific practice. This approach was known as the sociology of scientific knowledge (SSK). The approach developed along a variety of lines, emphasizing the social interests of scientists, the means by which scientists influence each other, and so on. But all of SSK had in common the view that science should be understood as a social phenomenon. Having been taken up also by philosophers and historians, it is now subsumed under the title of science studies.

One of the issues which arose within this approach was a feature of Bloor's (1976) early contribution, that the sociology of scientific knowledge should apply to itself, that is, be relexive. This highlights an important issue for economic methodology, which is that it too should be open to the same kind of scrutiny as its subject matter. The scope for a truly independent set of rules to be applied to economics was seen to be very limited (see our discussion in Chapter 6); from a science studies perspective, methodological knowledge is socially constructed just like economic knowledge. Put another way, methodologists come to their subject with their own (socially constructed) preconceptions. Indeed, for Fish (1985: 111–12) it is part of the critique of prescriptive literary theory that it serves the theorist's own interests:

[T]heory cannot reform practice because, rather than neutralizing interest, it begins and ends in interest and raises the imperatives of interest—of some local, particular, partisan project—to the status of universals.

Weintraub (1989) refers to this quote, drawing the similarity between literary theory for Fish and methodology for economics. It is not altogether surprising that Weintraub draws the conclusion that any attempt by methodologists to influence practice is misconceived and that they should concentrate solely on providing descriptive accounts.

Another tenet of the SSK programme identified by Bloor is that of symmetry between the investigator and the object of investigation. Thus when the investigator provides a reasoned sociological account of a set of theories, the account should apply equally to the theories, whether 'true' or 'false'. If the investigator were to assert a privileged position which allowed for judgements as to whether theories were good or not, there would be an asymmetry which would need to be justified (see Barnes and Bloor, 1982). Maintaining this symmetry has proved difficult in the application of SSK to economics, not least because it is readily apparent to sociologists that much of economics itself has no sociological content. It is hard for SSK to avoid being critical.

For example, in section 3.6 we highlighted the different way in which economists look at questions of health expenditure, compared to the general public, for example assigning a value to life. But, in constructing an SSK study of health economics, Ashmore, Mulkay, and Pinch (1989: 187) find that this exposes the problems of symmetry:

As symmetrical analysts in the sociology of scientific knowledge tradition ... we refuse, on principle, to evaluate the epistemological status [truth or falsity] of the knowledge claims we analyse. However, as applied sociologists of expertise we find that to avoid all evaluation of health economics is as unsatisfactory as it is impossible ... [I]t's not the epistemological status of applied economics in any abstract sense that concerns us but rather the specific moral and political implications of its underlying assumptions.

Can a sociological approach be truly neutral as to subject matter?

This issue arises also at the methodological level. We have come across the social dimension to methodology already in Chapter 6 when we encountered conventionalism. Conventionalism was the term used to apply to the methodological position which predominated in the absence of definitive rules for establishing truth. Blaug (1980: 6) defines it as the methodology whereby:

all scientific theories and hypotheses are merely condensed descriptions of natural events, neither true nor false in themselves but simply conventions for strong empirical information, whose value is to be determined exclusively by the principle of economy of thought:

Machlup (1978: 46) defined a conventionalist as:

one who accepts as meaningful and useful basic propositions that make no assertions but are conventions (resolutions, postulates) with regard to analytic procedure.

Conventionalism was the name given, for example, to Samuelson's arguments against Friedman's instrumentalism; particular theoretical structures may not predict noticeably well, but they may be preferred because they conform to what is conventionally understood to be the best way of constructing theory. The task of the 'progress' methodology literature was to decide on what were the best conventions.

The fullest discussion of conventionalism can be found in Boland (1989: ch. 1). He interprets conventionalist methodology more broadly, taking account, for example, of those for whom true statements about the real world are ruled out not only by the problem of induction but also by the absence of facts which are independent of theory, that is, facts which are not theory-laden. It is not clear then where conventionalism stops and postmodernism begins. Conventions too are central to the rhetoric approach—what is conventional is also *ipso facto* persuasive.

By taking a purely descriptive approach to economic methodology, the science studies approach has moved away from discussing which are the best conventions, and replaced it with a description of the prevailing conventions. But again, as with our discussion of postmodernism, we need to be wary of inappropriate dualisms—in this case the prescriptive/descriptive dual. 'Pure' description requires a set of independent facts—in this case, the practice of economics—yet the reflexivity of the science studies approach calls this independence into question.

The agenda in this new line of work in economic methodology is 'recovering practice', where practice is perceived in terms of communities rather than individual economists. Much of this analysis refers to sociological aspects of science, such as the incentive structures embedded in the society. If sophisticated mathematical skills are revered within the society of economists, for example, then employment and promotion prospects are enhanced by developing and applying these skills. Coats in particular has made a sociological study of the discipline of economics (see, for example, Coats, 1993). Similarly Mirowski (1989) focuses on sociological forces, as in the power of physics as the model for economics.

But there is a strong micro-element to much of the application of science studies to economics. Sent's (1998) study of Thomas Sargent provides a good example, using Pickering's (1992) science studies framework which looks for the free moves taken by the scientist and the forced moves taken when he comes up against constraints. The constraints may of course be social, and the free moves may be chosen according to outside influences from whoever happens to be a colleague at the time, for example, but the emphasis is on human agency. For example, Sargent's attempts to reconcile general equilibrium theory with econometrics (that is, establish a direct correspondence between theory and observation) produced a way of representing individuals' expectations formation. But he came up against the reflexivity problem: the models were not very good at predicting because they did not address the question of how individuals cope with a changing world; the techniques required the models to reflect a stable, unchanging world. He turned to bounded rationality for the solution, but found in turn that this approach now came up against the constraint that it could not deal with individuals' learning processes. So Sargent turned to the Santa Fe Institute and complexity theory. And so the saga continues.

For all its sociological emphasis, there is a strong move within science studies in the direction of micro-level analysis which tends to limit the scope for considering broad movements in thought, even as they impinge on the individual. As Weintraub (1999: 146) puts it:

Lost is the grand vision of revolutionary episodes, theories confronting data, and progress associated with greater and better knowledge about the external world. What replaces such stories are local narratives of laboratory life, of technological innovation, of ideas transformed by argument.

7.6 Conclusion

Having explored the problems encountered with applying rationalist philosophy to economic methodology in Chapter 6, in this chapter we have explored the reaction against rationalism and the new developments in methodology which have resulted. The key concept was Kuhn's incommensurability of paradigms, which arose from his descriptive accounts of development of thought in physics. This posed a challenge to the whole project of methodology as setting up rules for good scientific practice, as a basis for criticizing practice. The emphasis shifted over to trying to understand practice, by means of understanding the use of language, the social context of thought, and the motivation for new developments. This has been a good development for methodology, not least in promoting a better understanding of what economists do. It has also encouraged a greater degree of tolerance to different approaches to economics. The ideas explored in this chapter are now part of the methodological 'furniture', acknowledged even by those most closely associated with rationalism (see, for example, Blaug, 2001).

But doubts are often expressed as to how satisfactory this is as an end-state for economic methodology. Is that all there is? Among those who continue the rationalist approach to methodology, there is deep-seated discomfort that methodology might not be able to guide progress in economics. But even those who have taken an active part in developing the ideas discussed in this chapter see the ideas mattering for economic practice. Klamer (2001: 74) for example distances himself from Weintraub's denial of a role for methodology: 'In my experience reflection can matter for practice.'

There is further the issue of whether pure description is in fact feasible. The reflexivity argument applied to science studies points to the lack of independence of the economist studying economics. Science studies itself allows for a wide range of approaches: some are inclined to look for macro-influences, others for human agency, some seeing the consensus within economics, others seeing differences of view. The outcome is a multiplicity of accounts. The same applies to description of the economy: the science studies approach focuses on descriptions of the economy as being constructed by the economist (see, for example, Weintraub, 1999: 150).

In this age of political 'spin', there is in fact a general concern over the relation between reality and construction. The movie *The Matrix* touches on our fears that we live in a virtual world, constructed for us by some outside agency. The storyline is premissed on there being a 'true' account of what is happening, and a few humans have managed to access this truth. Take another piece of science fiction: *The X-Files*. We have here a representation of different scientific approaches. Dana Scully is portrayed as a traditional scientist who believes that all physical phenomena have an explanation within the existing scientific framework—although this belief is challenged by phenomena which cannot be explained in this way. Fox Mulder, on the other hand, extends the existing framework to allow for the possibility of alien life forms which intervene in our world. He allows for phenomena which cannot be explained by the existing scientific framework. 'The truth is out there', and he wants to find it. Further, Mulder believes that figures in authority are concealing knowledge, promoting the false representation of reality constructed by traditional science.

What should we as economists make of the argument that economic theories and models are constructions of a virtual world, with no independent facts against which to test them? Is the truth 'out there', still waiting to be found? Or is there no truth on which we can all agree, because there are different understandings of the real world and how we construct knowledge about it, and indeed differences as to what we mean by knowledge in the absence of truth?

By moving beyond the project of establishing rules for good science, we have come a long way in understanding how economics actually develops. But if, as economists, we are motivated to develop theory in order to address real-world problems, we have to take things a bit further. In the next chapter we consider ideas for retaining the understanding achieved on the basis of the ideas explored in this chapter, but going further in considering how methodology could actually assist practice.

7.7 Further Reading

For further reading on the topics explored here, see, by topic: Kuhn (1962, 1974, 1999), Hausman (1994), Dow (1996: ch.3) (economics as a social activity); McCloskey (1983, 1985, 1994), Klamer, Solow, and McCloskey (1988), Lavoie (1990), Henderson, Dudley-Edwards, and Backhouse (1993), Caldwell (1993: vol. iii, part III) (rhetoric); Samuels (1990), the symposium in the Summer 1991 issue of the *Journal of Post Keynesian Economics*, the chapters by Klamer, Amariglio, and Ruccio, and Backhouse in Dow and Hillard (1995), Cullenberg, Amariglio, and Ruccio (2001) (postmodernism); Weintraub (1989, 1999), Coats (1993), Hands (1994), Sent (1998) (SSK/science studies).

Endnotes

1. Adam Smith's ideas had much in common with those of Kuhn (see Skinner, 1979); we will come back in Ch. 8 to consider Smith's ideas and their context more fully.

2. Lakatos was also aware of the possibility of change in meaning of scientific terms, from his study of mathematics (Backhouse, 1998*b*); but he did not draw the same implications as Kuhn for the impossibility of objective appraisal of theories.

3. Adam Smith (1759) argued that people suffer from the illusion that wealth will bring happiness. But by following this illusion, hard work and the entrepreneurial spirit generate economic growth; this was one of his examples of the Invisible Hand at work.

4. Subsequently Feyerabend's views moderated somewhat; see Feyerabend (1978).

8

UNDERSTANDING THE ECONOMY

8.1 Introduction

What we have been grappling with is how difficult it is to demonstrate, using deductive logic and recorded data, that an economic theory is a good one. To the problems of proving even that a theory is false, far less true, we have now added the understanding that there is scope for different meanings of theoretical terms and also of observations. No wonder that Kuhn's ideas created a sense of unease. He seemed to have replaced the goal of firm (if only conventional) objective grounds for accepting or rejecting theories with what was widely understood as relativism, that is, no grounds at all for choosing one theory over another.

Nevertheless most of us believe that there is a reality which we are trying to understand (even if that reality involves human institutions, conventions, and expectations, and even if there are different understandings of that reality). There are economic theories which are accepted as good ones by a large proportion of the profession. And there are propositions which arise from economic theory on which many economists agree (see, for example, Alston, Kearl, and Vaughan 1992). Economists seem to be able to cope with deciding how to develop their own work. Policy makers seem to be able to adopt one theory or another to justify their policies. But on what basis? One answer is that these are the dominant conventions of the profession and we don't want to enquire into them too closely. The role of conventions has cropped up persistently, both in the prescriptive approach to methodology and the descriptive approach. But putting the focus on conventions is a powerful inhibitor to considering methodology—who knows what we might dig up once we start (Lawson, 1994b)? As Boland (1998a: 83) put it with respect to conventionalism: 'Perhaps it merely is, as Popper fears, an all-too-easy way to avoid criticism.'

One aspect of conventions is the tacit knowledge which is built up and embedded in routine behaviour. But, just as it is useful in a firm for routine behaviour to be open to scrutiny, so in economics the field of methodology exposes the methodological conventions of economists to scrutiny. In economics we have identified, as a leading convention, thinking in terms of ideal types. This convention has allowed for precise, consistent conclusions to be drawn. But as a basis for theorizing this may in fact mislead economists' expectations of the status of their own knowledge. The ideal-type economic agent makes choices on the basis of a complete information set (or specified limitations on information). If, rather than the benchmark of full information, we start from considering the human condition as entailing knowledge which is limited in a way which cannot be fully specified, the question can be turned around. Rather than asking how we cope without full information, we can ask how we nevertheless manage to build up enough knowledge as a basis for the choices we do make and the actions we do take. In other words, we can start with reality and work towards the abstract, rather than the other way round. The same issues apply to economists as to actors in the economy.

This is by no means untrodden ground. A similar debate was played out during the period of the Enlightenment. The rationalist tradition most closely associated with the French Enlightenment promoted the deductive approach to philosophy (and thus science). Yet the difficulty of proving logically that the real world existed seemed to undermine the very idea of science. David Hume, the eighteenth-century philosopher-economist, argued rather in favour of accepting the common-sense belief in the existence of the real world as a basis for science, and then building up knowledge by means of combining detailed observation and reason.[1] Scottish philosophy was explicitly addressed to the question of how to address practical problems (an important issue at a time of notable practical innovation). Not only did this put the philosophers' focus on how such innovation occurs in spite of the absence of a rationalist explanation, but also the notion of scientific progress itself was closely tied to success in dealing with practical problems.

Adam Smith, who came out of the same Scottish philosophical tradition as Hume, shared his view that true knowledge could not be demonstrated. So, like Hume, he focused on building up a theory of human nature which was prior to application to any science, or indeed mathematics (see Dow, 2001a). Hume and Smith regarded it as part of the human condition that we are not equipped fully to understand the workings of the universe—that capacity is reserved for the deity. Although Hume is commonly associated with the problem of induction as discussed in section 6.2.2, his statement of the problem was that humans, by their nature, cannot hope to understand the causal structure underlying their experience. The best we can do is to get the idea of cause from observing conjunctions of events—associating an increase in inflation with an increase in the quantity of money, for example. These associations are only manifestations of underlying processes, but they help us to intuit the notion of underlying causes. We cannot be sure at all of getting close to identifying underlying causal powers or tendencies, but it's a start. Further, as social beings, it was understood that our knowledge is socially, constructed. Smith (1983) accordingly explored rhetoric as a means of persuasion, as one aspect of his philosophy of science; it was through persuasion that new theories were adopted and knowledge was built up.

If as economists we are also concerned with dealing with practical economic problems, then ultimately it is with this in mind that we consider what the methodology literature offers. What does methodology say about our capacity to understand the real world? We saw in Chapter 6 that there is no reliable way of *demonstrating* the truth of theories. Chapter 7 explored the reasons for this, in the theory-ladenness of observation and the incommensurability of the language of different theories. These arguments are not peculiar to economics, but extend also to everyday life. But then, just as economists 'act' in the sense of developing and putting forward particular accounts of real-world problems and possible solutions, so as individuals we take action. If, rather than starting with philosophy, we start by studying how we take action in practice, with the awareness of the issues raised in Chapters 6 and 7 in mind, then we might be able to form judgements as to what are better or worse reasons on which to base action. This was what motivated Keynes's (1973a) work on probability: how to provide a basis in reason for courses of action when we do not have *certain* grounds for action. In this chapter we try to get back to some of the fundamental questions posed by economic practice which we introduced in Chapters 3 and 4.

We begin by looking at discussions in the methodology literature about realism, which zero in on this question of the connection between theory and the real world by putting the nature of the real world back at the centre of the picture. This leads into a discussion in section 8.3 of the concept of rationality, and the related concept of learning which is important when considering a changing economic environment. This discussion applies to our subject matter: the economy and the actors within it. But it also applies to economists, and methodologists (see, for example, Loasby, 1989; his work is notable for drawing parallels between knowledge in firms and knowledge among economists).

Since rationalism has been such a powerful force in economic methodology, we need to consider rationality at this level too. We have noted as we proceeded that how we understand rationality depends on the type of logic employed; in section 8.4 we consider a range of possibilities. Closely associated with rationalism applied to economics has been the notion of rigour, normally understood in relation to classical logic. So different notions of logic impact too on how we understand rigour, which we consider in section 8.5.

What all this implies specifically for economic methodology we discuss in the following section under the heading of pluralism. The direction which methodology has taken is on balance one towards greater openness to a plurality of methods; how open, and how we decide which among a range of methods to use, is considered here. Throughout this discussion we consider the realist approach, which addresses all these conceptual issues with the real world as the starting point.

8.2 Realism

8.2.1 Reality and our knowledge of it

We have already encountered the issue of realism when we discussed the debate sparked off by Friedman's argument, not only that realism of assumptions was not an issue for choosing between theories, but even that we should positively seek unrealistic assumptions in order to improve predictive power (section 5.3.1). It was pointed out that lack of realism of assumptions could be due to falsehood, idealization, or simplification. Since theory inevitably is unrealistic in the sense of simplification, the substantive issues of realism of assumptions really refer to the first two. The first might mean assuming away a feature that is known to exist in the real world, as a substitute for conducting experiments. As with experiments, the issue is how to apply the conclusions to the real world. Idealization means focusing on something which is not a feature of the real world. This too poses problems for application. A theory may have unrealistic assumptions in the third sense of simplification, like assuming that the working day is eight hours, when we know that there are variations. But that kind of lack of realism doesn't mean that a theory is non-realist. In other words it is important to distinguish between realism and realisticness (see Mäki, 1994, 1998c).

Realism as a philosophy can take many forms (see Mäki, 1998b). What these forms have in common is the affirmation of the real existence of the subject matter independent of the study of it. A realist economist agrees that the economy exists independently of economics. Well, of course, you might think. But then what do we mean by the economy? We have already seen that defining the subject matter of economics is not altogether straightforward. Does an economy defined in terms of scarce means and ends, as understood subjectively by the decision-maker, exist objectively, or is it a construction of the economist's mind? Does rational economic man exist objectively? If Robbins's definition of economics is, as Coase (1988: ch. 1) suggests, a method rather than a subject matter, then in what sense is it grounded in reality? From this point of view, the definition of economics as the study of production, consumption, distribution, and exchange does seem to connect much more with real economic life; the driving force may or may not be scarcity, but the subject matter is real economic processes.

Concern with the existence of an economy is a matter of *ontology*. A particular understanding of the nature of the real world can be established by different means. For example, Bhaskar (1975) arrives at his ontology of both social and natural systems using deductive logic applied to the observation of scientific practice. Hume (1739–40) arrived at his ontology of social and natural systems by means of common-sense belief (see Dow, forthcoming). It is important to distinguish this concern with the nature of the real world from how we build up knowledge about it. This means distinguishing ontology from *epistemology*, our theory of knowledge. This is because how we understand the real economy is relevant to how we construct knowledge about it.

In Chapter 7 we explored the implications of different uses of language, different perspectives, and different methodologies for developing knowledge, that is, learning in economics. McCloskey equated prescriptive, big 'm', Methodology with epistemology; it is concerned with how best to build up knowledge. Because this whole project has turned out to be unable to establish categoric rules for scientific behaviour, McCloskey and Weintraub argue that we should give up prescriptive epistemology and concentrate instead on understanding the way in which economics has evolved in practice. They focus therefore on giving a descriptive account of learning in economics, that is, of developing a descriptive epistemology. This approach is only realist in the sense that the aim is to represent the reality of economics, not the economy (see Mäki, 1988). We will continue to use the term 'epistemology' bearing in mind that it can be used descriptively as well as prescriptively.

But in considering the distinction between epistemology and ontology, the discussion is complicated in that, as a social system (of production, consumption, and so on), the economy is itself a product of, and producer of, knowledge (Searle, 1995). While it is reasonably straightforward to think of a real chair, for example, existing independently of the scientist,[2] economic subject matter is more fluid, and reflexive. Production for example is the outcome of decision-making based on the knowledge of the market, production conditions, working practices, and so on held by different members of the organization; how this knowledge generates a decision depends on the structure of the organization, the personalities involved, and so on. The decision may even be explicitly influenced by economic analysis. This is after all why we teach economics on MBA programmes.

This possibility of reflexivity is central to the Lucas critique; his critique of econometric models which assume fixed patterns of behaviour focuses on the response of decision-makers to new information. According to the rational expectations approach, the better-informed are decision-makers (by economists or anyone else), the less scope there is for the economy to deviate from the natural rate of unemployment. Rational expectations theorists have accommodated the reflexive interplay between economic theory and observation by tying expectations to the real world, putting theory and econometric analysis into the same logical framework. Because economic agents use the same model for forming expectations as the theorist uses for making predictions, there is a guaranteed internal consistency between the facts and the theory. The stochastic nature of expectations is simply picking up the stochastic nature of the real world (Lawson, 1988). However, the rational expectations epistemology for economic agents consists of absorbing new information about variables whose nature and role is already known; it is not clear that this constitutes learning in the sense in which we have talked about the economist's own epistemology; indeed Sargent was aware of this lack, and attempted to incorporate some form of learning (see Sent, 1998).

Another way of addressing the ontology–epistemology interface is taken by those referred to as 'constructive empiricists'. Compared with those who start with theory and see facts as theory-laden (see Chapter 7), constructive empiricists start at the other end, as it were, seeing descriptive 'facts' as what economists are aiming to establish, with the aid of theory (see Boylan and O'Gorman, 1995: ch. 6). For constructive empiricists, then, the purpose of theory is instead to build up a better description of the world—to construct the facts. Any explanation is an answer to a specific question within a specific context, so explanation within constructive empiricism is fragmented according to the variety of contexts. According to this approach, there is no universal explanation for slow economic growth, for example, or high inflation. But a 'thick' description allows these phenomena to be given particular explanations in different contexts. Theory is therefore not epistemological, separate from observation of the real world; it is simply an aid to observation.

A further way of dealing with the interplay between ontology and epistemology is to treat facts as well as theory as subjective (that is, to subsume ontology within epistemology). Subjective expected utility theory is an attempt to accommodate the subjective nature of expectations in this way, in the absence of the conditions necessary for objective probability estimates. These expectations are formed in a *theoretical* world which is specified in such a way that they can be expressed quantitatively. As Binmore (1987: 211) points out: 'Bayesian theory applies only to "closed universe" problems, i.e. to problems in which all potential surprises can be discounted in advance.' Expectations understood by the economist as being epistemic rather than about the real world can therefore allow for quantification and thus empirical analysis.

Since economists are generally concerned in their practice to address real-world problems, however, realists find this solution unsatisfactory. They put the focus on the subject matter of economics as determining how we build knowledge about it, rather than vice versa. For those who seek guidance for economic practice in terms of the progress agenda explored in Chapter 6, empirical testing is one expression of realism. Thus, when Backhouse (1997) doubts the usefulness of abstract theory which is not confronted with data, he is making the subject matter the determinant of epistemology. Theories are good if they are borne out by the 'facts'. Put another way, a realist decides whether a theory gets close to the truth or not according to how well it fits the facts.

8.2.2 What do we mean by 'reality'?

Within realism there is a wide disparity of view, as to how far there are facts independent of theory, and as to which type of fact represents the reality we are concerned with. Among those realists for whom the facts are not epistemological, that is, they are in some sense independent of theory, there are significant differences as to what we are talking about when we refer to 'facts'. In the tradition which has emerged from the concern with testing traced through logical positivism, then Popper, then Lakatos, the focus is on what Lawson (1997a) calls 'event regularities'. These are stable patterns among data series identified normally with the aid of econometric techniques. An example would be Friedman's work on monetary history, which identified a stable pattern between nominal income, or the general price level, and the money supply. Since predictive success is vulnerable to the problem of induction, it is generally accepted that it is important for theory to explain the regularity in such a way that changes in the structure underlying the stable relationship may be anticipated. So that structure needs to be modelled in a refined way, taking account of the foreign sector, for example, and allowing consideration of the likely effects of shocks. Tests for structural change, use of dummy variables, and backward prediction are all techniques to help us identify omitted variables and deal with our limited knowledge of the causes of structural change. The ultimate goal is to predict inflation. The philosophy of science from which this approach has emerged sees the purpose of science as being explanation (with a view to successful prediction); the facts help the scientist to check whether a good explanation has been found.

Realists see ontology (concern with the real world) as the primary focus of theory, and, for realists, there exists one reality.[3] Nevertheless, given our limitations in understanding that reality, there is a range of possible (socially constructed) knowledges about it. We can therefore combine the concern that economic theory address the real world, while taking account of the social constructedness of knowledge, in terms of there being 'one world and many theories' (Mäki, 1997). Our problem is in both accessing and theorizing about that one real world. But belief in the existence of an independent reality does provide a common reference point of sorts, which allows us to escape from pure relativism (the view that truth is only relative). It is generally agreed that we cannot establish truth in economics (our theories are fallible), but the realist approach focuses our attention on how we understand that reference point, which in turn can lead us in the direction of a wide range of views about the best way to build up knowledge.

The leading form of realism in the current literature is critical realism (Lawson, 1994a, 1997a). This approach sees the purpose of theory as going beyond the level of observation on the grounds that what we observe is governed by a collection of underlying causal mechanisms which not only change their form as economic institutions and behaviour evolve, but which also may well be pulling in different directions. Further, the mechanism may be potential rather than actual—what critical realists refer to as a 'capacity'. Critical realism thus breaks down what we might think of as 'the facts' (growth of GDP, the rate of inflation, and so on). There is the real level of generative mechanisms (such as upward pressure on wages from tight labour conditions, a changing institutional structure for wage bargaining, and the introduction of the euro), the actual (such as rising wages for some workers in some industries), and the empirical (labour force statistics measuring changing wages by a given definition for a sample panel of workers, with some measurement error). Focusing exclusively on the empirical (event regularities) is regarded as unsatisfactory on two counts. First, it does not address reality, which is the underlying causal mechanism. Second, since the underlying causal tendencies are normally operating intermittently and simultaneously, possibly pulling in different directions, critical realists argue that the project of precise prediction on the basis of event regularities cannot succeed.

8.2.3 Closed and open systems

For critical realists, as for all realists, the starting point is observation, with the aid of existing theories and beliefs. Then hypotheses about underlying causal mechanisms are derived from observation by a process of 'retroduction', 'abduction', or 'hypothetic inference' by means of the use of analogy and metaphor (Lewis, 1996; Runde, 1998).[4] How the process of retroduction works depends very much on ontology. The relevant distinction is between a closed-system ontology and an open-system ontology, that is, between an understanding of the economy as a closed system or an open system, respectively. A *closed system* is one for which all the relevant variables can be identified, for which the boundaries are specified such that these variables can be classified as endogenous or exogenous, and where relationships are either knowable or random. This entails further the condition of extrinsic closure, that only those specified exogenous variables can impact on the system, in a predetermined way, and the condition of intrinsic closure, that the components of the system are separable and constant in nature, and the structure of the relationship between the components is predetermined. This is the world of predetermination which Popper (1982) considered as the basis for deriving natural laws and which he rejected on the grounds that it undermined the whole project of science.

An *open system* on the other hand is one for which not all relevant variables are known (because of the complexity of the system), where the boundaries of the system cannot be specified (because of creative human behaviour for example, and also because we understand the system in terms of subsystems whose closure is only provisional); where interrelations within the system (between individuals) change; and where knowledge is rarely at the extreme of either being held with certainty or of being truly random—it is generally held with some degree of uncertainty. Further, since action stems from an 'internal' individual intentionality rather than an 'external' rationality, individuals themselves may change their nature (Rotheim, 1998). This was the world-view of Hume when he specified his problem of induction: the causal structure of the real world is ultimately inaccessible to the human mind.

If the economic system is closed in a way which we have some hope of grasping, then retroduction takes the form of hypothesizing about the determinate relationships in nature from observed regularities; after a sufficient number of goings back and forth between hypothesis and empirical testing, a firm view is formed of the relationship such that it can be held with some confidence as a basis for policy advice. This is the project of positivism. It is to build up knowledge as a closed system mirroring the closed system in nature. This is the approach adopted by rational expectations theory; only in this way can we make sense of the idea that expectations are objective, and yet the model on which the expectations are based is an 'analogue' rather than the real thing (Lucas, 1980: 700).

We have seen in Chapter 6 the difficulties faced by economics in terms of this approach. For many (with the support of Popper and Lakatos) the solution lay in defining the subject matter of economics in the form of an abstraction from the real world. The ideal type, rational economic man, supplied the axiomatic foundation for a logical structure which could be defined as a closed system, with a deterministic account of human behaviour. But this is a theoretical, or epistemological, closed system. The problem has been how to make the connection with the real economic system, not least because the economic system as defined for theory construction does not have a direct real-world counterpart. The whole point of the deductivist approach was to address the problem that human behaviour 'in the round' included a range of influences other than what was regarded as economic influences. These other influences introduced values which distorted what was seen as economic behaviour (see section 5.3.2). The need for abstraction to create a closed, virtual 'economic' world arose implicitly because of the view that the real world is an open system. As Lucas (1981: 271) puts it:

Any model that is well enough articulated to give clear answers to the questions we put to it will necessarily be artificial, abstract, patently 'unreal'.

8.2.4 Empirical regularities

Those such as Backhouse who point to the problems of confining economics to the abstract level argue for grounding theory in empirical work (econometrics), assessing abstract theory by reference to data. Effectively they rely on a closed-system ontology, that is, that the real economic system bears a correspondence to the closed theoretical system. But the data may not reveal causal mechanisms—indeed are unlikely to do so—if these mechanisms are neither deterministic (law-like), nor singular, nor in operation at that particular time. Generally, according to critical realism, several causal mechanisms are at work at any one time or potentially at work; the goal is to identify powers and tendencies which have the potential to be at work (Lawson, 1998). What we observe is not the outcome of any one mechanism. If we identify a pattern in empirical data (a 'demi-regularity', or 'demi-reg' for short, in the critical realist terminology), that is a signal for searching for an underlying causal mechanism which, in spite of any countervailing causal mechanisms, has got through the level of the actual to the level of the empirical. Econometrics faces difficulties because of the openness of the real world and the practical difficulties of isolating 'economic' relationships from empirical data.

Critical realists have been particularly critical of econometrics other than as a mechanism for identifying regularities for further study (Lawson, 1997a: ch. 7), although this continues as a matter for active discussion (see, for example, Downward, 2000). First, econometrics is all conducted at the level of the empirical, and much of it is directed to making forecasts for particular data series. It cannot identify the causal mechanisms of which the empirical data are single manifestations. Because critical realist ontology is of an evolutionary social system, with multiple causal mechanisms at work at any time, and some tendencies which may be in abeyance, it is unlikely that one mechanism would dominate for the full period of observation. Second, for the same reason, the structure of the economy within which that causal mechanism was working is unlikely to remain the same throughout, violating the necessity for econometrics to be expressed in terms of a fully specified (possibly stochastic) structure. Even though econometric techniques can identify a range of causal mechanisms operating simultaneously, they can only do so if the mechanisms operate deterministically. Third, the basic units of analysis to which the data series refer may change their nature during the period of reference. Attitudes to women in the labour force may change family and labour market behaviour, or the money supply definition may be rendered redundant by financial innovation, for example.

In fact, critical realists (following Keynes's use of negative analogy)[5] are more interested in a pattern which persists *despite* changing structure and variables. Keynes had identified a pattern between consumption and income which persisted over a long period despite other developments; this was a sign that there might here be an underlying causal mechanism, which he identified as a psychological law, captured in the consumption function. Econometrics therefore helps us identify regularities which persist regardless of other causal mechanisms and changing environment. But critical realists argue that, alone, it is inadequate as a basis for prediction; successful prediction requires the deterministic relationships of a closed real system. A realist analysis of causal mechanisms may allow prediction of tendencies at work in a particular context, but not prediction of particular values since generally tendencies push variables simultaneously in different directions.

The deductivist approach avoided these problems by explicitly denying empirical counterparts (see, for example, Hahn, 1981), but the need for abstraction held an important implication about the scope for economic knowledge—that certain knowledge was not possible on the basis of observation. What was not addressed was the knowledge problems facing economic actors themselves. A closed theoretical system has the great attraction of generating certain knowledge; we know within the usual general equilibrium framework, for example, that monetary policy is effective with flexible exchange rates, but not with fixed exchange rates. But in order to generate these conclusions from the axioms of rational individual behaviour, the theory must in turn assume certain knowledge on the part of individuals in the economy (as the basis for capital flows and foreign exchange transactions, for example). More generally, complete preferences can only be expressed if there is complete knowledge. As Lucas (1981: 224) concluded: 'in cases of uncertainty, economic reasoning will be of no value' (as quoted at the start of Loasby, 1999: 1). However, if uncertain knowledge is indeed the norm for economic actors, this feeds back into the (ontological) level of the real economy. The complexity of an open-system economy and the fallibility of human knowledge induce the formation and evolution of institutions which allow us to act in spite of complexity. These elements of stability further aid economists at the epistemological level to identify regularities in the economy and thus the basis for explanation. But, putting together the fallibility of human knowledge (for economists as well as economic actors) with the complexity of the subject matter also creates particular problems for economists building up knowledge about the real world (Loasby, 1999: ch. 1).

We have already encountered some of these issues in our discussion of Popper's three-worlds thesis (section 6.4.1); Popper distinguished between the real world, the psychological world, and the world of theory. Because of human intentionality and creativity, the economy cannot in reality be determined by laws, so theory should not be law-like either. Thus Popper's ontology is of the real world being open because it is governed by intentional individual behaviour; we saw that this individualistic view coloured his philosophy of science. Intentional individual behaviour also plays an important part in critical realism as a feature of the real world as an open system, but it is modified because individuals are situated in society. Society lends coherence and stability to social and economic relations; because of trust in the banking system we accept cheques in payment, and rather than labour auctions there is generally a 'rate for the job', for example. Knowledge about the economy is also socially constructed. This too lends stability. We tend to accept the opinions of pundits, for example, who forecast that inflation will be within certain bounds over the next year, and incorporate that in our planning. Credibility is an important factor in monetary policy. Rather than the potential anarchy of an individualistic ontology, therefore, the critical realist ontology is one of causal mechanisms at work within the enabling framework of social conventions and institutions (Hodgson, 1988).

If economic theory is to bear a correspondence with the real world, albeit by abstracting from it, then it must be the case not only that economic behaviour can be abstracted from other aspects of behaviour, but also that the essence of that behaviour is identified in the abstraction. The realist approach requires that abstraction be in the form of simplification, not of idealization—otherwise we cannot make the connection between theory and what we observe. When attempts have been made to make theory consistent with observation, the issues of human rationality in the face of uncertain knowledge, and of learning with experience, need to be addressed (as was recognized by Sargent; see Sent, 1998).

8.3 Rationality

8.3.1 The knowledge base for reason

Let us leave aside for the moment the issue of how far we can identify economic behaviour as separable from other aspects of behaviour and focus on the question of the correspondence between rational economic man and real behaviour, to see how far rational economic man is an ideal type and how far a simplification. Central to any such discussion is the concept of rationality, which has held a central place in the philosophy of science. Rationalists understand science as the exercise of the scientist's rationality. But, where the rational economic man axioms are employed we are extending the assumption of rationality in a particular form also to actors in the economy.

In what sense is our economic behaviour rational? To say that we are rationally optimizing when we make a particular choice (to buy this CD player rather than another, say) does not help—it is a matter of definition in an optimizing theoretical framework that what we choose to do is to optimize with respect to preferences, whatever they are. But the requirement of complete preferences means that we have fully specified preference functions in terms of all goods, services, and assets (as well as work and leisure), which requires full knowledge of what these are and also the utility to be derived from them.

No one would claim that we have perfect knowledge in this sense. There is only limited scope for certain knowledge in the world of experience as opposed to the world of theory. Knowledge of the actual is the closest we get; if we are made redundant, and thus unemployed, then (delusion aside) we can say that that is something we know. What the underlying causes were is generally uncertain (although we may have a good idea). Similarly, we may know that the Dow-Jones, or the FTSE, index fell 100 points yesterday, but we are normally uncertain as to how far this reflects the state of health of the companies in the index, and also about what this means for the index tomorrow. This is the normal state of affairs. If we were talking about quantifiable risk, then we could insure against it. It was the (mis)understanding that stock market risks could be insured against with derivatives products which led to the collapse of LCTM (see section 4.3). Those aspects of life where the causal structure is stable, such as mortality rates or incidence of damage to houses, for particular cohorts of the population, are the areas where frequency distributions can be constructed and probability statistics calculated; these are then used as the basis for our insurance premiums. Even then, premiums change with changing patterns of health or weather. This is the closest we get in real life to deterministic laws, albeit with a substantial stochastic variation.

But the norm is knowledge held with varying degrees of uncertainty. Clearly this does not generally impede action—although a high degree of uncertainty will do so. When we act, we often act as if we are certain, if not of the future then of the odds with respect to the future. When we buy stocks after a week of falling stock prices, we are acting as if we are certain that they will not fall much further, if at all. The only alternative to rationality based on complete information is not irrationality; clearly reason plays a large part in decision-making. Practical reason, suited to the situation, follows recognized strategies. We may be very knowledgeable about the company whose shares we buy, but we also need to have knowledge of market behaviour and broad economic trends to predict the direction of stock price changes. We therefore gather information about past behaviour of stock prices as a guide to the future, we consult the financial press to find out what the conventional opinion is, and we draw on tacit knowledge. If we recall Popper's notion of situated rationality as being a reasonable uncontestable basis for deductive reasoning in economics (see section 6. 4), we can see that it actually means something very different depending on the situation. In particular, it depends on whether or not there is complete information, or more generally whether decisions are being taken in a closed or open economic system. Situated rationality is thus a more general concept than the rationality of rational economic man (Lawson, 1997b).[6]

The techniques noted above for applying reason were some of those suggested by Keynes (1937) as ones we use to cope with uncertainty. He made this economic argument based on his prior work on probability (Keynes, 1973a), whose aim was to establish the grounds for belief in propositions when we do not have complete knowledge. We rely on what evidence is available in favour of a particular view, that the stock market is due to resume a secular upward path, for example. More evidence may not increase our optimism that this rise will take place; it may change the balance of view. Further, more evidence doesn't necessarily make us more sure that we are right; it may make us realize how little we know and reduce our confidence in our predictions. Beyond direct knowledge, we rely on theoretical knowledge which, as we have discussed, is fallible—it too is subject to uncertainty. A gap is left between what we have reason to believe and a demonstrable foundation for action. As Keynes (1936: ch. 12) pointed out, given unquantifiable risk with respect to the future, it is not rational for firms to commit themselves to illiquid investment projects. Here we use the term 'rational' in the special sense of 'rational economic man', as applying to a decision based on full knowledge. Yet businesses do invest. So they must make up the knowledge gap by various stratagems, which can be subsumed in the category of conventional judgement, buttressed by the will to act (animal spirits). When businesses are conscious of the shakiness of their knowledge, they lack the will to act—their preference to remain liquid is high.

8.3.2 Conventions

We have come back to the recurrent concept of conventions; here we have seen them playing an important part in providing a basis for action in the absence of complete knowledge. Subjective expected utility (SEU) theory states that our actions are effectively the placing of bets on the basis of subjective probability estimates. But Keynes argued effectively that there are (crucial) times at which we are unwilling to place bets because we are not willing to act as if we are certain about the odds (Runde, 1995).

We encountered conventions first as the procedure by which economists decide how to appraise and develop theory. We are now discussing conventions as the stratagem by which individuals in the economy assess situations and act. Choi (1993) draws a very direct parallel between the paradigms which determine the conventions of particular communities of scholars on the one hand and the conventions generated within society because of individuals' attempts to cope with uncertainty. It is because of our uncertainty as economists (due to the absence of objective rules for good economics) that we accept a disciplinary matrix (in Kuhn's terms) or a hard core (in Lakatos's terms) as a convention of the scientific community of which we are a part. The conventions of other scientific communities seem strange, just as do the conventions of foreign places we visit. But, without an external source of certain knowledge, some set of conventional judgement is necessary for theory to develop. This is rational, where 'rationality' is understood more broadly than applying reason to certain knowledge, that is, as situated rationality. This broader understanding of reason features strongly in modern philosophy. Hacking (1982), for example, explores different styles of reasoning, without allowing relativism or subjectivism to take over from rationalism. Even Feyerabend, according to Hacking, is a rationalist, an 'anarcho-rationalist'.[7]

Conventions have been understood differently in different parts of the economics literature (see Davis, 1998a). Simon (1982) sees conventions as the means by which we make decisions in practice, since we aren't capable of specifying a complete preference map; conventions then determine the bounds within which we are rational. Others such as Hayek (1960) see conventions as the unintended consequence of individual human action; the order of society arises from individual intentionality. Conventions may also be seen as what facilitates interdependent behaviour. This approach has been extended by game theory, which is an approach to economic behaviour built around conventions (see Sugden, 1989). However, as Hodgson (1988: 191–4) argues, game theory presumes knowledge of the rules of the game and the possible outcomes, ruling out the possibility of surprise, and thereby any basis for conventions to break down as they sometimes do in reality.

What these approaches have in common is the retention of rationality in its traditional economic form as the individual application of deductive reasoning to an external environment, but within the bounds (which may be facilitating) set by conventions. This approach owes much to what is termed 'methodological individualism', which is based on the ontological claim that 'society is composed of and does not exist over and above individual human beings' (Kincaid, 1998: 295). Knowledge may depend on social conventions, but it is the individual rather than society which is fundamental. A different view of conventions can be found in Keynes, and in Hume (who seems to have been a significant influence on him), because of a different view of humanity (a different ontology). If individuals are understood as essentially social beings, then it is not clear which should be given priority in analysis: individuals or social conventions, individual knowledge or social knowledge (Farmer, 1995). Again it is a matter of where we start. If complete certain knowledge is unattainable, we can start with that and discuss how far we fall short, as in the rationalist approach, or we can start with how we build up knowledge, which inevitably puts an emphasis on our grounding in common-sense social knowledge. Keynes's use of the concept of conventions therefore addressed the very nature of rationality and knowledge, and thus of logic.

8.4 Logic and Rigour

8.4.1 Deductivism again

A key feature of rationalism is that the logic employed is classical logic. This is a set of rules for deducing propositions on the basis of premisses, where premisses are either true or false. This type of logic is therefore well suited to an abstract theoretical structure where the premisses are taken to be 'as if' true. It has the three very appealing characteristics of internal consistency, precision, and definitive conclusions which are true if the premisses are true (see Hahn, 1973a). While drawing attention to the persuasive power of rhetoric, McCloskey (1985: 36) makes clear that the virtues associated with deductivist rhetoric are indeed persuasive (as quoted in section 7.3.3).

Adam Smith had similarly discussed the aesthetic appeal of deductive arguments, pointing to the success of Descartes's philosophy. We are disturbed if our experience of the world is at odds with a theory and seek relief in the form of a theory which is instead consistent with that experience. We are persuaded too by theories which accord with ideas with which we are already familiar. But simplicity and elegance can be dominant considerations:

> It gives us a pleasure to see the phaenomena which we reckoned the most unaccountable all deduced from some principle (commonly a wellknown one) and all united in one chain. . . . We need not be surprised then that the Cartesian Philosophy . . . tho it does not perhaps contain a word of truth . . . should nevertheless have been so universally received by all the Learned in Europe at that time. The Great Superiority of the method over that of Aristotle . . . made them greedily receive a work which we justly esteem one of the most entertaining Romances that has ever been wrote. (Smith, 1762–3, 1983: 146)

In what sense could Smith mean that Descartes's philosophy was perhaps not true? Smith distinguished between the communication of a theory (which could be persuasive if expressed in the form of deductive logic employing familiar principles) and the origins of the theory, which lay in reason applied to experience (Smith, 1795). Smith did develop principles (like the division of labour) from which to deduce conclusions (about trade policy, for example). But the principles had been derived by inductive logic from detailed historical observation. In other words, Smith, like Hume, saw reason applied to our experience of the world as more reliable than reason alone.

This difference in philosophical stance, between rationalism and common-sense philosophy, was a matter for much debate again early in the twentieth century in Cambridge (see Coates (1996) and Davis's (1999) review article). Here the focus of the philosophical debate was on the issue of precision of language. While rationalist argument aimed for precision, this precision was less clearly appealing when arguments were applied to the real world. Hahn (1973a), for example, supports deductivism in economics because it tells us precisely what must be the case, for full market coordination, for example (there must be complete knowledge, including complete futures markets, and so on). But this precision bears a cost. In applying abstract deductivist economics to real-world situations, the precision lies in explaining exactly what would have to be the case for a particular, precise conclusion to hold rather than in addressing the real conditions which do hold. It is a matter of choice which is preferable. Harcourt (1992: 276) suggests that Marshall made the choice in favour of real-world application at the cost of precision: 'it is better to be vaguely right than precisely wrong.'[8]

8.4.2 Vagueness

The vagueness of ordinary language may be seen to have the virtue of allowing greater scope for correspondence between reasoned argument and the real world. The scope for ambiguity allows for change in the subject matter, because meaning of verbal language is more flexible than the meaning of mathematical terms or data series. The meaning of verbal terms further tends to be complex rather than singular, incorporating a range of connotations.

We have already discussed the issue of finding empirical counterparts to theoretical concepts; part of the problem is that empirical measurement can involve too much precision. Much of this issue can be discussed in terms of 'vagueness'. In order to conduct a cost-benefit analysis, for example, we need to measure the utility attached to a particular good. In order to decide whether to replace single-species tree-planting with mixed woodland as a public service, for example, the Forestry Commission needs to estimate the monetary value of the aesthetic appeal of mixed woodland. A sampled population is asked how much they would be willing to pay for a change to mixed woodland. But it is notoriously difficult for people to convert a preference for one thing over another into a monetary sum. This is an example of 'degree vagueness'. But, as Coates (1996: 161) explains, many of these concepts in the social sciences 'display combinatory vagueness rather than degree vagueness'. In social systems, it is hard to separate one meaning of a term from another; it is hard to assess different styles of woodland in isolation; any definition of a term (like 'mixed woodland') is bound to leave something of relevance out of the account.

This is where the vagueness of ordinary language is helpful. It allows discussion and analysis to proceed. In elections, the package of prospects held out by any political party is inevitably vague. That does not mean that we do not seek as much information as possible as a basis for our voting decision. But if political leaders had to specify precise initial conditions and precise meanings of terms then the manifestos would be both interminable and also incomprehensible. Indeed, where precision has been sought, as in the setting of precise targets, many of the problems which have arisen have resulted from the juxtaposition between the language in which the policy was expressed, and the precision of the target measure, which may have unintended consequences. Thus, for example, a policy designed to encourage and reward good academic research, when expressed in precise terms, can divert attention from research activity which happens to fall outside those terms, even though that was not intended.

But surely, as scientists, we should seek a solution in even greater precision? In fact, terms even in mathematics and the physical sciences themselves are vague in the sense that their meaning has changed over the years (see, for example, Weintraub, 1998, on mathematics). The metaphors we use in economics benefit from their vagueness. Game theory, for example, draws on the metaphor of the game and the cluster of meanings attached to it (Coates, 1996: ch. 2). Similarly, the metaphor of the market benefits from its vagueness. That is what allows Becker to extend market analysis into the family context. It may be that the market is precisely defined for the purposes of deductive theory, in terms of preferences defined in a precise way with respect to the abstract concept of rational economic man. But what the rhetoric literature has taught us is that how we actually understand and discuss this theory and these concepts draws on our wider understanding of the world. This is made possible by the vagueness of our use of what are intended to be precise terms.

8.4.3 Probability and uncertainty

In economics, both Marshall and Keynes were involved in the early philosophical debates over language. In his *Treatise on Probability*, Keynes attempted to construct a logical basis for probable statements where there was no scope for quantifying probability. He considered quantified probability to be feasible as the exception rather than the rule, when there was scope for repeated instances within a stable structure (as in the tossing of a coin). This judgement as to the limited scope for certain knowledge arose from his ontology of social systems as being open; he saw them as extrinsically open in that we cannot identify *ex ante* all relevant causes, and intrinsically open because of the complex interrelationships within social systems which meant that they could not be understood as the sum of their parts. Our knowledge therefore is fallible, not only because of our human condition which means that we cannot hope to know the true causal processes, but also because of the complexity of the real world (see Davis, 1998*b*). Nevertheless, in general probability judgements have to be made if action is to be taken, so there needs to be some procedure for making judgements under conditions of uncertainty. Where Russell had classified any behaviour other than that guided by classical logic as irrational, Keynes sought a basis in reason for knowledge built up under conditions of uncertainty.

Keynes took classical logic as far as he could to apply to uncertainty, using the concept of weight of evidence to contribute to an assessment of a proposition as being more or less certain (precise quantification of probability being impossible in general). The two do not directly correspond: increased weight of evidence may make something less probable and vice versa. The more we know about current trends in international capital flows, for example, the less probable may be the proposition that a particular currency will rise in value. Further, as Runde (1990) points out, increased weight does not necessarily increase our confidence in our predictions. The more we know about international capital flows, the less confident we may feel in making any predictions about currency values at all. (This provides an answer to those who say 'those who can, do, those who can't, teach'—the more we know, the more we know we don't know . . .)

But the limitations of classical logic become apparent once we move beyond the realms of certainty; it then becomes a special case of a more general logic, called 'ordinary logic' or 'human logic' (Carabelli, 1988; Gerrard, 1992). Here the focus shifts to the basis for judgement where there are limited facts known with certainty, and true causal relations are not known. Having drawn as far as we can on existing knowledge and evidence, we make up the knowledge gap by falling back on conventions (such as extrapolating from the past, or taking the pundits' view). This theory of knowledge was built up to apply equally to scientific knowledge as to knowledge of actors in the economy. Keynes therefore saw ordinary logic as something to be employed by economists as well as their subjects in the economy.

Keynes therefore expressed particular doubts about the scope for mathematical analysis in economics (although he was by no means averse to its use where justified by the material: see O'Donnell, 1990). He was reacting to Russell's attempt to build up a rationalist system of knowledge. Russell's goal was to resolve the issue of language by making clear its logical structure:

The idea is to express in an appropriate symbolism what in ordinary language leads to endless misunderstandings. That is to say, where ordinary language disguises logical structure, where it allows the formation of pseudopropositions, where it uses one term in an infinity of different meanings, we must replace it by a symbolism which gives a clear picture of the logical structure, excludes pseudopropositions, and uses its terms unambiguously. (Russell, 1929: 163)

But Keynes (1921: 20, n. 1) expressed doubts as to whether formal logic would necessarily clarify meaning:

Confusion of thought is not always best avoided by technical and unaccustomed expressions, to which the mind has no immediate reaction of understanding; it is possible, under the cover of a careful formalism, to make statements, which, if expressed in plain language, the mind would immediately repudiate. There is much to be said, therefore, in favour of understanding the substance of what you are saying *all the time*, and of never reducing the substantives of your argument to the mental status of an *x* or *y*. (emphasis in original)

The question as to the precision of language as applied to the real world brings us back to questions of ontology, that is, the nature of the real world about which we are seeking linguistic counterparts. If the real world is a closed system, it consists of separable independent (atomistic) components which relate to each other in a deterministic manner, with predictable outcomes. The project of establishing a language which corresponds to that reality seems feasible. Even if the elements of reality change requiring a change in meaning of language counterparts, the causal mechanisms behind such change should be accessible and thus themselves amenable to language counterparts. But if the real world is an open system, then it consists of a social structure which evolves, and components whose interrelationships and nature evolve, in a manner which cannot be captured in deterministic laws. It is inevitable then that the language used to refer to this world will undergo changes in meaning.

So it boils down to the nature of the real world we are trying to analyse. Everything else follows. Critical realists argue, and deductivists would agree, that a formal abstract general equilibrium system represents the economy as a closed system. But critical realists argue further that empiricists who seek to predict the values of variables by means of empirical work which presumes a stable structure are going further by presuming, without adequate justification, that the real economy they are studying is itself a closed system. Some deductivists agree here as well, which is why they choose to restrict their theory to the abstract level. But critical realists make a different choice, in favour of allowing their (open-system) ontology to determine theory. Their theories therefore look very different to the closed-system theory of deductivist economics. As Cartwright (1999: 3) puts it:

It is a well-known methodological truism that in almost all cases there will be a trade-off between internal validity and external validity. The conditions that we need in order to increase the chances of internal validity are generally at odds with those that provide grounds for external validity.

8.4.4 Rigour

Cartwright proceeds to explore the concept of rigour. We are accustomed to associate rigour with formal mathematical argument. But the term has wider application, depending on whether the rigour is in terms of ensuring internal validity (the normal usage) or external validity. Rigour in the second sense requires aptness for application to the real world. As Cartwright argues, this requires that theory isolate in such a way as to identify tendencies. She gives an example from labour economics: the skill-loss model traces through the effects on future unemployment of the extent to which skills are lost in previous periods of unemployment. The outcome is a statement about tendencies, which would contribute to a case study analysis of unemployment. But the analysis would not justify a statement that in general a particular percentage of unemployment is due to skill loss. While critical realists might argue about whether a particular isolation ignored important interdependencies, they would share the aim as being to identify tendencies.

Cartwright proceeds to argue that much of abstract economic theory is overconstrained by assumptions to the point of allowing general conclusions which can only apply to real-world situations which correspond to the abstraction (that is, very rarely). The assumptions aren't designed to isolate a causal mechanism from other mechanisms in order to conduct a 'thought experiment' on a specific issue in the absence of real experimental conditions; they are designed rather to construct an analogue world which differs in important respects from the real world (Lucas, 1980). The results are model-dependent. Cartwright concludes that these models lack rigour in their capacity to allow conclusions about tendencies at work in the real world. In terms of the realism of assumptions discussion (section 5.3.1), assumptions do not just simplify or eliminate some functions which pertain in the real world—they create effectively new factors which do not pertain in the real world. Dennis (1995) similarly argues that, while mathematics may be internally rigorous, it is not clearly rigorous in its application, particularly when we focus on the intentionality (and thus lack of determinacy) of individual behaviour. In arguing likewise for rigour in terms of real-world applicability, Chick (1998) points out that this involves rigour in establishing the conditions under which formal mathematical analysis may play a constructive role.

The same type of argument applies to the notion of consistency. Within logical positivism, internal consistency is one of the criteria for a good theory. But again this is conditional on the type of logic used. The dual consistency/inconsistency is clear within classical logic. But in ordinary logic, where meaning is not absolutely fixed, and where the segmentation of the subject matter for purposes of analysis is only provisional, the dual does not apply internally (Dow, 1990b). Indeed, in any case priority is placed in realist analysis on external, rather than internal, consistency—consistency between the theory and the subject matter.

In the meantime, mathematics itself has become less closely associated with classical logic. Indeed, it has been evolving in ways which economists may find useful. As a subset of what we have been discussing as ordinary logic (or human logic), fuzzy logic is an example of a development which offers particular possibilities. Classical logic requires crisp definitions of sets, which contrasts with real-world vagueness of categories. However, in ordinary logic (or ordinary speech) we refer to someone as 'tall' without being precise as to where tall stops and medium height starts. Fuzzy logic gets away from absolute values by a generalization of classical logic from two values ('tall' or 'not tall') to the case of infinite values. Membership of a fuzzy set corresponds to a value somewhere in a range 0.0 to 1.0, and probabilities are assigned to membership of sets. This logical framework has the potential for application to economic methodology, in the sense that a preference for a particular theoretical explanation may be better understood as being positioned along a spectrum, rather than in the 'true/false' framework of rationalism. In this sense, as Mäki (1988) argues, the rhetoric approach can be understood as realist in its account of how economists behave. The unofficial rhetoric which McCloskey argues determines actual persuasion among economists is not rationalist, and does not accord with classical logic.

But then the same must be the case for our objects of study. Fuzzy logic therefore also has the possibility of allowing economic theory to represent human behaviour in a non-rationalist way, where 'non-rationalist' does not mean 'irrational' (note the departure from two-valued sets). Behavioural economics already sees decision-making as responding to perceived discrete jumps in observed values rather than the continuous optimizing of New Classical theory. Thus, for example, a firm may continue with a particular strategy, having made a commitment to it, until the reality of falling profitability breaks through in the form of a downward revision of expectations, and consequent structural change within the company (see Earl, 1984). Or international financial markets may persist in confidence in the US dollar until some high-profile public speech prompts a radical revision of expectations. Indeed, the concept of fuzzy sets is already incorporated in trading practice in capital markets; there is widespread use of algorithms to trigger trades when prices move outside specified ranges. More generally, in the absence of complete information, decision-makers rely on conventional views about the prospects for the economy (for example, which are more along the lines of 'higher growth' than '3.04 per cent growth'). Indeed, the realist emphasis on tendencies itself is employing fuzzy sets rather than crisp sets.

This is just one example of a logical framework which can address the issue of knowledge (and expectations) of an open-system economy (see Vercelli,

1999, for a wider discussion). If the real world is indeed an open system, with scope for all of institutional instability, structural change, and human creativity, then classical logic may not be up to the task. This was the view which Keynes came to. We have already discussed (section 3.2) how, in an essay on the evolution of his beliefs about human nature, Keynes (1972) gives an account of an encounter between himself, Bertrand Russell, the arch-rationalist, and D. H. Lawrence, the novelist. He evokes the conflict between them, and their espousal, respectively, of reason and emotion. Keynes concluded that human nature combined the two. He employed this insight when considering firms' investment behaviour (Keynes, 1936: ch. 12). He pointed out that no one would rationally (in the sense of rational economic man) commit a firm to long-term investment in the absence of reliable probabilities as to the outcome. If we lived in a world of quantifiable risk, firms could insure against failure of investment projects and therefore have a rational (in the narrow sense) basis for action. But if the real world is an open system where risks cannot be quantified, then the firm's owners cannot ultimately protect themselves against adverse developments. Russell's rationalism therefore could not explain real-world economic behaviour (see further, Elster, 1998).

Clearly as much knowledge is brought to the investment decision as possible, and measures taken to protect against risk (such as limited liability status, and contractual arrangements with employees, suppliers, and customers). The alternative to complete knowledge is clearly not ignorance. But in order to justify acceptance of unprotected risk, there is a role for what Keynes called 'animal spirits', or the urge to act. It requires the capacity to ignore ignorance. This perhaps is the key to the elusive quality of entrepreneurship so sought after by governments intent on promoting the growth of domestic industry. And sometimes that quality wanes. Sometimes we choose to hang back until we feel more confident in our capacity to make predictions; this was the basis for Keynes's theory of liquidity preference: money is the safe asset we hold until the fog clears enough, or our animal spirits surge enough, to warrant action.

We have been considering here the scope for rationalist logic to explain economists' choices as much as agents' choices, and explored some alternative forms of logic. The implication is that methodological judgements follow from our understanding of how the world works. We have considered in Chapter 6 the kind of methodology implied by a closed-system epistemology (whether or not justified by a closed-system ontology). We turn now to consider more explicitly the kind of methodology implied by an open-system ontology which steers economics towards an open-system epistemology. What does situated rationality consist of for economists—and for methodologists?

8.5 Pluralism

8.5.1 The general case for pluralism

The goal of methodology as discussed in Chapter 6 was to identify 'good' scientific practice, according to one, commonly held, set of criteria. By definition, all other practice fell short. This position is called *monism*, because of its emphasis on one best way of doing things. When it became apparent that no one best set of criteria, and therefore one best set of theories, could be substantiated, the alternative was pluralism: a plurality of criteria and a plurality of theories.

Methodological pluralism was the alternative which Caldwell advocated (1982: ch. 13) following his detailed account of the inability of positivism to provide a satisfactory philosophy of science for economics. Caldwell took on board the recognition that, in the absence of one set of choice criteria, different communities of economists (paradigms, research programmes) would converge around different sets of criteria. The task of the methodologist then was, first, to rationally reconstruct bodies of theory, identifying the methodological criteria employed, and, second, to offer critical advice, either in terms of the criteria employed (internal criticism), or in terms of other criteria (external criticism). This pluralism follows logically from a Kuhnian perspective, and is of tremendous importance for the role of methodology (Dow, 2001b). While there is considerable scope for debate about methodological pluralism (notably about the degree of pluralism, and about whether or not, and in what way, the real world imposes some constraints), there does seem to be a consensus in favour of some form of methodological pluralism. This is explicitly stated in Salanti's introduction to the volume of papers representing the range of views on pluralism (Salanti and Screpanti, 1997).

Methodological pluralism also carries forward to *pluralism in practice*, in the sense that it has implications for economists working within different paradigms (Dow, 1997). As economists we inevitably adopt a methodological position when we practise economics. What this position is is not readily apparent; it is one of the jobs of the methodologist to tease out what our methodological positions are and to explain their implications. But our methodology is expressed not only in how we do economics ourselves, but also in how we regard others' work. Inevitably methodological issues arise in communications between economists employing different methodologies; words are used differently, different issues are regarded as important, and different factors are regarded as decisive in choosing directions for theory development. The notion of a school of thought (or paradigm) is a good shorthand for expressing a commonly held set of methodological principles. Just as Kuhn (1999) faced the issue of Aristotle looking foolish in terms of later paradigms, so economists can make each other look foolish by translating ideas and practices from one paradigm into the language of another paradigm. From a rational expectations perspective, for example, adaptive expectations are irrational and thus indefensible. But in terms of rationality in the absence of complete information, perhaps slowly adapting expectations do indeed make sense.

Pluralism implies that economists should be tolerant of each other's principles, aware that none can claim absolute superiority. But what then? The rhetoric approach advocates playing down methodological differences, while being mutually tolerant, in order to promote communication. Certainly awareness of rhetoric alerts us to the possibility that language is being used differently by different participants in a conversation, and helps us to address it up to a point. But the bottom line is that the theory which succeeds is the one expressed most persuasively. So persuasive success creates its own pecking-order of theories and methodologies, allowing the possibility of the establishment of monism if that is most persuasive. McCloskey quite explicitly denies any critical role for methodologists with respect to persuasion. Postmodernists on the other hand stress the plurality of knowledge at a very micro-level and the absence of any basis for choosing one theory over another, other than the demands of a very particular problem, as understood in a very particular way. So postmodernists are pluralist in an extreme way; there is no limit to the feasible number of theories nor any basis for choosing between them other than on a case-by-case basis, and only then by the analyst concerned.

8.5.2 Moderate pluralism

There is however an intermediate position, a moderated form of pluralism, which lies between monism on the one hand and pure pluralism on the other. We confine our discussion now to this intermediate form of pluralism, which involves some restrictions on the range of methods used. We start with methodological pluralism and consider the nature and source of these restrictions.

Kuhn's theory of paradigms as social/language structures makes it clear that economists will tend to coalesce around a fairly limited range of paradigms, which entail an ontology and epistemology, and thus methodological principles. In order to practise economics, we need to exercise judgement as to which methodological principles we want to employ (or which paradigm we are most closely associated with). Situated rationality for the economist consists of employing reason to justify that choice. Inevitably this means employing reason for not choosing another paradigm, so that there is implicitly or explicitly the basis for criticism of alternatives. If we accept, with Popper, that criticism is one of the hallmarks of science, then extraordinary science can make a contribution through (constructive) criticism of one paradigm by another. Indeed, many of the great advances in economics have occurred as a result of operating at the boundaries of paradigms (as, for example, in the case of Hicks's work). Further, understanding the controversies in economics is a great way to understand what underpins different theories, since debates across paradigms, if successful, focus on the methodological level. The important point, though, that we take from recent developments in method-ology is that no paradigm can lay any absolute claim to truth; we just choose what we judge to be the best set of principles.

But what about practice itself? Here too there have been arguments for a moderate pluralist methodology, that is a methodology which advocates use of a range of methods. In fact, methodological pluralism (based on the view that there is no scope for monism in economics) lends itself to a pluralist methodology in practice (Dow, 1997). If we understand the real world to be an open system, requiring an open-system knowledge, then inevitably we are accepting that no one method will generate certain knowledge about the real world. Certainly, the choice can be made to construct an abstract formal system as a virtual closed economy which would generate certain conclusions within that economy. Internal consistency, elegance, and so on are being given precedence over applicability. But, as with any method, there is still no basis for claiming any absolute superiority for this method over any other. McCloskey argues in any case that even those most strongly in favour of such an approach in practice employ other methods to persuade, ranging from the language used within the formal system to the informal arguments used to persuade others to accept its conclusions.

So, if we accept McCloskey's account, economists are in practice unofficial (if not official) pluralists in terms of method. We can use the methodological discussion developed so far here to understand why this should be the case, and to consider its implications. Just as in Keynes's theory of behaviour under uncertainty, individuals in the economy employ a range of methods as a basis for action, economists themselves can be seen as employing a range of methods to generate conclusions about the economy. Empirical evidence is employed where it exists, other types of evidence (from historical texts, or from sociological studies, for example) are brought to bear, models are chosen to address the situation at hand, conventional judgements are employed as to which variables to consider, verbal arguments are constructed with carefully chosen metaphors and telling analogies, and the whole put together, with careful choice of language and the exercise of judgement, in order to reach a conclusion.

8.5.3 Judgement

The role of judgement is crucial, and we will return to consider its implications in the next chapter. Keynes instead used the word 'art' when he referred to the crucial stage of applying abstract reasoning to the real world:

Economics is a science of thinking in terms of models joined to the art of choosing models which are relevant to the contemporary world. (Keynes, 1973c: 296)

The significance of judgement is that it is something different from the rationality of rational choice models; if it were not, then there would be little to discuss as far as methodology is concerned. Judgement is often thought to be inferior to formal methods because of the scope for human bias to creep in. But while this bias was at one stage identified with reference to the 'rational' choice implied by formal Bayesian models, there has been increasing interest in trying to understand the exercise of judgement as situated rationality, against which the formal rationality of choice theory is judged (see, for example, Kahneman and Tversky, 1984). For economic theory, a formal closed-system model does not leave much room for judgement. For many this is part of its appeal, that the conclusions follow from the internal logic rather than (fallible) judgement (Fitzgibbons, 2000).

But when policy issues are to be addressed, judgement potentially plays a large part in framing the way in which theory is applied to reality. The issue of judgement has arisen most in the forecasting literature, with discussion of judgemental forecasting. As Makridakis and Wheelwright (1979: 348) put it:

Of course it must be remembered that just as it is impossible to say which methodology is always best, it is impossible to conclude that quantitative methods are always better than subjective or judgementally based methods. Human forecasters can process much more information than most of the formalized quantitative methods, and such forecasters are more likely to have knowledge of specific near-term events that need to be reflected in current forecasts.

It is clear that judgement is an important element both in the use of, and development of, econometric forecasting techniques more generally (see, for example, the various accounts in Hendry, 1993). The Bank of England (1999) explicitly refers to the crucial role of judgement in putting together forecasts and policy decisions on the basis of a plurality of modelling approaches.

While the exercise of judgement is required by a plurality of methods, it is also assisted by knowledge gleaned from a plurality of methods. Colander (1994) points out that controversy helps the formation of judgement, so that arguing across paradigms helps economists in their practice. He argues therefore for the benefits of bringing to the surface the methodological differences which are present in economics but are normally suppressed in communications.

Not all economists employ the same range of methods. It depends on the economist's understanding of the nature of the economy (her ontology) which methods will be employed. A neo-Austrian economist, being a methodological individualist, will tend to focus on methods for building up knowledge at the very micro-level—case studies, questionnaire surveys to find out the (subjective) knowledge of the individuals concerned, and so on. Someone who understands the world in terms of stages of development will focus on aggregate data series and employ historical methods in order to understand the context from which the data were drawn as a basis for theory construction. Someone who sees individuals as independent, optimizing entities will be more inclined to employ mathematics based on classical logic, while someone else who sees individuals more as social beings may employ a different logic, which may or may not allow for mathematical expression.

8.5.4 The mathematical method

The role of the mathematical method is one which has tended to raise most controversy. The attraction of mathematics is that it promotes internal consistency because it makes all arguments commensurate. If, indeed, all arguments could be made commensurate by mathematical expression, then there would be a strong case for all argument to be mathematical. But the argument for pluralism is based on the view that not all arguments are commensurate. Put another way, the issue is whether mathematizing an argument is neutral, that is, the meaning is preserved (see Chick and Dow, forthcoming). For some (for example, Weintraub, 1985: 179) all reasoning is at root mathematical, so mathematics is neutral. For others mathematics is best suited to closed-system reasoning; to mathematize open-system reasoning is to change its nature. For example, the model uncertainty literature represents an attempt to mathematize the uncertainty of the economist as to whether or not the best model is being used (see section 3.5). In Keynesian terms this type of uncertainty is not quantifiable, and is better analysed in terms of the procedures employed to cope with the uncertainty. To express that uncertainty in an error distribution is to provide a conclusive answer as to how the economist should behave, but at the cost of ignoring the unquantifiable nature of the uncertainty, which arises from the inability of methodology to help us determine conclusively which is the best model.

The attractions of mathematics are powerful, and there is clearly scope for developing different forms of mathematics more suited to a system which is not fully determined. And indeed particular parts of an open system can be studied separately, segmented off as if they were closed, and thus amenable to standard mathematical treatment. Care needs to be taken to make sure that such segmentation for theoretical purposes is justified by the subject matter. Further, any such closure is provisional, in the awareness that the real economic system evolves, and may do so in a way which no longer justifies this particular closure; the subsystem is not in reality extrinsically closed. It is also provisional in the sense that what is treated as exogenous for that partial analysis may be endogenous in another partial analysis, and a policy question might require the two analyses to be combined. Again we are drawing here on the notion of situated rationality. We may well understand the economy to be organic (and thus interdependent in a complex way). But, as in daily life, we need to start somewhere and put together (provisional) knowledge one piece at a time. As far as the status and scope of mathematical argument is concerned, pluralism suggests that, for all its undoubted attractions, it is a partial method and requires combination with other methods in order to construct a complete argument.

This raises the issue of consistency, since one of the attractions of making the entire argument mathematical was that it ensured consistency. But again consistency in terms of classical logic, which is ensured by mathematical treatment, is not the same as consistency in a broader logical framework. For example, a partial analysis of the effect of monetary policy might take the money supply to be exogenous for that purpose, while a partial analysis of bank behaviour might take the money supply to be endogenous. This methodology involves consistency with the subject matter rather than internal consistency.

8.6 Conclusion

In this chapter we have explored the implications of letting the goal of addressing real-world problems have the greatest influence on how we do economics. Those who choose the deductivist approach believe that that way is the most rigorous and scientific, and offers the best way of addressing real economic problems. What is achieved is results which are precise, internally consistent, and definitive—all appealing attributes. But, unless it is believed that the deductivist model captures the essential nature of the real world, the cost is a lack of precision, consistency, and definitiveness in application to the real world. The realist approach explored in this chapter makes a different choice, which allows for much greater correspondence with reality, but at the cost of not generating precise, definitive results which are consistent in the sense of classical logic.

In considering the realist approach we have seen that there is much to discuss, with respect to the nature of economic reality and the knowledge we build about it. The same is true of the pluralist methodology which arises from realism. By its nature, pluralism raises more issues than it resolves. There is clearly much room for debate, about the extent of pluralism and whether there is scope for conventional agreement about its scope, what range of methods is suggested by different ontologies, how different types of know-ledge should be combined, about the role of mathematics, which type of mathematics, and so on. In other words, pluralism, as opposed to monism, opens up a huge area for methodological analysis. We now step back in the final chapter to assess where the methodology literature has taken us, and what its implications are.

8.7 Further Reading

For further reading on the topics explored here, see, by topic: Mäki (1989), Boylan and O'Gorman (1995), Lawson (1997), Fleetwood (1999) (realism); Elster (1988), Hargreaves Heap (1989), Mäki, Gustafsson, and Knudsen (1993), Dow and Hillard (1995), Dennis (1998) (rationality); Gerrard (1992), Coates (1996), Chick (1998) (logic and rigour); Caldwell (1982: ch. 13), Salanti and Screpanti (1997), Morgan and Rutherford (1998a), Fitzgibbons (2000) (pluralism); and Davis, Hands, and Mäki (1998) (particular concepts).

Endnotes

1. The term 'common sense' is being used here to refer to common-sense philosophy. This philosophy has arisen in different forms over the years, with a particular impact on economics; see Comim (1999).

2. Straightforwardness is relative. Apart from the physical make-up of the chair, which might be understood differently by a physicist and a manufacturer, for example, the concept of the chair might be understood differently by a teacher and a therapist, while the word itself can refer to a physical object or a position (as in 'committee chair'). See Rossetti (1990).

3. Physicists may understand reality as consisting of simultaneous universes, but what is meant here by 'one reality' is a universe, or universes, which exist independently of human understanding.

4. Retroduction was a key feature also of the methodology advocated by the pragmatist Pearce (Hoover, 1994).

5. Keynes in turn developed the idea of negative analogy put forward by Hume. Hume's (1777: 31) example was of eggs: all eggs are different, but we can recognize something held in common despite the differences, which allows us to use the category of 'egg' (see Carabelli, 1988).

6. Others, such as Rorty, are less willing to retain even this broad notion of rationalism:

On the pragmatist view, rationality is not the exercise of a faculty called 'reason'—a faculty which stands in some determinate relation to reality. Nor is it the use of a method It is *simply* a matter of being open and curious, and of relying on persuasion rather than force. (Rorty, 1980. /1)

7. There is a large literature on the issue of rationality in economics, with a range of classifications of rationality. See, e.g. Hargreaves-Heap (1989, 1998), the special issue (June 1997), on rationality and methodology, of the *Journal of Economic Methodology*, and Vercelli (forthcoming).

8. Shove (1942: 323) attributes this saying to Wildon Carr.

9

ISSUES FOR METHODOLOGY AND ECONOMICS

9.1 Introduction

In the foregoing chapters, we have explored the reasons why economists make simplifying and idealizing assumptions, why it is difficult to predict the future, why it is impossible to demonstrate in any absolute sense which is the best theory, why there tends to be a range of theoretical approaches, and why those who pursue these different approaches often talk past each other. We have also seen how the field of methodology has evolved, from attempting to establish a single set of ground rules for practice, to an attempt at describing practice and its foundations, using methodological concepts. We have explored the reasons why neither prescription nor description can be achieved in any pure form—there is no basis for a universal set of rules, nor is there any neutral ground from which to describe. But much has been achieved over the years, in the pursuit of these two projects, by way of understanding both methodology and economics.

The real challenge lies in exploring the middle ground, having accepted that a range of perspectives is likely to persist, in methodology as in economics. For some this plurality is regrettable—inevitable, perhaps, given the inability to establish universal principles, but nevertheless regrettable. But there are overwhelmingly positive benefits from pluralism. First, it is through controversy that judgement develops. In the absence of absolute rules for good practice, judgement is crucial. If classical logic alone cannot produce the answers, then we as economists evolve our own situational logic, which is well served by having access to a range of methods and methodologies. Second, it is through diversity that new developments arise. Here the biological analogy is instructive; protection against unforeseen shocks lies in diversity in nature. If one strain succumbs to a particular shock, another survives. We have seen that the economic system is not static any more than nature is; it inevitably changes its form as history is played out. So some sets of economic ideas will attract attention because they are particularly apt for some contexts, and will therefore be developed further, but then may cease to be relevant as the context changes.

While we have raised some doubts about scarcity as being the defining characteristic of economics, it is clearly an important concept. It can be applied also to methodology. In choosing to do economics one way, we are making the choice not to do it another way. There are trade-offs: the precision of idealized abstract theory is gained at the expense of direct applicability, the realism of a case-by-case approach is gained at the expense of generality, and so on. So what the field of methodology can do is spell out the nature and implications of these choices. It also involves a raising of consciousness as to what exactly we are doing in our economic practice (and judgements) and what methodology is implied. Since there are different approaches, each holds different implications and involves different underpinnings. In the next section we explore one aspect of human nature as embodied in economists, in order to understand something about what underpins our judgement—our modes of thought. We then proceed to consider the choice of methodology.

In the following sections we consider the implications of this methodological discussion for economics, focusing first on the relationship between economics and other disciplines: philosophy, history, and the other social sciences. We then consider the implications for the use of economics for policy advice, and for the way in which economists are educated. The chapter concludes with some discussion of methodology and the future of economics.

9.2 Sociology, Modes of Thought, and Visions of Reality

The field of methodology encourages us to reflect on why we make the choices we do when pursuing our research and when forming judgements about other theories. What we have seen is that there is a range of methodological choices: economists can choose monism—reliance on one method (abstract mathematical formalism, or prediction based on a particular econometric methodology, or historical analysis), or pluralism in the form of a particular range of methods out of the full range of possibilities. Similarly, methodologists make choices as to which methodological approach to pursue (falsificationism, science studies, critical realism, and so on).

But it is worthwhile to reflect further on what underlies those choices. Much can be explained by the sociology of scientific knowledge (SSK) literature. The education process, the institutional arrangements for university economics departments, the locations within particular communities of key creative thinkers, all influence the development and perpetuation of conventions as to use of language, range of acceptable methods, and so on. But we are not completely programmed by our environment, although the environment clearly can be very influential in encouraging the support for, or rejection of, particular methodologies. Sometimes economists feel uncomfortable in particular environments, or openly reject the dominant methodology of that environment.

What is it that makes us comfortable or uncomfortable with a particular methodology? Major contributory factors are first how we view the economy (our ontology) and second how we habitually think (the two being not unrelated). If we are inclined to think of the economy as something separable from the rest of social life, then we will be more inclined to adopt a deductivist methodology. If we are inclined to think of the economy in terms of data series, we will be inclined to adopt a positivist methodology whereby we test theory according to the 'facts'. If we think of the economy as the manifest-ation of universal laws, we will adopt a methodology designed to identify those laws, whereas if we see the economy as fragmented and in flux, we will adopt a methodology which focuses on specific contexts without seeking to identify laws. More generally, if we understand the economy as a closed system we will be more inclined to adopt a closed-system methodology, and vice versa for an open-system ontology.

But what our vision of reality is is closely tied into how we think. Within how we think, or our mode of thought, lies the way in which we exercise judgement, both with a view to constructing arguments and with respect to reacting to others' arguments. Some economists tend to think in duals (either/or categories) while others feel more comfortable with more open and fluid categories, where the borders change according to the problem at hand. Simi-larly, some economists tend to think in terms of atomistic individuals, independent units which retain their characteristics despite interactions with other units, while others think in terms of organic interaction, whereby the nature of the units is shaped by and evolves as a result of interactions.[1]

Why this should be the case is not something we even attempt to explore here—in particular how mode of thought interacts with ontology. But it does help us to understand, not only why some methodologies appeal more to some economists than others, but also the different reactions we have to economists whose methodologies differ from our own. A pluralist methodology, for example, is more likely to appeal to someone whose mode of thought is non-dualist and organicist. The clear-cut categories and fully specified interactions of a general equilibrium model, which is the ideal for a dualistic atomist, seem inappropriate as a basis for knowledge for a non-dualistic organicist. On the other hand, the incommensurability of methods and vagueness of language associated with pluralism seem unsatisfactory to a dualistic atomist.

Further, awareness of difference in mode of thought helps us to understand the interactions between economists. We have already suggested that there is considerable scope for economists to talk past each other when they are using language in different ways and referring to different understandings of the way the world is. Difference in mode of thought itself is another barrier to constructive communication. Chick (1995) identifies four possible reactions to this kind of fundamental clash of perspective. When we come across an argument which conflicts with our own we can deal with it in four possible ways: rejection, containment, paradox, and synthesis.[2]

Rejection is a dualistic reaction combined with the judgement that our own argument is right and therefore the other is wrong. This strategy denies the fallibility of knowledge and presumes that it is legitimate to state categorically that an alternative discussion, either about the argument or about criteria for appraisal, is wrong. It is intended to put an end to argument. Of course, someone's argument may well be wrong, either in their own terms or in the terms of the rejecter. But in a field where the criteria for theory acceptance are not established, the relevant distinction is the one made by Keynes (1973*b*: 470, emphasis in original):

In economics you cannot *convict* your opponent of error; you can only *convince* him of it. And, even if you are right, you cannot convince him, if there is a defect in your own powers of persuasion and exposition or if his head is already so filled with contrary notions that he cannot catch the clues to your thought which you are trying to throw to him.

And if the argument is only wrong in terms of one of the frameworks, then rejection still is not necessarily legitimate; it needs to be qualified by specifying which framework justifies rejection. For example, an argument not couched in terms of an equilibrium end-state (for example, about the motion in financial markets) may strike someone as 'wrong' who adopts the positive heuristic 'construct theories that make predictions about equilibrium states' (section 6.4.2), but nevertheless have some useful insights to offer. But rejection means no discussion and therefore no scope for sharing insights.

Containment involves seeing one argument as a special case of the other. When Keynes published his *General Theory of Employment, Interest and Money* in 1936, he saw the prevailing market-clearing theory as a special case, where aggregate demand just happened to be at the full-employment level. But then Hicks and Modigliani proceeded to argue that it was Keynes's theory which was the special case, where the demand for money was perfectly interest-elastic, or where nominal wages were sticky downward, or where the saving and investment schedules do not intersect at a positive rate of interest. This illustrates that the notion of containment, and what is general and what special, itself depends on methodology. So, in this example, both were right in their own terms. Keynes was right that the market-clearing model itself relied on special conditions being met, like full information; his was a more general framework which allowed for uncertainty which is the more general case. But within the market-clearing model itself, if, unlike Keynes, we take its applicability as given, then Keynes's argument could indeed be shown to be a special case. So, containment is a possible constructive strategy, but cannot be definitive because what is understood as containment differs depending on methodological stance.[3]

The third strategy is to accept both arguments simultaneously, as a paradox. This is in fact one of the characteristic features of postmodernism, the capacity to accept two (or more) apparently contradictory views on a subject. Up to a point, paradox is a necessary feature of pluralism. Incommensurability of methods means not being able to put all arguments on the same footing, in the same terms. And it is possible for some of the arguments to conflict. Supposing we are concerned to understand how the economy is behaving following a change in tax policy. One economist constructs a macro-model which shows that output and expenditure will be stimulated, another conducts a historical analysis of similar circumstances, concluding that this will not be the case. Each has good reasons for her conclusions. And each may be right within the terms of the methodology employed. Similarly, Keynes (1936) offered two apparently incompatible analyses of the investment decision, in terms of the marginal efficiency of capital (ch. 11) and of animal spirits (ch. 12) (Dow and Dow, 1985). This is what happens because of the limitations to our understanding: choosing any one method means taking a path to building knowledge which involves costs and benefits. The macro-modeller takes the structure of the economy as given, for example, in order to generate conclusions. The historian does not, but may be unable to predict on the basis of past experience exactly how structure may change.

So far we have considered paradox as a result of the perspective of any one method or methodology. But it may in fact be a feature of reality if what the different methods are picking up is different underlying causal mechanisms; in other words the paradox reflects counteracting tendencies in the real world. Suppose, for example, that extrapolating from the past using econometric techniques suggests that expenditure on petrol should rise at a certain rate. There are good reasons to rely on what we have learnt from past patterns of behaviour. But a questionnaire survey suggests that car-owners have decided to cut back consumption. There has just been a public debate about non-renewable energy consumption, and the government has raised fuel taxes. Do we ignore the survey on the grounds that people misrepresent their own intentions? Or do we pay attention to it as the harbinger of behavioural change? To entertain the latter is to allow for paradox, at least in the interim.

The fourth strategy is synthesis: to take both opposing arguments seriously and try to put them together in a new framework. It is perhaps natural, if we want to build up some general understanding of the economy (as opposed to very specific understanding of particular contexts in isolation) that paradox is only something which may be accommodated as an interim position. To accommodate two apparently opposing points of view is to incorporate features of both in order to resolve the paradox, and thereby to create a different, third argument. Thus Keynes's two analyses of the investment decision can be seen to be complementary. Similarly, in money and banking theory, there are those who focus on the asset side of banks' balance sheets as being what makes banks distinctive: bank loan contracts are generally fixed term, and non-marketable. It is through the creation of such contracts that bank deposits (the money supply) come into being, so the focus is on the credit market. Others see bank liabilities as what makes them distinctive; bank deposits are used in payment, so that the rate at which deposits are redeposited in the banking system is high. The focus here is on the money market, and liquidity preference. A synthesis of these two apparently opposing arguments is to consider both sides of the balance sheet as being distinctive together, and indeed interdependent—it is the high redeposit ratio, because deposits are used in payment, which allows banks to take on such illiquid assets.

Our discussion of the field of methodology itself can be understood in terms of a tension between dualistic and non-dualistic modes of thought. Methodological discussion has often focused on duals: induction/deduction, rationalism/empiricism, prescription/description, modernism/postmodernism. What we have seen, however, is that none of these purist positions is actually sustainable. Induction requires some deduction and vice versa; neither reason alone nor experience alone is sufficient for knowledge; there is no general basis for prescription, nor for description; neither modernism nor postmodernism provides a satisfactory basis for knowledge. The rhetoric literature has made it clear that economists in practice actually use a wide range of persuasive techniques, of which classical logic and empirical evidence form only a part.

In order to practise economics, the purist (dualistic) methodologies provide guidance, but not adequate guidance. So there has been a tendency for economists to bypass explicit methodological discussion, which has been understood to require pure categories, and (implicitly) construct their own methodological frameworks. Methodology has tended to be called upon only as rhetorical ammunition in arguments, or as isolated injunctions to test theories empirically, or in isolated preliminary sections of introductory textbooks. The categories discussed above for analysing reactions to methodological difference can be used equally to analyse the confrontation of methodology with practice. One reaction is for practising economists to reject methodological discussion, another to contain it by suggesting that methodology is all embodied in practice anyway. Where there is some dissonance between methodology and practice, as pointed out for example by Blaug (1980), then many economists seem to have been content to accept this as a paradox and proceed as normal.

But what is suggested by the modern methodology literature is instead a process of engagement between methodology and practice; the pluralist approach to methodology allows the latitude for much more correspondence between methodology and practice. The science studies approach provides some basic material in the form of accounts of methodologies actually employed in practice. By formulating a synthesis from the old dualisms, methodology is now going forward by mapping out the territory within which we can analyse the specific methodologies employed. Not that there is any neutral analytical ground, but there is a good understanding of the parameters for such an analysis. In particular, attention has been drawn to the distinction between ontology and epistemology, which is important if the ultimate goal is to address real-world problems.

9.3 Our Choice of Methodology

One of the key features of modern methodology has been the corollary of accepting that we cannot identify one best way to do economics, which is that there may well at any time be several ways of doing economics, for each of which good reasons can be given. This means that it is open to the economist to choose a methodological approach for which the reasons are most appealing. It is then the role of the methodologist to spell out what is involved at the methodological level, to make constructive suggestions as to further developments which would be consistent with that methodology, and criticism of inconsistencies between methodology and practice.

Blaug (1980) looked at the practice of economists who tended to profess a positivist methodology and pointed out that the two were not consistent. Economists were not in general actively seeking to falsify their theories. Within the methodology literature there is greater understanding now of why economists are not falsificationist. But then what methodologies do we actually use? There is scope for teasing out the methodologies implicit in practice, exposing them to reasoned debate, and considering their implications. Since economists work in scientific communities, within university departments, in cross-university groupings, in research institutes, or government organizations, we tend to coalesce around a limited range of methodologies which we can most usefully understand in Kuhnian or Lakatosian terms.

There have been various exercises in identifying the characteristics of schools of thought in economics: Mair and Miller (1991), Snowdon, Vane, and Wynarczyk (1994), Dow (1996). For example, there is neo-Austrian economics which adopts the position of methodological individualism. There is institutional economics which seeks regularity in evolutionary long-term trends, and a focus on the detail of particular institutional structures. There is Post-Keynesian economics which focuses on the interplay between macroeconomic trends and microeconomic behaviour under institutional arrangements conditioned on the uncertainty with which knowledge is held. Although mainstream economics apparently encompasses a wide range of approaches—New Classical, New Keynesian, game theory, and so on—there are sufficient methodological characteristics in common to consider it all as a school of thought (one scientific community with shared underpinnings). We encountered these common characteristics in Chapter 6 in Weintraub's specification of the Lakatosian hard core. The key features are the axiomatic structure of theory, where the axioms specify rational choice by independent individuals with given information sets, and where conclusions are specified in relation to equilibrium.

Since mainstream economics is the dominant paradigm, it has been natural for non-mainstream schools of thought to focus on methodological differences, so that many of the statements of alternative methodologies are expressed also as critiques of mainstream methodology (see, for example, Lawson, 1997a). Further, since explicit expressions of methodological principle within mainstream economics tend to be positivist (as in introductory textbooks, such as Parkin, Powell, and Matthews, 1997: ch. 1), non-mainstream economists have also paid particular attention to the argument that there is only one best (positivist) methodology. While some non-mainstream economists have also adopted the rejection approach, the most prevalent approach is to advocate open-mindedness and mutual tolerance.

It has been a particular impediment to reasoned discussion that there has been a fairly widespread acknowledgement of positivist methodological principles (in introductory textbooks, for example) which encourage rejection of the espousal of alternative methodologies. How far mainstream economists would actually subscribe to a positivist methodology as a ruling principle for their own research if the matter were brought to the surface and thoughtfully addressed is open to question. The work of Blaug and McCloskey suggests some significant dissonance between positivism and actual practice in economics; the problem may lie more in the profession of positivism than in a falling short of practice. And, indeed, our discussion of positivism in Chapter 6 provides good reason for economists to be wary of professing it. But until the question is addressed not much progress can be made.

9.4 Relationships with Other Disciplines

9.4.1 Philosophy

In introducing the various ideas about economic methodology, reference was made to the philosophical positions on which the ideas were based. Hutchison (1996, 1997) argues, not only that economists should be methodologically aware, but also that we should be philosophically aware. In order to understand how we do economics, and the source of many of the debates in economics, we need to dig deep. But if awareness among economists of what has been happening within the field of methodology has been hampered by the increasing specialization within the field, how reasonable is it to advocate philosophical awareness?

Certainly any methodological discussion is enhanced by use of philosophical concepts, such as ontology and epistemology, rationalism and empiricism, and so on. It is important to understand the (hedonistic) philosophy behind the axioms of rational economic man for discussions about the role of values in economic theory. Awareness of the philosophy implicit in our economics cannot but improve our capacity to address issues within economics, and the application of economics to policy issues. If there were no philosophical issues about building knowledge about the real world as the basis for action, then we could just get on with it. But the philosophical literature clearly shows that this is not an unproblematic exercise, so we are better to take that on board in economics if we are to do the job well.

Traditionally, methodology drew directly on the philosophy of science, applying that philosophy to economics. But we have seen that methodology has been changing, paying more attention to what economists actually do rather than imposing a set of guidelines from outside. In this, as we have seen, methodology has been drawing on changes within the philosophy of science which have made that field itself more aware of actual practice. Just as it is no longer the case that there is a unidirectional influence from methodology to practice, so there is no longer a unidirectional influence from philosophy to methodology. Philosophy itself changes as a result of change in practice and in methodology. The subject matter of philosophy, as for economics, is after all ultimately the real world. So what is crucial is that there be effective communications between the three levels (see Dow, 2001b).

The argument that there is no ultimate means of establishing the best theory, or the best methodology, also applies to philosophy. That too is up for discussion; there is a range of philosophies to draw on. So economists must also choose their philosophy. This may seem to place an unreasonable burden on economists, but we are not talking about choosing a philosophy from scratch. Philosophies are embedded in paradigms, so that philosophy-methodology-theory tends to come as a package; economists examining the paradigm within which they operate will be able to identify the philosophy on which it is based, with the aid of the methodology literature. On the other hand, philosophical injunctions need to be appraised like anything else. The argument that economists should pay more attention to philosophy doesn't mean that economists have to accept philosophical instruction without discussion. Thus, for example, suppose a philosophical argument is presented against the general use of econometrics. Taking philosophy seriously means that the econometrician would neither immediately drop econometrics nor ignore the argument. It would mean rather that the econometrician would attempt to engage with the argument, to learn more about it, and to formulate counter-arguments as appropriate which might in turn encourage revision of the original argument.

If, as the methodology literature has tended to conclude, building knowledge in economics is not a straightforward matter of applying an agreed logic to an agreed set of facts, then the role of judgement takes on great importance. Judgement is what we use when there is no clearly demonstrated conclusion; we need to apply judgement in providing an account of reality, in choosing a methodology to address it, including a form of logic; as Hacking (1982) points out, it is possible to retain a rationalist philosophy (broadly defined) and yet have a range of styles of reasoning. Judgement is of particular importance for a social science, because the subject matter keeps changing, and also because theorizing requires an abstraction from aspects of social life, and a means of making the argument concrete in order to turn it into a policy conclusion. We have discussed the pluralist approach, which involves building up knowledge of a complex subject matter by means of a range of incommensurate methods and lines of reasoning (if they were not incommensurate, there would be no need for a range). This argument extends also to disciplinary range; it suggests that the application of judgement in economics might benefit from knowledge built up in other disciplines. One other discipline which can make a particular input into our formulation of judgement is history.

9.4.2 Relationship with history

History can contribute to economics in a variety of forms. First, there is economic history. One way of looking at it is that economic history provides the largest possible data set against which to test theory. Curiously, Popper (1944–5) explicitly ruled out falsification on the basis of historical evidence; he associated historical analysis, or 'historicism' with absence of criticism. However, Lakatos did not restrict the range of evidence in this way, and both Hutchison and Blaug included historical evidence in applying positivism to economics (see Boylan and O'Gorman, 1995: 22). From this point of view, it is worthwhile to incorporate economic history into positive economics.

Economic history performs a somewhat different function in non-positivist methodology. If it is the case that theory develops to address the problems raised by a particular historical context, then it is important to understand the context along with the theory. If theory has to be adapted to future changes in the context, then judgement needs to be applied to the way in which theory is changed. By understanding better how theory adapted to fit a context in the past, there will be a sounder basis for future developments. Or it may be that there are important factors in common between historical contexts and modern ones. Thus, for example, it is possible to analyse the financial system in South-East Asia by drawing on the experience of Western financial systems at a similar stage of development, and the way in which institutional arrangements—and indeed lengthy experience—served to build up confidence. In the absence of experimental evidence, economists can look to history to assess the reactions, in different contexts, to policy measures. It is a means of building up weight of evidence. The exercise of judgement comes into weighing up the similarities with historical contexts and the differences. For example, unlike the UK in the nineteenth century, the financial system of South-East Asia is developing in the context of an existing sophisticated international financial system. The history of the US financial system, which also developed in an international context where there were already developed financial systems, could yield insights for South-East Asia, although other differences would need to be assessed for significance.

A field of history of particular interest to economists is the history of economics itself. It is a field which has been undergoing some heart-searching along with methodology. Indeed, in the case of the science studies approach to methodology, the two have converged. Methodology-as-description is understood to be history of economics, so that methodology is subsumed into history of economics (Weintraub, 1989). But issues impinge on the history of economics similar to those we have discussed in relation to methodology. What is the role, for example, of history told from a modern perspective rather than from a reconstruction of the perspective of the author? Should history of thought be an account of progress? Should history of economic thought be as close as possible to the intentions of the author and the context of writing, and can it contribute to modern discussions around particular themes? The pendulum has swung in favour of the first of these approaches, echoing developments in methodological thinking. However, it is acknowledged that it is not completely possible to shed our modern perspective and be sure that we have identified the intentions of the author. Nevertheless, in making this argument, Winch (1997) argues that it is important that we try.

However, we have noted that many important developments in economics have occurred because of ideas crossing from one paradigm to another. It may not be regarded as good history of thought, but there is a role for historical ideas to inspire, even if they are not understood as the author intended. For example, it is now generally accepted in the history of thought literature that general equilibrium theory represents a misunderstanding of what Smith meant by the invisible hand. But Smith's inspiration is important as the instigator of the development of the framework, even though the inspiration was based on a misunderstanding.

The least controversial argument for studying the history of thought is that it helps us to understand modern economics (Blaug, 2001). Since economic thought does not develop according to set rules, as we have seen, it is helpful, in using and extending modern theory, to understand why it is set up in the way it is. It would be hard, for example, to understand why choice theory is set up as it is without understanding its origins in the mechanical methodology of the physical sciences in the late nineteenth century. From the point of view of understanding, and the capacity to exercise judgement, this is undoubtedly an important argument.

But there is a further dimension, since, in social systems, knowledge in turn impacts on reality. The institutional arrangements of central banking stem only in part from past practice; they are also changed according to economic theory. It was a particular theory of inflation which encouraged the idea of controlling the supply of bank reserves in the nineteenth century, and a particular theory which encouraged making central banks independent of government in the late twentieth century. These arrangements in turn impact on reality. Monetary policy in the UK and the USA switched from a focus on interest rates to a focus on monetary aggregates from 1979. The result was greater interest rate instability which impacted on firms' planning framework, and thus on investment, output, and employment. This is also an illustration of what happens when a theory employs an assumption (money supply exogeneity) in order to demonstrate a causal mechanism, when this is at odds with reality. Since in practice it was difficult to control the money supply, other measures (such as fiscal tightening) may have to be employed to squeeze inflation out of the economy.

So, the historian is interested in understanding the development of theory against the background of its context. The methodologist is interested further in the reflexive nature of the interplay between reality, theory, and the institutional arrangements indicated by theory, and the possibility that these may be out of phase (see the Dow and Dow (2002) discussion of Chick on Niebyl, who analysed monetary economics in this way). A context may suggest a methodological approach which produces theory which encourages institutional change which changes the context, and so on. So theory is part of the reality we analyse.

However, we have touched from time to time on the way in which economics abstracts from the reality of the social system to focus on economic behaviour as distinct from other social behaviour. This poses particular issues for the relationship between economics and other social sciences.

9.4.3 Relationship with other social sciences

In its origins in the enlightenment period, modern economics evolved alongside the other social sciences; indeed all saw their beginnings as case studies in moral philosophy. The emergence of economics as a scientific discipline in the nineteenth century saw an effort at separating economics from other social sciences, with a sentiment that economics was the social science most close to the physical sciences. Increasingly now there is a consciousness that that separation has gone too far. In the centennial issue of the *Economic Journal*, this issue was raised, and it was predicted that, over the next century, we would see the need to reduce the separability of economics. For example, Hahn (1991: 47) predicted that 'instead of simple transparent axioms there looms the likelihood of psychological, sociological and historical postulates'.

One approach has been the Becker 'imperialist' approach whereby the issue is resolved by subsuming other social sciences within economics. Indeed, some within other social sciences are attracted to the benefits of representing human behaviour in an individualistic, deterministic fashion, as with rational economic man. These benefits include the scope for mathematical formalism and for statistical testing. Others have sought to qualify the picture of economic behaviour presented by rational economic man. There is a large and growing literature in combining psychology with economics (see Earl, 1990; Rabin, 1998). In particular, behavioural economics, which is attracting increasing attention, has always included analysis of individuals, within institutions or social contexts, being motivated by emotion as well as some narrow notion of rationality. Thus, for example, it is arguably an emotional, or psychological, willingness to ignore ignorance which underpins entrepreneurial decision-making; similarly, it is arguably an emotional, or psychological, unwillingness to face reality which allows companies to persist with a business strategy which, to the outside world, no longer makes sense from the traditional economic point of view.

We have seen how sociology has been employed in helping us to understand the society of economists. Similarly, sociology can be employed to help us understand our subject matter (see, for example, Farmer's (1995) sociological analysis of knowledge itself). If indeed much of our behaviour is influenced by the social setting, then that is worthy of study. If workers are more concerned with relative wages than absolute wages, or if consumers are more concerned with 'keeping up with the Jones's' than meeting specific independent needs, then theory based on individualism, optimization, and incentives is missing something important. Thus, for example, new work in labour economics suggests that incentive schemes have a stronger effect on labour productivity if they are accompanied by clusters of human resource management practices (see, for example, Ichniowski, Shaw, and Prennushi, 1997). Equally interesting is the 'happiness' literature which attempts to identify different levels of happiness across countries, and the factors that seem to explain these differences. While economics has separated off the economic realm for study, it is presumed that economic wealth is a good proxy for well-being from all sources, since wealth provides the buying power for happiness. But the studies do not bear out a positive relationship between earnings and happiness, suggesting that there are other socio-psychological factors to be taken into account (see, for example, Oswald, 1997). Clearly such analysis raises all sorts of methodological issues; it is an example of an area in which methodology, and the issue of separation between disciplines, is at the core and can provide insight.

9.5 What all this Means for Applying Economics to Policy Issues

We have been concerned so far with the issues raised by developing economic theory, albeit with the goal of developing the basis for addressing real-world problems. We have seen that the economist has to make choices, explicitly or implicitly, about methodology, and exercise judgement. Here we zero in on the particular issues which arise in actually applying theory to policy issues, both from the point of view of the economist, and of the recipient of the advice.

We have seen a range of possibilities. At one end of the spectrum is the search for universal laws which can be brought to bear on any question. The economist is then in a position to offer advice at arm's length, as it were, without too much concern with the particular details of the case. This is the much maligned case of the economist giving advice immediately on stepping down from the plane in some developing country. If economic theory abstracts from other aspects of reality, and the details of the reality involve an amalgam of influences, some economic and some non-economic, then the advice stems purely from the abstract argument. The model is a substitute for an experiment, and yields conclusions along the lines of 'indirect taxes reduce utility more than direct taxes, *ceteris paribus*'. If there are other considerations, such as the social impact of different types of taxation, that is not the concern of the economist.

At the other end of the spectrum is the view that knowledge is context-specific, so that policy advice cannot be given without detailed study of the context, and there is little scope for generalization. This approach tends to be associated with the view that economic behaviour is not separable from other types of behaviour, so that a good study would be done by an interdisciplinary team. The contribution of the economist is to bring a set of tools of analysis, and to focus more on such variables as prices and incomes than other disciplines.

But for most economists the preferred approach lies somewhere in between, where it is accepted that we do not have the scope to identify universal laws, but on the other hand there is some scope for general principles to be established, albeit provisionally. This is where the unsettled questions lie. For those who bring economic theories based on choice theory to a problem, it is not clear how that is to be combined with an acceptance of the role of society in shaping actual individual behaviour. For those who adopt a pluralist methodology, how is it decided which methods to employ? While incommensurate methods inevitably mean some form of inconsistency, this does not mean that the notion of inconsistency is redundant. Each inconsistency needs to be examined for whether or not it matters. For example, there is an inconsistency between modelling individuals as fully informed within a pluralist framework, when the methodology itself is justified by the lack of knowledge of the economist. This type of inconsistency within a pluralist methodology might matter.

In the meantime, how is the user to choose between competing theories? As far as macroeconomic models are concerned, you would think that it would be relatively straightforward to work out which was the most successful model in terms of predictive success. There are periodic exercises in reviewing the competing models of the UK economy (see, for example, Church et al., 1997) but, while highly informative, the comparison does not lend itself to simple conclusions. In any case, as Smith (2000) points out, predictive success is only one criterion used by governments in choosing models; providing a clear analysis as input to the bureaucratic and political process may be just as important.

Another factor relevant to the policy maker's choice of economic input is the conclusion which has emerged from much of the methodology literature that economics is not value-free. Rather, any paradigm embodies a set of core values and an accepted mode of reasoning, coloured by an understanding of how the economy works (a focus on markets, on social relations, on production, on its fragmented nature, and so on). What is rational is for the policy maker to identify the paradigm which mirrors the value system and understanding of the real world of the government, and to see what economic theory within that paradigm throws up. But that is not sufficient. Being aware of the inability of any paradigm to provide a definitive account of an economic problem, it is also rational to find out what alternative paradigms and their theories suggest, in order to retain a critical attitude. Thus, for example, the fact that the UK's Monetary Policy Committee represents a range of approaches to monetary policy is to be welcomed. The policy which emerges is based on a synthesis of sometimes competing views.

9.6 Implications for Economics Education

In all of this discussion the role of judgement is central: judgement in choosing a paradigm, judgement in choosing methods where the methodology is pluralist, judgement in applying theoretical conclusions to real problems, and judgement on the part of the policy maker in choosing and interpreting the economic advice which is to be followed. We have argued that engaging in debate across paradigms, being aware of the different perspectives and methodologies which economists adopt, and having a good knowledge of history (of the economy, of economic institutions, and economic ideas) all contribute to the formation of judgemental capabilities. Much of this can be an exercise in learning-by-doing. The implication of the methodological material we have been discussing is that methodological awareness can make the task of dealing with fundamental issues easier, since much of the ground has been gone over many times before. But here we consider what this implies for the content and purpose of economics education.

In this age of teaching transferable skills, economics is notable for teaching analytical skills: the ability to take a problem and address it rigorously. What is hoped for is that economics graduates have learned how to formulate a problem in such a way as to apply a chosen theory to it. Thus in job interviews an economics graduate should be able to address such questions as 'should the UK join EMU?', or 'should fuel taxes be reduced?', drawing on theory and evidence explored in the degree programme. A good training will equip the student to exercise the judgement necessary to choose the most appropriate theory, and then express the conclusions in such a way as to address the policy question. Further, since the conclusion will generally include the '*ceteris paribus*' clause, judgement has to be applied here too; what factors would the policy maker need to be alert to which are currently subsumed in this clause? So the training needs to foster judgement as well as knowledge of theories and empirical techniques.

Along the lines we have already been discussing, this requires an awareness of the range of possibilities within which choice of methodology is to be made, and a knowledge of history (of the economy, and of economic thought). There is a danger that the benefits from learning sophisticated technique may be gained at the expense of equipping students to exercise judgement over the application of technique, and in what domain it may legitimately be applied. This was something noted by the American study into higher education in economics (Krueger *et al.*, 1991). Further, it is not necessarily a straight trade-off. If there is a lack of awareness of the range of approaches that may be taken in economics, of the history of the subject, and of the real-world context to which the techniques are to be applied, then there may be undue confidence in the knowledge gained. As in Keynes's probability theory, confidence in knowledge can go down as well as up when new knowledge is gained. The modern methodology literature promotes an awareness of fallibility, and thus both modesty with respect to our chosen approach and tolerance of alternative approaches, which provide the basis for good judgement to be formed.

In Chapter 2 we referred to some studies of economics programmes conducted by economists. Earlier, Colander and Klamer (1987) had surveyed US graduate students, who expressed some disaffection from the emphasis on technique rather than policy relevance. More recently, there has been a push to debate the issues coming from the students themselves. Thus students first in France, then in the USA and the UK, have been petitioning for a change in the content of economics teaching in the direction of a greater degree of pluralism—involving a focus on debate as a means of promoting understanding, and specifically debate on methodological issues. The expression of these views, and the responses to them, have indicated several areas for methodological debate. Kirman's (2001) report on the discussion in France, for example, highlights the importance of such questions as whether or not mathematics is neutral, and the relationship between ideology and economics. This reinforces the argument that methodological discussion is important, for students as well as practising economists. Yet there seems to be some reluctance among other economists to embark on such an exercise. It is possible that, through a lack of methodological discussion, those who benefited from a broader education themselves do not appreciate its benefits adequately. But now there is clearly a groundswell of opinion among many students themselves that these matters warrant debate.

9.7 Conclusion: Methodology and the Future of Economics

The students of today represent the future of economics, so the implications of our methodological discussion apply equally to the future of economics. Methodology now is a field which opens up the discipline to debate about fundamentals rather than closing it off. To engage in such debate is important for a social science where it is generally agreed that there are no external rules we can draw on to decide how we proceed. Our knowledge of the economy is fallible. But we can nevertheless build up knowledge (albeit held with greater or lesser degrees of uncertainty) within our chosen frameworks, as a basis for policy advice. These frameworks in turn embody a set of values, a vision of reality and a methodology. But since there is no one framework which can claim supremacy, other than by mutual consent, there is scope for a range of bodies of knowledge to be built up on different foundations. Methodology makes explicit the foundations which economists implicitly build on, and provides the basis for discussion between frameworks. There is no neutral language, but we can still learn to communicate more effectively.

In a rapidly changing economic environment, with new policy problems arising, economists need to be open to different possibilities for the future development of the discipline. It may be that the way forward is to synthesize two or three existing frameworks to create another more suited to new economic circumstances. But an initial condition is that the awareness of what is currently going on in economics needs to be there. This involves the open-mindedness necessary for us to explore each other's frameworks on their own terms, just as we may adopt different habits to conform to a foreign country in which we are travelling, and which we want to understand. Normally we want to get on with our economics in our chosen framework. But if we are conscious, through methodological discussion, of the fallibility of any framework, then we need to keep our minds open whenever we come up against problems. Methodological knowledge further helps us to see what the problems are, and also the possibilities for advance by drawing on different frameworks.

Exposing to critical discussion those conventions by which we unconsciously operate (in economics or in any walk of life) is inevitably uncomfortable. But to avoid doing so, particularly in a social science where no set of conventions has any absolute claim to superiority, is to endanger the discipline even more. Economics has a tremendous amount to offer both the policy maker and the simply curious in terms of an understanding about powerful forces at work in society. But this offering is not necessarily seen in its best light if expressed in terms of a discipline apparently driven by internal concerns arising from the process of abstraction, rather than by concerns arising from real-world problems. In order to demonstrate the power of economics more effectively, we need to develop better the capacity to discuss openly questions about the foundations of the discipline. Maybe if the public understood better the methodological issues posed by an attempt to understand the economy they would be less inclined to tell jokes about us!

In conclusion, this volume has been an exercise in drawing attention to what has been happening within the field of methodology, to indicate where it is relevant to the practice of economics, and to provide signposts through the growing mass of literature on the subject. For those new to this area, it is hoped that you will now see the practice of economics, and the issues posed by practice, in a new light.

9.8 Further Reading

For further reading on the topics explored here, see by topic: Chick (1995), Dow (1996: ch. 2) (sociology, modes of thought, and visions of reality); Mair and Miller (1991), Snowdon, Vane, and Wynarczyk (1994), Dow (1996), Cole, Cameron, and Edwards (1991) (choice of methodology); Hausman and McPherson (1996), Mini (1974), Kindleberger (1990), Blaug (2001), Farmer (1995) (relationship with other disciplines); Blendon et al. (1997), Bank of England (1999) (application to policy issues); Colander and Klamer (1987), Sept., 1991 issue of the *Journal of Economic Literature* (economics education); more generally, the centennial issue in vol. 101 of the *Economic Journal* (1991), Gordon (1991), Fox (1997), the millennial issue (14.1) of the *Journal of Economic Perspectives* (2000), and the March 2001 issue of the *Journal of Economic Methodology*.

Endnotes

1. These two modes of thought are discussed, as Cartesian/Euclidean thought and Babylonian thought, respectively, in Dow (1996).

2. Chick expresses the framework in terms of how we deal with duals; we are adapting the argument here to how we deal with conflicting arguments.

3. See Chick and Dow (forthcoming) for a discussion of different meanings of generality.

BIBLIOGRAPHY

AGHION, P., and HOWITT, P. (1998), *Endogenous Growth Theory* (Cambridge, Mass: MIT Press).

AKERLOF, G. (1982), 'Labor Contracts as Partial Gift Exchange', *Quarterly Journal of Economics*, 97: 543–69.

AKHTAR, M. A. (1995), 'Monetary Policy Goals and Central Bank Independence', *Banca Nazionale del Lavoro Quarterly Review*, 158: 423–40.

ALCHIAN, A. A. (1950), 'Uncertainty, Evolution and Economic Theory', *Journal of Political Economy*, 57: 211–21.

ALESINA, A., and SUMMERS, L. (1993), 'Central Bank Independence and Macroeconomic Performance: Some Comparative Evidence', *Journal of Money, Credit and Banking*, 25: 151–62.

ALSTON, R. M., KEARL, J. R., and VAUGHAN, M. B. (1992), 'Is There a Consensus among Economists', *American Economic Review*, 82: 203–9.

AMARIGLIO, J. (1998), 'The Body, Economic Discourse, and Power', *History of Political Economy*, 20: 583–613.

—— and RUCCIO, D. F. (1995), 'Keynes, Postmodernism, Uncertainty', in S. C. Dow and J. Hillard (eds.), *Keynes, Knowledge and Uncertainty*, 334–56 (Cheltenham: Elgar).

ARESTIS, P., and GLICKMAN, M. (forthcoming), 'Financial Crisis in South-East Asia: Dispelling Illusion the Minskian Way', *Cambridge Journal of Economics*.

ASHMORE, M., MULKAY, M., and PINCH, T. (1989), *Health and Efficiency: A Sociology of Health Economics* (Milton Keynes: Open University).

BACKHOUSE, R. E. (1991), 'The Neo-Walrasian Research Programme in Macroeconomics', in N. de Marchi and M. Blaug (eds.), *Appraising Economic Theories* (Cheltenham: Elgar).

—— (1995), 'Should Economists Embrace Postmodernism?', in S. C. Dow and J. Hillard (eds.), *Keynes, Knowledge and Uncertainty*, 357–66 (Cheltenham: Elgar).

—— (1997), *Truth and Progress in Economic Knowledge* (Cheltenham: Elgar).

—— (1998a), 'If Mathematics Is Informal, then Perhaps We Should Accept that Economics Must Be Informal too', *Economic Journal*, 108: 1848–58.

—— (1998b), 'Imre Lakatos', in J. B. Davis, D. W. Hands, and U. Mäki (eds.), *The Handbook of Economic Methodology*, 270–2 (Cheltenham: Elgar).

—— (forthcoming), 'How do Economic Theorists use Empirical Evidence?', in S. C. Dow and J. Hillard (eds.), *Post Keynesian Econometrics, Microeconomics and the Theory of the Firm: Beyond Keynes*, i (Cheltenham: Elgar).

BALLS, E. (1998), 'Open Macroeconomics in an Open Economy', *Scottish Journal of Political Economy*, 45: 113–32.

BANK OF ENGLAND (1999), *Economic Models at the Bank of England* (London: Bank of England).

BARNES, B., and BLOOR, D. (1982), 'Relativism, Rationalism and the Sociology of Knowledge', in Hollis and Lukes, 21–47.

BARRO, R. J., and SALA-i-MARTIN, X. (1995), *Economic Growth* (New York: McGraw-Hill).

BECKER, G. S. (1965), 'A Theory of the Allocation of Time', *Economic Journal*, 80: 493–517.
—— (1976), *The Economic Approach to Human Behavior* (Chicago: University of Chicago Press).
—— (1991), *A Treatise on the Family* (Cambridge: Harvard University Press).
BEED, C. (1991), 'Philosophy of Science and Contemporary Economics', *Journal of Post Keynesian Economics*, 13: 459–94.
—— and KANE, O. (1991), 'What is the Critique of the Mathematisation of Economics?', *Kyklos*, 44: 581–612.
BELL, D. N. F. (2000), 'Higher Education in Scotland: An Economic Perspective', in Independent Committee of Inquiry into Student Finance, *Student Finance: Fairness for the Future, Research Report*, ii, annex O, 345–73.
BENSUSAN-BUTT, D. (1978), *On Economic Man* (Canberra: Australian National University).
BERG, A., and PATTILLO, C. (1999), 'Are Currency Crises Predictable? A Test', *IMF Staff Papers*, 46: 107–38.
BERGER, H., DE HAAN, J., and EIJFFINGER, S. C. W. (2001), 'Central Bank Independence: An Update of Theory and Evidence', *Journal of Economic Surveys*, 15: 3–40.
BHASKAR, R. (1975), *A Realist Theory of Science* (Leeds: Leeds Books).
—— (2000), *From East to West* (London: Routledge).
BINMORE, K. (1987), 'Modelling Rational Players: Part I', *Economics and Philosophy*, 3: 179–214.
BLANCHARD, O., and FISCHER, S. (1989), *Lectures in Macroeconomics* (Cambridge, Mass: MIT Press).
BLAU, F. D. (1998), 'The Well-Being of American Women', *Journal of Economic Literature*, 36: 112–65.
BLAUG, M. (1976), 'Kuhn versus Lakatos on Paradigms versus Research Programmes in the History of Economics', in S. J. Latsis (ed.), *Method and Appraisal in Economics*, 149–80 (Cambridge: Cambridge University Press).
—— (1980), *The Methodology of Economics; Or How Economists Explain* (Cambridge: Cambridge University Press).
—— (1991), 'Afterword', in N. de Marchi and M. Blaug (eds.), *Appraising Economic Theories: Studies in the Methodology of Research Programs*, 499–512 (Oxford: Blackwell).
—— (1994), 'Why I am not a Constructivist: Confessions of an Unrepentant Popperian', in R. E. Backhouse (ed.), *New Directions in Economic Methodology*, 109–36 (London: Routledge).
—— (1998), 'The Positive-Normative Distinction', in J. B. Davis, D. W. Hands, and U. Mäki (eds.), *The Handbook of Economic Methodology*, 370–4 (Cheltenham: Elgar).
—— (1999), 'The Formalist Revolution or What has Happened to Orthodox Economics after World War II', in R. E. Backhouse and J. Creedy (eds.), *From Classical Economics to the Theory of the Firm: Essays in Honour of D. P. O'Brien*, 257–80 (Cheltenham: Elgar).
—— (2001), 'No History of Ideas, Please, We're Economists', *Journal of Economic Perspectives*, 15: 145–64.
BLENDON, R. J., BENSON, J. M., BRODIE, M., MORIN, R., ALTMAN, D. E., GITTERMAN, D.,

BROSSARD, M., and JAMES, M. (1997), 'Bridging the Gap between the Public's and the Economists' Views of the Economy', *Journal of Economic Perspectives*, 11: 105–18.

BLINDER, A. (1976), 'On Dogmatism in Human Capital Theory', *Journal of Human Resources*, 11 (Winter): 8–22.

BLOOR, D. (1976), *Knowledge and Social Imagery* (London: Routledge & Kegan Paul).

BOADWAY, R. W., and BRUCE, N. (1984), *Welfare Economics* (Oxford: Blackwell).

BOLAND, L. A. (1979), 'A Critique of Friedman's Critics', *Journal of Economic Literature*, 17: 503–22.

—— (1982), *The Foundations of Economic Method* (London: George Allen & Unwin).

—— (1989), *The Methodology of Economic Model Building: Methodology after Samuelson* (London: Routledge).

—— (1998*a*), 'Critical Rationalism', in J. B. Davis, D. W. Hands, and U. Mäki, (eds.), *The Handbook of Economic Methodology*, 86–8 (Cheltenham: Elgar).

—— (1998*b*), 'Conventionalism', in J. B. Davis, D. W. Hands, and U. Mäki (eds.), *The Handbook of Economic Methodology*, 79–83 (Cheltenham: Elgar).

BOULDING, K. E. (1991), 'A Note on the Meaning of "Scientific"', *Methodus*, 3: 32–3.

BOYLAN, T. A., and O'Gorman, P. F. (1995), *Beyond Rhetoric and Realism in Economics: Towards a Reformulation of Economic Methodology* (London: Routledge).

BRAINARD, W. (1967), 'Uncertainty and the Effectiveness of Policy', *American Economic Review*, 57, *Papers and Proceedings*: 411–25.

BRENNAN, H. G., and WATERMAN, A. M. C. (eds.), (1994), *Economics and Religion: Are They Distinct?* (Boston: Kluwer).

BRONFENBRENNER, M. (1971), 'The "Structure of Scientific Revolutions" in Economic Thought', *History of Political Economy*, 3: 136–51.

BROWN, V. (1994), 'The Economy as Text', in R. E. Backhouse (ed.), *New Directions in Economic Methodology*, 368–82 (London: Routledge).

CALDWELL, B. J. (1980), 'A Critique of Friedman's Methodological Instrumentalism', *Southern Economic Journal*, 47: 366–74.

—— (1982), *Beyond Positivism: Economic Methodology in the Twentieth Century* (London: Allen & Unwin).

—— (ed.) (1984), *Appraisal and Criticism in Economics: A Book of Readings* (London: Allen & Unwin).

—— (1988), 'Situational Analysis', in Davis, Hands, and Mäki (eds.), 462–8.

—— (1991), 'Clarifying Popper', *Journal of Economic Literature* 29: 1–33.

—— (ed.) (1993), *The Philosophy and Methodology of Economics*, i–iii (Cheltenham: Elgar).

CARABELLI, A. (1988), *On Keynes's Method* (London: Macmillan).

CARTWRIGHT, N. (1998), 'Capacities', in Davis, Hands, and Mäki (eds.), 45–8.

—— (1999), 'The Vanity of Rigour in Economics: Theoretical Models and Galilean Experiments', LSE Centre for Philosophy of Natural and Social Science, *Discussion Paper* 43/99.

CHICK, V. (1995), '"Order out of Chaos" in Economics?', in S. C. Dow and J. Hillard (eds.), *Keynes, Knowledge and Uncertainty*, 25–42 (Cheltenham: Elgar).

—— (1998), 'On Knowing One's Place: The Role of Formalism in Economics', *Economic Journal*, 108: 1859–69.

CHICK, V., and DOW, S. C. (1997), 'Competition and Integration in European Banking', in
A. Cohen, H. Hagemann, and J. Smithin (eds.), *Money, Financial Institutions and
Macroeconomics*, 253–70 (Boston: Kluwer).

—— —— (forthcoming), 'Formalism, Logic and Reality: A Keynesian Analysis',
Cambridge Journal of Economics.

CHOI, Y. B. (1993), *Paradigms and Conventions: Uncertainty, Decision Making, and
Entrepreneurship* (Ann Arbor: University of Michigan Press).

CHURCH, K. B., MITCHELL, P. R., SAULT, J. E., and WALLIS, K. F. (1997), 'Comparative
Properties of Models of the UK Economy', *National Institute Economic Review*, 161:
91–100.

CLARK, S. (1999), 'Law, Property, and Marital Dissolution', *Economic Journal*, 109: C41–54.

CLEMENTS, M. P., and HENDRY, D. F. (1995), 'Macro-economics Forecasting and
Modelling', *Economic Journal*, 105: 1001–13.

COASE, R. H. (1937), 'The Nature of the Firm', *Economica*, 4: 386–405.

—— (1988), *The Firm, the Market and the Law* (Chicago: University of Chicago Press).

COATES, J. (1996), *The Claims of Common Sense* (Cambridge: Cambridge University
Press).

COATS, A. W. (1969), 'Is There a "Structure of Scientific Revolutions" in Economics?',
Kyklos, 22: 289–96.

—— (1993), *The Sociology and Professionalization of Economics* (London: Routledge).

CODDINGTON, A. (1975), 'The Rationale of General Equilibrium Theory', *Economic
Inquiry*, 13: 539–58.

—— (1979), 'Friedman's Contribution to Methodological Controversy', *British Review of
Economic Issues*, 2(4): 1–13; repr. in Caldwell (1993), i.

COLANDER, D. C. (1994), 'Vision, Judgment, and Disagreement among Economists',
Journal of Economic Methodology, 1: 43–56.

—— and KLAMER, A. (1987), 'The Making of an Economist', *Journal of Economic
Perspectives*, 1: 95–113.

COLE, K., CAMERON, J., and EDWARDS, C. (1991), *Why Economists Disagree*, 2nd edn.
(London: Longman).

COMIM, F. (1999), *Common Sense Economics: Essays on the Role of Common Sense in the
History of Economic Thought*, Cambridge University, Ph.D. thesis.

COOLEY, T. F., and LEROY, S. F. (1981), 'Identification and Estimation of Money Demand',
American Economic Review, 71: 825–43.

CROSS, R. (1982), 'The Duhem–Quine Thesis, Lakatos and the Appraisal of Theories in
Macroeconomics', *Economic Journal*, 92: 320–40.

CUBEDDU, R., (1993), *The Philosophy of the Austrian School* (London: Routledge).

CUKIERMAN, A., WEBB, S., and NEYAPTI, B. (1992), 'Measuring the Independence of
Central Banks and its Effect on Policy Outcomes', *World Bank Economic Review* (Fall):
353–98.

CULLENBERG, S., AMARIGLIO, J., and RUCCIO, D. F. (eds.) (2001), *Postmodernism,
Economics and Knowledge* (London: Routledge).

DARNELL, A. C., and EVANS, J. L. (1990), *The Limits of Econometrics* (Aldershot: Elgar).

DAVIS, J. B. (1998a), 'Conventions', in J. B. Davis, D. W. Hands, and U. Mäki (eds.), *The
Handbook of Economic Methodology*, 83–6 (Cheltenham: Elgar).

—— (1998b), 'Organicism', in J. B. Davis, D. W. Hands, and U. Mäki (eds.), *The Handbook of Economic Methodology*, 349–51 (Cheltenham: Elgar).

—— (1999), 'Common Sense: A Middle Way between Formalism and Post-structuralism?', *Cambridge Journal of Economics*, 23: 503–13.

—— HANDS, D. W., and MÄKI, U. (eds.) (1998), *The Handbook of Economic Methodology* (Cheltenham: Elgar).

DEAN, J. M., and WATERMAN, A. M. C. (eds.) (1999), *Religion and Economics: Normative Social Theory* (Boston: Kluwer).

DEANE, P. (1978), *The Evolution of Economic Ideas* (Cambridge: Cambridge University Press).

DEBREU, G. (1991), 'The Mathematization of Economic Theory', *American Economic Review*, 81: 1–7.

DENNIS, K. (1995), 'A Logical Critique of Mathematical Formalism in Economics', *Journal of Economic Methodology*, 2: 181–99.

—— (ed.) (1998), *Rationality in Economics: Alternative Perspectives* (Boston: Kluwer).

DOBB, M. (1973), *Theories of Value and Distribution since Adam Smith: Ideology and Economic Theory* (Cambridge: Cambridge University Press).

DOW, A. C., and DOW, S. C. (1985), 'Animal Spirits and Rationality', in T. Lawson and H. Pesaran (eds.), *Keynes' Economics: Methodological Issues*, 46–65 (London: Routledge).

—— —— (2002), 'The Relevance of Historical Experience for Economics', in P. Arestis, M. Desai, and S. Dow (eds.), *Methodology, Microeconomics and Keynes: Essays in Honour of Victoria Chick*, ii. 39–50 (London: Routledge).

DOW, S. C. (1990a) 'Post-Keynesianism as Political Economy: A Methodological Discussion', *Review of Political Economy*, 2: 345–58.

—— (1990b), 'Beyond Dualism', *Cambridge Journal of Economics*, 14: 1434–58.

—— (1991), 'Are There Signs of Postmodernism in Economics?', *Methodus*, 3: 81–5.

—— (1996), *The Methodology of Macroeconomic Thought* (Cheltenham: Elgar).

—— (1997), 'Methodological Pluralism and Pluralism of Method', in A. Salanti and E. Screpanti (eds.), *Pluralism in Economics*, 89–99 (Cheltenham: Elgar).

—— (1998), 'Knowledge, Information and Credit Creation', in R. Rotheim (ed.), *New Keynesian Economics*, 214–26 (London: Routledge).

—— (2000), 'Rationality and Rhetoric in Smith and Keynes', in R. R. Favretti, G. Sandri, and R. Scazzieri (eds.), *Incommensurability and Translation: Kuhnian Perspectives on Scientific Communication and Theory Change*, 189–200 (Cheltenham: Elgar).

—— (2001a), 'Hume: A Reassessment', in R. Scazzieri, P. L. Porta, and A. S. Skinner (eds.), *Knowledge, Division of Labour and Social Institutions*, 75–92 (Cheltenham: Elgar).

—— (2001b), 'Methodology in a Pluralist Environment', *Journal of Economic Methodology*, 8: 33–40.

—— (forthcoming), 'Historical Reference: Hume and Critical Realism', *Cambridge Journal of Economics*.

—— and HILLARD, J. (eds.) (1995), *Keynes, Knowledge and Uncertainty* (Cheltenham: Elgar).

DOWNWARD, P. (2000), 'A Realist Appraisal of Post-Keynesian Pricing Theory', *Cambridge Journal of Economics*, 24: 211–24.

DRAKOPOULOS, S. (1991), *Values in Economic Theory* (Aldershot: Avebury).

DUISENBERG, W. F. (1999), 'Monetary Policy-making under Uncertainty: Introductory Statement' (3 Dec.), *http://www.ifk-cfs.de/pages/ecb/papers/duisenberg/conten_e.htm*.

DURLAUF, S. N. (1996), 'On the Convergence and Divergence of Growth Rates: An Introduction', *Economic Journal*, 106: 1016–18.

EARL, P. E. (1984), *The Corporate Imagination: How Big Companies Make Mistakes* (Brighton: Wheatsheaf).

—— (1990), 'Economics and Psychology', *Economic Journal*, 100: 718–55.

—— (1995), *Microeconomics for Business and Marketing* (Aldershot: Elgar).

—— (ed.) (2000), *The Intellectual Legacy of Herbert A. Simon* (Cheltenham: Elgar).

EDWARDS, J., and FISCHER, K. (1994), *Banks, Finance and Investment in Germany* (London: CEPR).

EICHNER, A. S. (ed.) (1983), *Why Economics is not yet a Science* (London: Macmillan).

ELSTER, J. (1988), 'Social Norms and Economic Theory', *Journal of Economic Perspectives*, 3: 99–117.

—— (1998), 'Emotions and Economic Theory', *Journal of Economic Literature*, 36: 47–74.

ENGLAND, P. (1993), 'The Separate Self: Androcentric Bias in Neoclassical Assumptions', in M. A. Farber and J. A. Nelson (eds.), *Beyond Economic Man: Feminist Theory and Economics*, 37–53 (Chicago: Chicago University Press).

EUROPEAN COMMISSION (1990), 'One Market, One Money: An Evaluation of the Potential Benefits and Costs of Forming an Economic and Monetary Union', *European Economy*.

FARMER, M. (1995), 'Knowledgeability, Actors and Uncertain Worlds', in S. C. Dow and J. Hillard (eds.), *Keynes, Knowledge and Uncertainty* (Cheltenham: Elgar).

FEYERABEND, P. K. (1975), *Against Method: Outline of an Anarchist Theory of Knowledge* (London: New Left Books).

—— (1978), *Science in a Free Society* (London: New Left Books).

FINCH, J., and MCMASTER, R. (forthcoming), 'On Non-Parametric Statistical Inference in the Pursuit of Causal Explanations', *Cambridge Journal of Economics*.

FISH, S. (1980), *Is There a Text in This Class? The Authority of Interpretive Communities* (Cambridge: Cambridge University Press).

—— (1985), 'Consequences', in W. J. T. Mitchell (ed.), *Against Theory*, 106–31 (Chicago: University of Chicago Press).

FISHER, I. (1965), *Mathematical Investigations in the Theory of Value and Prices* (New York: Augustus M. Kelley [1897]).

FITZGIBBONS, A. (2000), *The Nature of Macroeconomics: Instability and Change in the Capitalist System* (Cheltenham: Elgar).

FLEETWOOD, S. (ed.) (1999), *Critical Realism in Economics: Development and Debate* (London: Routledge).

FOOT, M. D. K. W., GOODHART, C. A. E., and HOTSON, A. C. (1979), 'Monetary Base Control', *Bank of England Quarterly Bulletin*, June.

FOSS, N. J. (1999), 'Incomplete Contracts and Economic Organization: Brian Loasby and the Theory of the Firm', in S. C. Dow and P. E. Earl (eds.), *Contingency, Complexity and the Theory of the Firm: Essays in Honour of Brian J. Loasby*, ii. 40–66 (Aldershot: Elgar).

—— and MAHNKER, V. (eds.) (2000), *Competence, Governance, and Entrepreneurship* (Oxford: Oxford University Press).

FOX, G. (1997), *Reason and Reality in the Methodologies of Economics* (Cheltenham: Elgar).

FRENKEL, J. A., and ROSE, A. K. (1996), 'Currency Crashes in Emerging Markets: An Empirical Assessment', *Journal of International Economics*, 41: 351–66.

FRIEDMAN, M. (1953), 'The Methodology of Positive Economics', in *Essays in Positive Economics*, 3–43 (Chicago: Chicago University Press).

—— (1956), 'The Quantity Theory of Money: A Restatement', in M. Friedman (ed.), *Studies in the Quantity Theory of Money*, 3–21 (Chicago: Chicago University Press).

—— and SCHWARTZ, A. (1963), *A Monetary History of the United States: 1867–1960* (Princeton: Princeton University Press, for NBER).

—— —— (1982), *Monetary Trends in the United States and the United Kingdom: Their Relation to Income, Prices, and Interest Rates, 1867–1975* (Chicago: Chicago University Press, for NBER).

FURMAN, J., and STIGLITZ, J. E. (1998), 'Economic Crises: Evidence and Insights from East Asia', *Brookings Papers on Economic Activity*, 2: 1–135.

GARNETT, R. F. Jr. (1999), 'Economics of Knowledge, Old and New', in R. F. Garnett Jr. (ed.), *What do Economists Do? New Economics of Knowledge*, 1–15 (London: Routledge).

GERRARD, B. (1992), 'Human Logic in Keynes's Thought: Escape from the Cartesian Vice', in P. Arestis and V. Chick (eds.), *Recent Developments in Post-Keynesian Economics*, 1–16 (Cheltenham: Elgar).

—— (ed.) (1993), *The Economics of Rationality* (London: Routledge).

—— (1995), 'The Scientific Basis of Economics: A Review of the Methodological Debates in Economics and Econometrics', *Scottish Journal of Political Economy*, 42: 201–20.

GOODHART, C. A. E. (1999), 'Central Bankers and Uncertainty', *Bank of England Quarterly Bulletin*, 39: 102–14.

GORDON, D. M., EDWARDS, R., and REICH, M. (1982), *Segmented Work, Divided Workers* (Cambridge: Cambridge University Press).

GORDON, S. (1991), *The History and Philosophy of Social Science* (London: Routledge).

GRAHAM, E. (1992), 'Postmodernism and Paradox', in J. Docherty, E. Graham, and M. Malek (eds.), *Postmodernism and the Social Sciences*, 148–61 (London: Macmillan).

GREENWALD, B., and STIGLITZ, J. E. (1993), 'New and Old Keynesians', *Journal of Economic Perspectives*, 7: 22–44.

GRILICHES, Z. (1977), 'Estimating the Returns to Schooling: Some Econometric Problems', *Econometrica*, 45: 1–22.

GRILLI, V., MASCIANDARO, D., and TABELLINI, G. (1991), 'Institutions and Policy', *Economic Policy* (Oct.): 341–92.

GROENEWEGEN, P. (1995), *A Soaring Eagle: Alfred Marshall 1842–1924* (Cheltenham: Elgar).

GROSSMAN, S., and HART, O. (1986), 'The Costs and Benefits of Ownership: A Theory of Lateral and Vertical Integration', *Journal of Political Economy*, 94: 691–791.

GRUBEL, H. G., and BOLAND, L. A. (1986), 'On the Effective Use of Mathematics in Economics', *Kyklos* 39: 419–42.

HACKING, I. (1982), 'Language, Truth and Reason', in M. Hollis and S. Lukes (eds.), *Rationality and Relativism*, 48–66 (Oxford: Blackwell).

HAHN, F. H. (1973a), 'The Winter of our Discontent', *Economica*, 40: 322–30.

—— (1973b), *On the Notion of Equilibrium in Economics* (Cambridge: Cambridge University Press).

—— (1981), 'General Equilibrium Theory', in D. Bell and I. Kristol (eds.), *The Crisis in Economic Theory* (New York: Basic Books).

—— (1991), 'The Next Hundred Years', *Economic Journal*, 101: 47–50.

HALL, S. (1995), 'Macroeconomics and a Bit More Reality', *Economic Journal*, 105: 974–88.

HANDA, J. (2000), *Monetary Economics* (London: Routledge).

HANDS, D. W. (1985), 'The Structuralist View of Economic Theories: A Review Essay', *Economics and Philosophy*, 1: 303–35.

—— (1990), 'Thirteen Theses on Progress in Economic Methodology', *Finnish Economic Papers*, 3: 72–6.

—— (1991), 'The Problem of Excess Content: Economics, Novelty and a Long Popperian Tale', in N. de Marchi and M. Blaug (eds.), *Appraising Economic Theories* (Cheltenham: Elgar).

—— (1998), 'Positivism', in J. B. Davis, D. W. Hands and U. Mäki (eds.), *The Handbook of Economic Methodology*, 374–8 (Cheltenham: Elgar).

—— (2001), 'Economic Methodology is Dead – Long Live Economic Methodology: Thirteen Theses on the New Economic Methodology', *Journal of Economic Methodology*, 8: 49–64.

HANLEY, N., SHOGREN, J. F., and WHITE, B. (1997), *Environmental Economics in Theory and Practice* (London: Macmillan).

HANSEN, W. L. (1991), 'The Education and Training of Economics Doctorates', *Journal of Economic Literature*, 29: 1054–87.

HARCOURT, G. C. (1992), 'Marshall's *Principles* as Seen through the Eyes of Gerald Shove, Dennis Robertson and Joan Robinson', in C. Sardoni (ed.), *On Political Economists and Modern Political. Economy: Selected Essays of G. C. Harcourt*, 265–80 (London: Routledge).

HARDING, S. G. (ed.), (1976), *Can Theories be Refuted?* (Dordrecht, Boston: Reidel).

HARGREAVES-HEAP, S. (1989), *Rationality in Economics* (Oxford: Blackwell).

—— (1998), 'Rational Choice', in J. B. Davis, D. W. Hands, and U. Mäki (eds.), *The Handbook of Economic Methodology*, 400–4 (Cheltenham: Elgar).

HAUSMAN, D. M. (1989), 'Economic Methodology in a Nutshell', *Journal of Economic Perspectives*, 3: 115–27.

—— (1992), *The Inexact and Separate Science of Economics* (Cambridge: Cambridge University Press).

—— (1994), 'Kuhn, Lakatos and the Character of Economics', in R. E. Backhouse (ed.), *New Directions in Economic Methodology*, 195–215 (London: Routledge).

—— (1997), 'Theory Appraisal in Neoclassical Economics', *Journal of Economic Methodology*, 4: 289–96.

—— (1998), 'Separateness, Inexactness and Economic Method: A Brief Response', *Journal of Economic Methodology*, 5: 155–56.

—— and McPHERSON, M. S. (1996), *Economic Analysis and Moral Philosophy* (Cambridge: Cambridge University Press).

HAYEK, F. (1960), *The Constitution of Liberty* (London: Routledge & Kegan Paul).

HEILBRONER, R. L. (1998), 'Rhetoric and Ideology', in A. Klamer, D. N. McCloskey, and R. M. Solow (eds.), *The Consequences of Economic Rhetoric*, 38–43 (Cambridge: Cambridge University Press).

HENDERSON, W. (1994), 'Metaphor and Economics', in R. E. Backhouse (ed.), *New Directions in Economic Methodology* (London: Routledge).

—— DUDLEY-EVANS, T., and BACKHOUSE, R. E. (eds.) (1993), *Economics and Language* (London: Routledge).

HENDRY, D. F. (1993), *Econometrics: Alchemy or Science?* (Oxford: Blackwell).

—— and ERICSSON, N. R. (1991), 'An Econometric Analysis of *UK Money Demand in Monetary Trends in the United States and the United Kingdom* by Milton Friedman and Anna Schwartz', *American Economic Review*, 81: 8–38.

HODGSON, G. M. (1988), *Economics and Institutions* (Oxford: Policy Press).

HOLLIS, M., and LUKES, S. (1982), *Rationality and Relativism* (Oxford: Basil Blackwell).

HOOVER, K. D. (1994), 'Pragmatism, Pragmaticism and Economic Method', in R. E. Backhouse (ed.), *New Directions in Economic Methodology*, 286–315 (London: Routledge).

HORWITZ, S. (1995), 'Feminist Economics: An Austrian Perspective', *Journal of Economic Methodology*, 2: 259–79.

HUME, D. (1739–40), *A Treatise of Human Nature*, ed. by L. A. Selby-Bigge (Oxford: Clarendon Press, 1978).

—— (1777), *Enquiries Concerning Human Understanding and Concerning the Principles of Morals*, ed. by L. A. Selby-Bigge (Oxford: Clarendon Press, 1975).

HUTCHISON, T. W. (1938), *The Significance and Basic Postulates of Economic Theory* (London: Macmillan).

—— (1964), *'Positive' Economics and Policy Objectives* (London: Allen & Unwin), repr. in Caldwell (1993. ii).

—— (1996), 'On the Relations between Philosophy and Economics, Part I', *Journal of Economic Methodology*, 3: 187–214.

—— (1997), 'On the Relations between Philosophy and Economics, Part I', *Journal of Economic Methodology*, 4: 127–51.

—— (1998), 'Ultra-deductivism from Nassau Senior to Robbins and Daniel Hausman', *Journal of Economic Methodology*, 5: 43–92.

—— (2000) '"Crisis" in the 1970s: The Crisis of Abstraction', ch. 4 of *Knowledge and Ignorance in Economics* (Oxford: Blackwell, 1977), repr. in *On the Methodology of Economics and the Formalist Revolution*, ch. 4 (Cheltenham: Elgar).

ICHNIOWSKI, C., SHAW, K., and PRENNUSHI, G. (1997), 'The Effect of Human Resource Management Practices on Productivity: A Study of Steel Finishing Lines', *American Economic Review*, 87: 291–313.

JENKINS, M. A. (1996), 'Central Bank Independence and Inflation Performance: Panacea or Placebo?', *Banca Nazionale del Lavoro Quarterly Review*, 159 (June): 241–70.

JEVONS, W. S. (1871), *The Theory of Political Economy* (London: Macmillan).

JOHNSON, H. G. (1971), 'The Keynesian Revolution and the Monetarist Counter-Revolution', *American Economic Review*, 61: 1–14.

KAHNEMAN, D., and TVERSKY, A. (1984), 'The Psychology of Decision Making', *Naval Research Reviews*, 36: 20–4.

KAMINSKY, G., LIZONDO, S., and REINHART, C. (1998), 'Leading Indicators of Currency Crises', *IMF Staff Papers*, 45: 1–48.

KANTOR, B. (1979), 'Rational Expectations and Economic Thought', *Journal of Economic Literature*, 17: 1422–41.

KASPER, H., *et al.* (1991), 'The Education of Economists: From Undergraduate to Graduate Study', *Journal of Economic Literature*, 29: 1088–109.

KATZNER, D. W. (1991), 'In Defence of Formalization in Economics', *Methodus*, 3: 17–24.

KAY, J. (2000), 'Finance and Fiction', *Financial Times*, 27 Dec.: 8.

KAY, N. M. (1995), 'Alchian and "the Alchian Thesis"', *Journal of Economic Methodology*, 2: 281–6.

KEIZER, W., TIEBEN, B., and VAN ZIJP, R. (eds.) (1997), *Austrian Economics in Debate* (London: Routledge).

KEYNES, J. M. (1936), *The General Theory of Employment, Interest and Money* (London: Macmillan).

—— (1937), 'The General Theory of Employment', *Quarterly Journal of Economics*, 51 (1937), repr. in Keynes (1973c).

—— (1972), 'My Early Beliefs', *Essays in Biography. Collected Writings*, x (London: Macmillan, for the Royal Economic Society).

—— (1973a), *A Treatise on Probability, Collected Writings*, viii; first published 1921. (London: Macmillan, for the Royal Economic Society).

—— (1973b), *The General Theory and After*, pt. i: *Preparation, Collected Writings*, xiii (London: Macmillan, for the Royal Economic Society).

—— (1973c), *The General Theory and After*, pt. ii: *Defence and Development, Collected Writings*, xiv (London: Macmillan, for the Royal Economic Society).

KEYNES, J. N. (1890), *The Scope and Method of Political Economy* (London: Macmillan).

KINCAID, H. (1998), 'Methodological Individualism/Atomism', in J. B. Davis, D. W. Hands, and U. Mäki (eds.), *The Handbook of Economic Methodology*, 294–300 (Cheltenham: Elgar).

KINDLEBERGER, C. P. (1990), *Historical Economics: Art or Science?* (Hemel Hempstead: Harvester Wheatsheaf).

KING, J. E. (1995), *Conversations with Post Keynesians* (London: Macmillan).

KIRMAN, A. (2001), 'The Teaching of Economics: Signes d'Alarme', *RES Newsletter*, 112: 7–8.

KLAMER, A. (1983/4), *Conversations with Economists* (Totowa, NJ: Rowman & Allanhold, 1983); also published as *The New Classical Macroeconomics* (Brighton: Wheatsheaf, 1984).

—— (1995), 'The Conception of Modernism in Economics: Samuelson, Keynes and Harrod', in S. C. Dow and J. Hillard (eds.), *Keynes, Knowledge and Uncertainty*, 318–33 (Cheltenham: Elgar).

—— (2001), 'Making Sense of Economics: From Falsification to Rhetoric and Beyond', *Journal of Economic Methodology*, 8: 69–76.

—— SOLOW, R. M., and McCLOSKEY, D. N. (eds.) (1988), *The Consequences of Economic Rhetoric* (Cambridge: Cambridge University Press).

KLANT, J. J. (1994), *The Nature of Economic Thought: Essays in Economic Methodology* (Cheltenham: Elgar).

KNIGHT, F. H. (1940), '"What is Truth" in Economics?', *Journal of Political Economy*, 158 (1): 1–32.

KRUEGER, A. O., *et al.* (1991), 'Report of the Commission on Graduate Education in Economics', *Journal of Economic Literature*, 29: 1035–53.

KRUGMAN, P. (1998), 'Two Cheers for Formalism', *Economic Journal*, 108: 1829–36.

KUHN, T. S. (1962), *The Structure of Scientific Revolutions* (Chicago: University of Chicago Press; 2nd, enlarged edn., 1970).

—— (1970), 'Reflections on my Critics', in I. Lakatos and A. Musgrave (eds.), *Criticism and the Growth of Knowledge* (Cambridge: Cambridge University Press).

—— (1974), 'Second Thoughts on Paradigms', in F. Suppe (ed.), *The Structure of Scientific Theories*, 459–82 (Urbana: University of Illinois Press).

—— (1999), 'Remarks on Incommensurability and Translation', in R. R. Favretti, G. Sandri, and R. Scazzieri (eds.), *Incommensurability and Translation: Kuhnian Perspectives on Scientific Communication and Theory Change* (Cheltenham: Elgar).

KUNIN, L., and WEAVER, F. S. (1971), 'On the Structure of Scientific Revolutions in Economics', *History of Political Economy*, 3: 391–7.

KYDLAND, F. E., and PRESCOTT, E. C. (1990), 'Business Cycles: Real Facts and Monetary Myths', *Federal Reserve Bank of Minneapolis Quarterly Review*, Spring; repr. in J. E. Hartley, K. D. Hoover, and K. D. Salyer (eds.), *Real Business Cycles: A Reader* (London: Routledge, 1998).

LAIDLER, D. E. W. (1981), 'Monetarism: An Interpretation and an Assessment', *Economic Journal*, 91: 1–28.

—— (1999), *Fabricating the Keynesian Revolution* (Cambridge: Cambridge University Press).

LAKATOS, I. (1970), 'Falsification and the Methodology of Scientific Research Programmes', in I. and A. Musgrave (eds.), *Criticism and the Growth of Knowledge* (Cambridge: Cambridge University Press).

—— (1974), 'The Role of Crucial Experiments in Science', *Studies in History and Philosophy of Science*, 4: 309–25.

LASH, S. and URRY, J. (1987), *The End of Organised Capitalism* (Cambridge: Polity Press).

LAVOIE, D. (1990*a*), 'Hermeneutics, Subjectivity, and the Lester/Machlup Debate: Toward a More Anthropological Approach to Empirical Economics', in W. J. Samuels (ed.), *Economics as Discourse*, 167–84 (Boston: Kluwer).

—— (ed.) (1990*b*), *Economics and Hermeneutics* (London: Routledge).

LAWSON, T. (1988), 'Probability and Uncertainty in Economic Analysis', *Journal of Post Keynesian Economics*, 11: 38–65.

—— (1994*a*), 'A Realist Theory for Economics', in R. E. Backhouse (ed.), *New Directions in Economic Methodology*, 257–85 (London: Routledge).

—— (1994*b*), 'Why are so many Economists so Opposed to Methodology?', *Journal of Economic Methodology*, 1: 105–33.

—— (1995), 'Economics and Expectations', in S. C. Dow and J. Hillard (eds.), *Keynes, Knowledge and Uncertainty*, 77–106 (Cheltenham: Elgar).

—— (1997*a*), *Economics and Reality* (London: Routledge).

—— (1997*b*), 'Situated Rationality', *Journal of Economic Methodology*, 4: 101–25.

—— (1998), 'Tendencies', in Davis, Hands, and Mäki (eds.), 493–8.

LEIJONHUFVUD, A. (1981), 'Life among the Econ', in *Information and Coordination: Essays in Macro Theory*, ch. 12 (Oxford : Oxford University Press).

LEVIN, A., WIELAND, V., and WILLIAMS, J. C. (1998), 'Robustness of Simple Monetary Policy Rules under Model Uncertainty', *Federal Reserve Board Finance and Economics Discussion Series*, 45.

LEWIS, P. (1996), 'Metaphor and Critical Realism', *Review of Social Economy*, 54: 487–506.

LIPSEY, R. G., and LANCASTER, K. (1956/7), 'The General Theory of Second Best', *Review of Economic Studies*, 24: 11–32.

LOASBY, B. J. (1976), *Choice, Complexity and Ignorance* (Cambridge: Cambridge University Press).

—— (1982), 'On Scientific Method', *Journal of Post Keynesian Economics*, 6: 394–410.

—— (1989), *The Mind and Method of the Economist: A Critical Appraisal of Major Economists in the Twentieth Century* (Cheltenham: Elgar).

—— (1995), 'Acceptable Explanations', in S. C. Dow and J. Hillard (eds.), *Keynes, Knowledge and Uncertainty*, 6–24 (Cheltenham: Elgar).

—— (1999), *Knowledge, Institutions and Evolution in Economics* (London: Routledge).

LOOMES, G. (1999), 'Experimental Economics: An Introduction', *Economic Journal*, 109: F1–F4.

LUCAS, R. E. Jr. (1972), 'Expectations and the Neutrality of Money', *Journal of Economic Theory*, 4: 103–24.

—— (1980), 'Methods and Problems in Business Cycle Theory', *Journal of Money Credit and Banking*, 12: 696–715.

—— (1981), *Studies in Business Cycle Theory* (Cambridge, Mass. MIT Press).

—— (1988) 'On the Mechanics of Economic Development', *Journal of Monetary Economics*, 22: 3–42.

—— (1990), 'Why Doesn't Capital Flow from Rich to Poor Countries?', *American Economic Review*, 80: 92–6.

McCALLUM, B. T. (1980), 'Rational Expectations and Macroeconomic Stabilization Policy', *Journal of Money, Credit, and Banking*, 12: 716–46.

MACHLUP, F. (1967), 'Theories of the Firm: Marginalist, Behavioral, Managerial', *American Economic Review*, 57.

—— (1978), *Methodology of Economics and Other Social Sciences* (New York: Academic Press).

—— (1993), 'Positive and Normative Economics: An Analysis of the Ideas', in R. L. Heilbroner (ed.), *Economic Means and Social Ends: Essays in Political Economics*, 99–129 (Englewood Cliffs, NJ: Prentice-Hall, 1969), repr. in Caldwell (1993, ii).

McCLOSKEY, D. N. (1983), 'The Rhetoric of Economics', *Journal of Economic Literature*, 21: 434–61.

—— (1985), *The Rhetoric of Economics* (Brighton: Wheatsheaf).

—— (1988), 'Two Replies and a Dialog in the Rhetoric of Economics: Mäki, Rappoport and Rosenberg', *Economics and Philosophy*, 4: 150–66.

—— (1994), *Rhetoric and Persuasion in Economics* (Brighton: Wheatsheaf).

MAIR, D., and MILLER, A. G. (1991), *A Modern Guide to Economic Thought* (Cheltenham: Elgar).

Mäki, U. (1988), 'How to Combine Rhetoric and Realism in the Methodology of Economics', *Economics and Philosophy*, 4: 89–109.

—— (1989), 'On the Problem of Realism in Economics', *Ricerche Economiche*, 153: 176–98, repr. in B. J. Caldwell (ed.), *The Philosophy and Methodology of Economics*, 193–215 (Cheltenham: Elgar, 1993).

—— (1992), 'On the Method of Isolation in Economics', in C. Dilworth (ed.), *Idealization IV: Intelligibility in Science, Poznan Studies in the Philosophy of the Sciences and the Humanities*, xxvi (Amsterdam and Atlanta, Ga.: Rodopi).

—— (1994), 'Reorienting the Assumptions Issue', in R. E. Backhouse (ed.), *New Directions in Economic Methodology*, 236–56 (London: Routledge).

—— (1996), 'Two Portraits of Economics', *Journal of Economic Methodology*, 3: 1–38.

—— (1997), 'The One World and the Many Theories', in A. Salanti and E. Screpanti (eds.), *Pluralism in Economics: New Perspectives in History and Methodology*, 37–47 (Cheltenham: Elgar).

—— (1998a), 'Separateness, Inexactness and Economic Method', *Journal of Economic Methodology*, 5: 147–54.

—— (1998b), 'Realism', in J. B. Davis, D. W. Hands, and U. Mäki (eds.), *The Handbook of Economic Methodology*, 404–9 (Cheltenham: Elgar).

—— (1998c), 'Realisticness', in J. B. Davis, D. W. Hands, and U. Mäki (eds.), *The Handbook of Economic Methodology*, 409–13 (Cheltenham: Elgar).

—— Gustafsson, B., and Knudsen, C. (eds.) (1993), *Rationality, Institutions and Economic Methodology* (London: Routledge).

Makridakis, S., and Wheelwright, S. C. (1979), 'Forecasting the Future and the Future of Forecasting', in S. Makridakis and S. C. Wheelwright (eds.), *Forecasting* (Amsterdam: North-Holland).

de Marchi, N. (ed.) (1993), *Non-Natural Social Science: Reflecting on the Enterprise of More Heat than Light, History of Political Economy Annual Supplement*, xxv (Durham, NC: Duke University Press).

—— and Blaug, M. (eds.) (1991), *Appraising Economic Theories* (Cheltenham: Elgar).

Marshall, A. N. (1920), *Principles* (London: Macmillan, 8th edn., 1920; reissued ed. with annotations, by C. W. Guillebauld, 1961).

Mayer, T. (1993), *Truth versus Precision in Economics* (Cheltenham: Elgar).

—— (1994), 'Why is There so much Disagreement among Economists?', *Journal of Economic Methodology*, 1: 1–14.

Medema, S., and Samuels, W. J. (eds.) (1996) *Foundations of Research in Economics: How do Economists do Economics?* (Cheltenham: Elgar).

Mill, J. S. (1863), *Utilitarianism* (Glasgow: Collins, [1979]).

—— (1874), *Essays on Some Unsettled Questions of Political Economy* (London: Longmans, Green & Oyer).

Mincer, J. (1974), *Schooling, Experience, and Earnings* (New York and London: Columbia University Press for NBER).

Mini, P. V. (1974), *Philosophy and Economics* (Gainesville: University Presses of Florida).

Minsky, H. P. (1982), *Inflation, Recession and Economic Policy* (Brighton: Harvester, and Armonk, NY: M. E. Sharpe).

Mirowski, P. (1989), *More Heat than Light: Economics as Social Physics. Physics as Nature's Economics* (Cambridge: Cambridge University Press).

—— (1991), 'The When, the How and the Why of Mathematical Expression in Economics', *Journal of Economic Perspectives*, 5: 145–58.

Mishkin, F. (1992), *The Economics of Money, Banking and Financial Markets* (New York: HarperCollins).

Morgan, M. S. (1990), *The History of Econometric Ideas* (Cambridge: Cambridge University Press).

—— (1999), 'Learning from Models', in Morgan and Morrison (1999).

—— and Morrison, M. (eds.), (1999), *Models as Mediators: Perspectives on Natural and Social Science* (Cambridge: Cambridge University Press).

—— and Rutherford, M.(eds.), (1998a), *From Interwar Pluralism to Postwar Neoclassicism* (Durham, NC: Duke University Press).

—— —— (1998b), 'American Economics: The Character of the Transformation', in Morgan and Rutherford (1998a: 1–28).

Morre, B. (1998), *Horizontalists and Verticalists: The Macroeconomics of Credit Money* (Cambridge: Cambridge University Press).

Morrison, M., and Morgan, M. S. (1999), 'Models as Mediating Instruments', in Morgan and Morrison, ch. 2.

Muth, J. F. (1961), 'Rational Expectations and the Theory of Price Movements', *Econometrica*, 29: 315–35.

Myrdal, G. (1995), *The Political Element in the Development of Economic Thought*, P. Streeton (trans.) (Cambridge, Mass: Harvard University Press).

Nagel, E. (1963), 'Assumptions in Economic Theory', *American Economic Review Papers and Proceedings*, 53: 231–6.

Nelson, J. (1993), 'Value-free or Valueless? Notes on the Pursuit of Detachment in Economics', *History of Political Economy*, 25: 121–45.

—— (1996), *Feminism, Objectivity and Economics* (London: Routledge).

O'Donnell, R. M. (1990), 'Keynes on Mathematics: Philosophical Foundations and Economic Applications', *Cambridge Journal of Economics*, 14: 29–48.

Oswald, A. J. (1997), 'Happiness and Economic Performance', *Economic Journal*, 107: 1815–31.

Pagan, A. R. (1987), 'Three Econometric Methodologies: A Critical Appraisal', *Journal of Economic Surveys*, 1: 3–24.

Papps, I. (1980), 'For Love or Money?', *Hobart Paper*, 86 (London: IEA).

Pareto, V. (1927), *Manual of Political Economy*, A. S. Schwier (trans.), A. S. Schwier and A. N. Page (eds.) (London: Macmillan, [1971]).

Parkin, M., Powell, M., and Matthews, K. (1997), *Economics*, 3rd edn. (London: Addison-Wesley).

Partington, I. (1989), *Applied Economics in Banking and Finance*, 4th edn. (Oxford: Oxford University Press).

Pasinetti, L. (2000), 'Critique of the Neoclassical Theory of Growth and Distribution', *Banca Nazionale del Lavoro Quarterly Review*, 53: 383–432.

Phelps, E. S. (1990), *Seven Schools of Macroeconomic Thought* (Oxford: Oxford University Press).

PHILLIPS, A. W. H. (1958), 'The Relationship between Unemployment and the Rate of Change of Money Wage Rates in the United Kingdom, 1861–1957', *Economica* 25: 283–99.

PICKERING, A. (1992), 'From Science as Knowledge to Science as Practice', in A. Pickering (ed.), *Science as Practice and Culture* (Chicago: University of Chicago Press).

POPPER, K. (1944–5), *The Poverty of Historicism* (London: Routledge).

—— (1959), *The Logic of Scientific Discovery* (London: Hutchinson).

—— (1963), *Conjectures and Refutations* (London: Routledge).

—— (1970), 'Normal Science and its Dangers', in I. Lakatos and A. Musgrave (eds.), *Criticism and the Growth of Knowledge* (Cambridge: Cambridge University Press).

—— (1974), 'Autobiography of Karl Popper', in P. A. Schilp (ed.), *The Philosophy of Karl Popper* (La Salle, Ill: Open Court).

—— (1982), *The Open Universe: An Argument for Indeterminism* (London: Routledge).

—— (1994), 'Models, Instruments and Truth', in *The Myth of the Framework* (London: Routledge).

PORTER, M. E. (1980), *Competitive Strategy: Techniques for Analysing Industries and Competitors* (New York: Free Press).

PRICE, B. B. (ed.) (1997), *Ancient Economic Thought* (London: Routledge).

QUINE, W. V. O. (1951), 'Two Dogmas of Empiricism', in *From a Logical Point of View* (Cambridge, Mass: Harvard University Press).

RABIN, M. (1998), 'Psychology and Economics', *Journal of Economic Literature*, 36: 11–46.

REDMAN, D. A. (1991), *Economics and the Philosophy of Science* (Oxford: Oxford University Press).

RICKETTS, M., and SHOESMITH, E. (1992), 'British Economic Opinion: Positive Science or Normative Judgement', *American Economic Review*, 82, Papers and Proceedings: 210–15.

ROBBINS, L. (1932), *An Essay on the Nature and Significance of Economic Science* (London: Macmillan).

RORTY, R. (1979), *Philosophy and the Mirror of Nature* (Princeton: Princeton University Press).

—— (1988), 'Is Natural Science a Natural Kind?', in E. McMullin (ed.), *Construction and Constraint: The Shaping of Scientific Rationality* (South Bend, Ind.: University of Notre Dame Press).

ROSENBERG, A. (1986), 'Lakatosian Consolations for Economics', *Economics and Philosophy*, 2: 127–140.

—— (1988), 'Economics is too Important to be left to Rhetoricians', *Economics and Philosophy*, 4: 129–49.

ROSSETTI, J. (1990), 'Deconstructing Robert Lucas', in W. J. Samuels (ed.), *Economics as Discourse: An Analysis of the Language of Economics*, 225–43 (Boston: Kluwer).

ROTHEIM, R. J. (1998), 'On Closed Systems and the Language of Economic Discourse', *Review of Social Economy*, 56: 324–34.

ROWTHORN, R. (1999), 'Marriage and Trust: Some Lessons from Economics', *Cambridge Journal of Economics*, 23: 661–91.

ROYAL SWEDISH ACADEMY OF SCIENCES (1997), *http://www.kva.se/eng/pg/prizes/economics/1997/ecoback97.html*

Ruccio, D. F. (1991), 'Postmodernism and Economics', *Journal of Post-Keynesian Economics*, 13: 495–510.

Rudebusch, G. D. (1999), 'Is the Fed Too Timid? Monetary Policy in an Uncertain World', *Working Paper* 99–05, Federal Reserve Bank of San Francisco.

Runde, J. (1990), 'Keynesian Uncertainty and the Weight of Arguments', *Economics and Philosophy*, 6: 275–92.

—— (1995), 'Risk, Uncertainty and Bayesian Decision Theory: A Keynesian View', in S. C. Dow and J. Hillard (eds.), *Keynes, Knowledge and Uncertainty*, 197–210 (Cheltenham: Elgar).

—— (1998), 'Assessing Causal Economic Explanations', *Oxford Economic Papers*, 50: 151–72.

Russell, B. (1929), 'Some Remarks on Logical Form', *Proceedings of the Aristotelian Society*, supp. ii.

Sachs, J., Tornell, A., and Velasco, A. (1996), 'Financial Crises in Emerging Markets: The Lessons from 1995', *Brookings Papers on Economic Activity*, 1: 147–215.

Sack, B. (1998), 'Uncertainty, Learning and Gradual Monetary Policy', *Federal Reserve Board Finance and Economics Discussion Series*, 34.

Salanti, A. (1987), 'Falsificationism and Fallibilism as the Epistemic Foundations of Economics: A Critical View', *Kyklos*, 40: 368–91.

—— and Screpanti, E. (eds.) (1997), *Pluralism in Economics* (Cheltenham: Elgar).

Samuels, W. J. (ed.) (1990), *Economics as Discourse: An Analysis of the Language of Economics* (Boston: Kluwer).

Samuelson, P. (1938), 'A Note on the Pure Theory of Consumer Behaviour', *Economica*, 5: 61–71.

—— (1963), 'Problems of Methodology–Discussion', *American Economic Review Papers and Proceedings*, 53: 231–6.

Sargent, T. J. (1998), 'Discussion of "Policy Rules for Open Economies" by L. Bell', papers presented at the NBER Conference on Monetary Policy Rules, Islamorada, Florida, January.

Schoemaker, P. J. H. (1991), 'The Quest for Optimality: A Positive Heuristic of Science?', *Behavioral and Brain Sciences*, 14(2): 205–15, repr. in Caldwell (1993, ii).

Schultz, T. W. (ed.) (1974), *The Economics of the Family* (Chicago: Chicago University Press, for NBER).

Schumacher, E. F. (1975), *Small is Beautiful: A Study of Economics as if People Mattered* (London: Sphere Books).

Screpanti, E., and Zamagni, S. (1993), *An Outline of the History of Economic Thought* (Oxford: Oxford University Press).

Searle, J. R. (1995), *The Construction of Social Reality* (London: Free Press).

Sent, E.-M. (1998), *The Evolving Rationality of Rational Expectations* (Cambridge: Cambridge University Press).

Shove, G. (1942), 'The Place of Marshall's *Principles* in the Development of Economic Theory', *Economic Journal*, 52: 294–329.

Siegel, S., and Castellan, N. J. (1988), *Nonparametric Statistics for the Behavioral Sciences*, 2nd edn. (London: McGraw-Hill).

Simon, H. (1982), *Models of Bounded Rationality* (Cambridge, Mass.: MIT Press).

SIMS, C. A. (1980), 'Macroeconomics and Reality', *Econometrica*, 48: 1–48.

SKINNER, A. S. (1979), 'Adam Smith: An Aspect of Modern Economics', *Scottish Journal of Political Economy*, 26: 109–25.

SMITH, A. (1759), *The Theory of Moral Sentiments*, ed. by A. L. Macfie and D. D. Raphael (Oxford: Clarendon, [1976]).

—— (1762–3), *Lectures on Rhetoric and Belles Lettres*, ed. by J. C. Bryce (Oxford: Oxford University Press, [1983]).

—— (1795), 'History of Astronomy', in W. P. D. Wightman (ed.), *Essays on Philosophical Subjects* (Oxford: Clarendon, [1980]).

SMITH, R. (2000), 'Emergent Policy Making with Macroeconomic Models', in M. Morgan and F. den Butter (eds.), *Empirical Models and Policy Making* (London: Routledge).

SNOWDON, B., and VANE, H. R. (1999), *Conversations with Leading Economists* (Cheltenham: Elgar).

—— —— and WYNARCZYK, P. (1994), *A Modern Guide to Macroeconomics* (Cheltenham: Elgar).

SOLOW, R. M. (1988), 'Comments from Inside Economics', in A. Klamer, D. N. McCloskey, and R. M. Solow (eds.), *The Consequences of Economic Rhetoric*, 31–7 (Cambridge: Cambridge University Press).

—— (1994), 'Perspectives in Growth Theory', *Journal of Economic Perspectives*, 8: 45–54.

—— (2001), 'The Neoclassical Theory of Growth and Distribution', *Banca Nazionale del Lavoro Quarterly Review*, 53: 349–82.

STIGLER, G. J., and BECKER, G. S. (1977), 'De Gustibus Non Est Disputandum', *American Economic Review*, 67 (2): 76–90; repr. in Caldwell (1993, ii).

STIGLITZ, J., and WEISS, M. (1981), 'Credit Rationing with Markets with Imperfect Competition', *American Economic Review*, 71: 22–44.

SUGDEN, R. (1989), 'Spontaneous Order', *Journal of Economic Perspectives*, 3: 85–97.

SWALES, J. (1993), 'The Paradox of Value: Six Treatments in Search of the Reader', in W. Henderson, T. Dudley-Evans, and R. E. Backhouse (eds.), *Economics and Language*, 225–39 (London: Routledge).

TIEBEN, W., and KEIZER, W. (1997), 'Introduction' to W. Keizer, B. Tieben, and R. van Zijp (eds.) *Austrian Economics in Debate* (London: Routledge).

TRAUTWEIN, H.-M. (2000), 'The Credit View, Old and New', *Journal of Economic Surveys*, 14: 155–89.

VAN REIJEN, W., and VEERMAN, D. (1988), 'An Interview with Jean-Francois Lyotard', *Theory, Culture and Society*, 5: 277–309.

VERCELLI, A. (1991), *Methodological Foundations of Macroeconomics: Keynes and Lucas* (Cambridge: Cambridge University Press).

—— (1999), 'The Recent Advances in Decision Theory under Uncertainty: A Non-technical Introduction', in L. Luini (ed.), *Uncertain Decisions: Bridging Theory and Experiments* (Dordrecht: Kluwer).

—— (forthcoming), 'Uncertainty, Rationality and Learning: A Keynesian Perspective', in S. C. Dow and J. Hillard (eds.), *Keynes, Uncertainty and the Global Economy: Beyond Keynes*, ii (Cheltenham: Elgar).

WEINTRAUB, E. R. (1985), *General Equilibrium Analysis* (Cambridge: Cambridge University Press).

—— (1989), 'Methodology Doesn't Matter, but the History of Thought Might', *Scandinavian Journal of Economics*, 9: 477–93.

—— (1992), 'Roger Backhouse's Straw Herring', *Methodus*, 4: 53–7.

—— (1998), 'Axiomatisches Missverständnis', *Economic Journal*, 108: 1837–47.

—— (1999), 'How Should We Write the History of Twentieth-Century Economics?', *Oxford Review of Economic Policy*, 15: 139–52.

WHEELOCK, J. (1990), *Husbands at Home: The Domestic Economy in a Post-Industrial Society* (London: Routledge).

WHITLEY, J. (1997), 'Economic Models and Policy-making', *Bank of England Quarterly Bulletin*, 37: 163–71.

WILLIAMSON, O. E. (1975), *Markets and Hierarchies* (New York: Free Press).

—— and MASTEN, S. E. (1999), *The Economics of Transactions Costs* (Cheltenham: Elgar).

WILLIS, R. J. (1986), 'Wage Determinants: A Survey and Reinterpretation of Human Capital Earnings Functions', in O. Ashenfelter and R. Layard (eds.), *Handbook of Labor Economics*, i (Amsterdam: Elsevier).

WINCH, D. (1997), 'Adam Smith's Problem and Ours', *Scottish Journal of Political Economy*, 44: 368–83.

WORKING GROUP ON FINANCIAL MARKETS (1999), 'Hedge Funds, Leverage, and the Lessons of Long-Term Capital Management', *Report to the President* (April).

INDEX